CARRY ON COPING

*Cover: First page of Joan Hickson's wartime diary and
Joan pictured at Green Gables in the 1940s*

Frontispiece: Joan as a medical student, circa 1918

CARRY ON COPING

Diary of a Doctor
1942–1945

Joan F. Hickson

Edited by Ruth Skrine

EX LIBRIS PRESS

Published in 2013 by
EX LIBRIS PRESS
11 Regents Place
Bradford on Avon
Wiltshire
BA15 1ED

www.ex-librisbooks.co.uk

Origination by Ex Libris Press

Typeset in 11/13.75 Minion Pro

ISBN 978-1-906641-61-0

Printed by CPI Anthony Rowe
Chippenham

CONTENTS

PREFACE

by Ruth Skrine (*née* Hickson)

The author of these diaries, my mother Joan Hickson, was born at the end of the nineteenth century into a professional Birmingham family. Her father was a solicitor whose firm expanded to London, and when Joan was a medical student they moved to Whitchurch near Reading. The whole family had a deep love of the River Thames. Trips in a punt or one of the two family skiffs, as well as visits to Henley for the Regatta, provided some of her happiest memories. Her mother came from a traditional well-to-do family. She was a keen gardener with a sparkling personality and dancing blue eyes, who captured the heart of all those who met her, especially men of all ages.

Joan was sent to St Felix School in Southwold, Suffolk, where she developed a deep admiration for the forward-looking headmistress Miss Silcox. She qualified as a doctor from University College Hospital, where she met Eric Hickson, who became a general practitioner in Chippenham, Wiltshire. They lived for a short time in Morley House, a terraced house on the Bath Road, before building the family home, Green Gables. This house contained a consulting room, waiting room and well-stocked dispensary, as well as room for three children and two live-in maids.

At the beginning of her marriage Joan helped her husband in the practice, but she also trained in non-operative ophthalmology and worked in the Supplementary Ophthalmic Services in schools and seeing patients at home. For almost all her professional life she spent two mornings a week at the Eye Infirmary in Bath, completely unpaid until the introduction of the National Health Service in 1948.

How can we understand the passionate, often conflicted person Joan grew to be? After her death there was a box marked 'My most precious letters for my family to read'. Among them were three from her father addressed to 'Dear Johnnie'. Was there an unspoken regret that the first born had not been a boy, her parents unconsciously giving out mixed messages about what sort of person she should be? Certainly she competed with men on more than equal terms, maintaining that women in medicine always had to be better. Yet this record suggests that her hard head was won at some cost, for it is clear that she had an instinctive dislike for the messiness that is an integral part of looking after people's bodies. Perhaps her choice of ophthalmology was more than just a convenience, for eyes are a long way away from the dirtier parts of the body.

Her papers contained scraps of writing from an early age, but when it came to editing the diaries I found that they only started in a coherent way from the day after the Bath blitz in 1942, when she was 43 years old. As soon as peace returns in 1945 the fire goes out of them. The drama of the times, and her wish to record it for posterity, released her to write about some of her inner passions.

The most difficult of these passions to understand is her intense hatred of the church. My sister points out that the fury seems to be a gut response to clergymen and the panoply and symbols of the church, rather than a well worked-out intellectual atheism. I do not know when her feelings became so fixed, but I suspect that a deep dislike of all forms of hypocrisy and dishonesty was reinforced by her experiences of the First World War. At the beginning of that war clergymen were not expected or encouraged to enter the front lines and she felt they used the church as a shield. She and her sister both lost young men who were dear to them. Working as a medical student she must have been surrounded by mangled bodies and destroyed lives. Like so many of her generation she did not talk much about it.

During the editing process I have omitted some repetitive passages and regularised some stylistic details such as capitalisation, but I have refrained from imposing an artificial consistency on the text and have added nothing of substance. Real names are left as they appeared, with single initials for patients. The list of principal characters provides a key to members of her family, friends and colleagues at the time. In the notes I explain medical terms and give a short description of some of the places and people connected with the progress of the war, which the author followed with such great interest.

Here then is part of one person's long and mainly successful life story. As a postscript I have included a vignette of my mother in old age, written by my sister. The book is also a contemporary record of one middle-class family at an extraordinary time in the history of England.

ACKNOWLEDGEMENTS

I am grateful to my brother, Dr Arthur Hickson of Alsager, Cheshire, and my sister Elizabeth Murray (Bess/Biz) of Charlottesville, Virginia, USA, for allowing me to publish our mother's words. Bess and her husband Jim have provided support and advice, especially to the endnotes, but any mistakes are my own.

Sonia Dickinson of Bath suggested I should return to this record which had lain in a drawer for 15 years since I first worked on the hand-written source material.

Roger Jones of Ex Libris Press accepted the manuscript with encouraging enthusiasm.

My warmest thanks must go to my friend Hannah Hyam, whose advice has been invaluable and who has generously given so much of her time and professional expertise to copy-editing the final draft.

*Four generations: Joan looking out of the
picture; her mother sitting beside her and
cradling her great granddaughter. Joan's
daughter Ruth, the baby's mother,
is standing behind*

PRINCIPAL CHARACTERS

Family

Joan Whitelock, b. 1899, the author
Eric Hickson, b. 1895, her husband

Their children

Arthur, b. 1925   Ruth, b. 1929   Elizabeth (Biz), b. 1932

Joan's family

Her parents lived at Underwood, Whitchurch-on-Thames.
Mother (Mummy or FM)
Father (D)
Scoot, younger sister
Miles, younger brother
Hugh Meredith, a cousin of Joan's mother, Professor of
    Economics at Queen's University Belfast and a friend of
    E.M. Forster

Eric's family

Mother (Granny), Elizabeth Hickson (née Beck), who started and
ran Oldfeld, a private school in Swanage, Dorset
Jo, Eric's elder sister
Marcus, younger brother, who was disabled
Pip, younger sister, married to Robert Timberlake (Tim),
    headmaster of Lancaster Grammar school who was also
    housemaster of the school house for boarders
Arthur, youngest brother, married to Vera
Gundred, widow of Horace Beck, Granny's youngest brother
Conrad Beck, one of Granny's brothers, married to Aunt Annie
Sylvia Guthrie, one of Eric's cousins, a respected paediatrician in
Manchester

Others working or living in the household, past and present
Daisy, started as parlour maid in 1932 and became long-term
  housekeeper
Lucy, second maid
Simmy, Eric's secretary
Daphne Bryant, Eric's previous secretary
Mr Harlow, gardener
Mrs Harlow, one of Daisy's sisters
Mrs Bridgeman (Mrs B), another of Daisy's sisters.
Mrs Gillard, an elderly evacuee from Portsmouth

Family pets
Dogs, Jimmy, Gerda and Bertha
Cat, Mima

Joan's school friends
Frankie Lowe (née Champion)
Polly Furse
Helen Mcgillivray
'Squibs' (Mrs Mitchelmore)

Doctors and other medical staff
Mr John Bastow, consultant orthopaedic surgeon at the Royal
  United Hospital, Bath (RUH)
Mr Belsey, South-West Region chest specialist
Dr Boschi, GP with a practice in Great Pulteney Street, Bath
Dr Broomhead, army doctor who lived opposite Joan
Mr Richard Colley, consultant ophthalmologist, RUH; wife Mary
Dr and Mrs Eastes, both doctors running a practice in Marshfield
Nurse England, district nurse in Chippenham
Dr Hargreaves, psychologist (psychiatrist?) living in London
Dr Hirst, Eric's salaried assistant
Dr Kersley, consultant rheumatologist, RUH
Mr Kindersley (Charles), consultant surgeon, RUH; wife Peg

Dr Lawrence, GP in the rival practice in Chippenham
Mr Leech-Wilkinson, consultant obstetrician, RUH; wife Joan
Mr Leigh, honorary ENT consultant, RUH
Dr McKaigue (Mac), consultant physician, RUH; wife Mary
Mr Mitchell, honorary gynaecologist and obstetrician, RUH
Dr Nixon, Eric's senior partner in general practice
Dr Royal, GP who ran a practice in Castle Combe
Dr Spong, GP with a practice in a nearby village
Dr Tangye, Medical Officer of Health for Wiltshire
Mr Tizzard, consultant ophthalmologist, RUH
Dr Wheeler, Eric's GP partner in Corsham

Friends

The Awdrys, Eddie a solicitor in Chippenham, his wife Daphne
and children Daniel and Biddy
Basil Fletcher, one-time headmaster of Chippenham Grammar
School and then Professor of Education at Bristol University
Mr Hale, local vet related to Avice, who kept his children's pony
at Mr Self's farm
Sir Eric and Lady Holt-Wilson, friends and also patients. He
worked for the Secret Service in various capacities
Margaret Rudman, widow of the architect who designed Green
Gables
Avice Rita Wilson (*née* Dickinson), lived opposite and has
remained a good friend to all the family
Lina Wood, widow of previous vicar of a Chippenham parish

Joan and Eric on their wedding day, 1923

A camping and boating holiday on the Thames – see chapter 6

Green Gables in Chippenham; family home and doctor's surgery

Sisters and brother: Elizabeth (Biz), Ruth and Arthur at Green Gables

1

THE BATH BLITZ

27 April–7 May 1942

Monday 27 April 1942

After two noisy nights, which rumour said were centred on Bath, decided I must make contact with the Eye Infirmary,[1] and also our friends in the Circus. Thinking to minister to tired doctors and their wives deprived of cooking apparatus, I took four thermoses and two extremely small spirit stoves in the back of the car, over-optimistically as it turned out.

I shall never forget a blitzed town the morning after or regret that I had the experience of seeing it, though it was a good deal worse than I anticipated. Nothing much till Walter's nurseries[2] where there was a colossal crater. After that, glass and debris all over the road with occasional signs of greater damage. Traffic diverted down Walcot St with many fire hoses and engines and great activity by Civil Defence and rescue works etc. Made my way over endless hoses to the Guildhall and Abbey. A good deal of traffic so had to keep going in a stream. Tried to ask a policeman if it was possible to get round to the Circus and Eye Hospital, but he didn't know and waved me on.

I had my 'Doctor' notice down for once which helped to get through. Passed Boschi going in opposite stream so couldn't stop. He is the first doctor I have seen alive. It struck me that he was in a smaller shabbier car than usual and afterwards heard that his garage had fallen on his car, and that this was his wife's.

Abbey seems intact except for windows, but could not look round much owing to traffic jams (a good many cars with labels on obvious business). Turned up past Colmers and up Milsom St, which was practically intact, even the windows were in place. Tried to get to the Circus up Gay St but was deflected round Queen's Sq. where several houses demolished and fire hoses and static water in use and nearly empty. Up to the right through the park. Still streams of traffic – no one asking for a lift and everyone following their own business grimly. Tried to cut away to the right after the park, but held up some time by a burning church and people coping with it. Tried to cut round by the Circus but a big bomb crater in middle of road. Crescent looked shattered – not a window left. Many roofs damaged but standing, very desolate. Several cars outside with people piling in suitcases and obviously evacuating. No one to direct traffic and difficult to turn. I was obviously a nuisance to the Fire people but none of them asked 'Why the hell are you here?' or shouting for me to get out of the way. Was it my doctor notice, or was it not their business? Got into St James Sq. and could not get out again. Tried four or five roads – all blocked. Many fires raging, houses completely demolished, pathetic bits of furniture in the road, and people looking oh so tired. Quite the worst part so far. I began to feel despairing of ever getting anywhere and that I was merely in the way and it was not fair to block the traffic any more – but I dare not leave the car. Ultimately on trying the last road out I did get to a policeman on a crossroads who waved me on, so I went on and soon found myself passing the Cranhill Hotel[3] the wrong way! Whereupon I gave up and decided to get out of Bath anyway I could and work round afterwards. (Fortunately I had a full petrol tank.)

Reached the Eye Infirmary eventually after two and a half hours driving. Practically no windows, blood on the steps and devastation all round. Went in and found Matron rendering first aid and the waiting hall full of beds with recumbent forms. She said they were all alive but only just, and it had been pretty grim. Most of the in-patients had been sent home the day before and they were merely acting as a first aid point. Dirt, dust, broken glass and mess indescribable. Cooking on open fires. She refused my hot drinks and stoves, though she regretted this later. There seemed to be nothing medical to do. She was in the stage when she couldn't stop, and there were only a few trickling in and out. The WVS[4] were getting them away as soon as possible. Colley had been in and was OK, but he said everyone had been turned out of the Circus owing to a time bomb, so it was no good my attempting to get there. Some doubt about the safety of some doctors, but Mac and Charles OK and at RUH, with their wives at various places. I had assumed they would have come to us with no invitation if they had wanted somewhere to escape but apparently this idea was erroneous. It did not strike me as possible that after ten years or so people could know me so little.

News that there was a team of surgeons from Bristol, also a resuscitation team at the RUH, so there didn't seem to be much for me to do medically, so I decided to go home. Guinea Lane seemed to have a narrow space between the heaps of glass at each side, so got out quicker than I got in.

At Batheaston passed Colley who it turned out had just been to Chippenham to arrange with me for five children and three adults for the night. He had interviewed Daisy who had risen splendidly to the occasion and said 'of course' and didn't think where to put them first. She has her faults but is trumps in an emergency. Actually we had the five Colleys, but someone else made an offer for the other three out of their house, so everyone had a bed in the end. Arthur and Ruth not too keen on turning out of their rooms, but tolerably pleasant. Didn't see why it should be they to turn out, but they were occupying one large room each (spare room and nursery) which were the obvious ones in which to accommodate refugees. Came home with thermoses and stoves.

Tuesday 28 April
A quiet night and everyone feels better. An incredible amount of glass swept up, and many fire hoses removed, though a few still there, and rows of engines outside the Fire Station on Cleveland bridge. Few OPs[5] at the Eye Inf., and nurses all in trousers and still

rather shattered as had been expecting another raid so had not slept much for three nights. One basin of water for all the washing all morning. Telephones and electricity working. Windows starting to be boarded up. Matron nearly at the end of her tether, had not been able to keep warm or get any hot drinks in night as had to let out coal fires at night, and cold north east wind blowing through. Would have loved my stoves and thermoses today and of course I hadn't brought them.

Place still a frightful mess and everyone standing about swapping stories. Half the nurses have been sent home on holiday. Wards closed as no possibility of cooking or sterilising. A few OPs but not more than Colley could deal with easily. The obvious job that wanted doing seemed to be to clear up the mess, so I found brooms and a duster and swept and swept and swept, emptying piles of glass and dirt. Cleaned Matron's room which I think she appreciated, also swept all stairs and passages, much to the amazement of nurses and domestic staff who were all standing about gossiping instead of getting on with the work. I heard an amazed whisper go round – 'Dr Hickson is sweeping the stairs!' Felt I had really done a good job when I had finished, but half an hour later it was as bad as ever owing to cold north east wind blowing in bits of the pulverised Bath stone.

Stayed to scratch lunch with Matron and staff and then evacuated the last in-patient to Calne. Driving back to Chippenham I suddenly remembered to call in and say goodbye to the Nixons who were leaving the next day. All very polite and friendly if rather distant. Could whip up no emotion over it all, even jubilation, even after 17 years of suppressed animosity, though really becoming senior partner must be one of the biggest things that has ever happened to us. But somehow having got down to fundamental brass tacks of life and death in Bath, personal issues don't seem to count any more, and anyway the future of private practice is so uncertain. Colleys came to us again for the night.

Wednesday 29 April
A quiet day packing for children who decided to go to Whitchurch the day before and up to London to join school trains there, so as to be with the others if alternative routes had to be used.

Thursday 30 April
Devizes school clinic in morning and pushed off children in pm. Have never been so glad to see them go though at the last minute we all silently thought we might have been nicer to each other during the holidays. They have been appallingly adolescent all the time, touchy and inclined to take offence at anything said to them or any criticism or request to do anything. Don't see why they should or why the beastly old war should spoil things for them. I can remember feeling like it myself in the last war so ought to be sympathetic. But a perpetual state of busyness and fatigue drives me to chronic irritability, and though they understood the cause of it and would cope occasionally, it is naturally difficult for them to do so permanently, so it is a vicious circle.

They have had dreadful ructions with Daisy culminating in their 'leaving home'. A note said they would not return unless something drastic was done about her. A dreadful bombshell as both sides were quite sure they were completely right. Daisy vowed she had hardly spoken to them the whole holidays and only asked them to go up the town once. They said she nagged at them incessantly and made home not worth living in. All very difficult as Daisy is quite invaluable and irreplaceable to me and by her complete charge of housekeeping and menage generally, enables me to keep on pretty full-time work which I should simply have to chuck if she went. Eric finally intervened and talked to both camps and patched things up for the moment, and next holidays they are both to have outside jobs. I can't bear them not to feel that home is a peaceful place and a refuge even if they are in the wrong. I suppose that after the war she will have to go, and I shall have to put up with a dirty house for the sake of peace, but at the moment it would be impossible to manage without her.

Friday 1 May

To Bath Eye Inf. again and did see some OPs though rather gloomily with windows felted up and only a poor battery in my torch. Forgot to put my personal raid story for Tuesday. Colley had gone, and Matron, Sister and I had collected in the most dishevelled out-patients at the last gasp, wondering if we could tackle another job before eating the communal stew, when in blows a well-dressed and shaved, clean, fat, aggressive man with a pipe of good tobacco. Obviously had slept all night (not in Bath) and had a hot bath and shave and eggs and bacon for breakfast.

Man: Please send an ambulance to remove two bodies at once, Sister.

Sister: I am afraid we don't have any ambulances here. We are a first aid point only.

Man: You don't, don't you – but you can get in touch with them and get one sent.

Matron: Yes, you may use our telephone. It is over there.

Man: I am not going to phone. That is your business. I am from the Ministry of Works. I am busy.

We were so taken aback and all so done in that there was a horrified silence and no one said a word. Then Matron said very quietly 'Very well, I will phone for you.'

As he went out I said in a very loud voice 'Well, I never heard the like of that before', but I wished afterwards I had said 'What damned bloody hell of a cheek.' I was absolutely boiling that anyone should speak like that to Matron who had spent three nights without sleep on duty continuously and responsible for everyone there. She said everyone would do exactly as she told them but wanted to be told every little thing and guided and overseen. The first night she had 40 people to look after, patients and staff, though they gradually diminished and as many as possible went home.

A show like this brings out acutely those who can lead and those who must be led, and it is not always those in authority who come up to scratch.

Another Bath story concerns a quite inconspicuous little man from Chippenham, no one we knew or had ever heard of. He happened on a heap of rubble that had been a house where he had reason to believe there were people buried. He at once organised a party and started digging. The aimless, sightseeing crowd became a nuisance and would not keep back. Ultimately a special constable appeared and was greeted with joy by man, who asked him to control the crowd. 'Dunno as I can do that' was the reply, 'dunno as I am allowed to.'

And another. The first aid point at the house of an ex-nurse who had shut up and gone off without a word, and the husband very annoyed that casualties arrived there. Also, various WVS ladies had been driving about the town with labels on their cars getting extra petrol, just went off without a word, with the result that the conscientious ones left behind worked day and night on feeding, evacuation etc. These people did extremely well by all accounts.

And then there was John Bastow who was fire-watching in the Circus and was so busy putting out incendiary bombs that his own house was completely burnt out. His wife escaped with exactly what she stood up in and nothing more.

The feeding and fire arrangements seem to have been excellent from all accounts. Strings of fire engines and hoses from all over the country were sent and fresh teams with their own food to take over every few hours. If a house was too far gone for hope they soaked the adjacent ones and stopped it spreading.

Food was rushed into the town from all quarters, wholesalers etc., and as many people left town there was no lack. Several Queen's Messenger canteens[6] did noble work, butchers set up stalls in the roads and squares and seemed to acquire meat and sausages which were selling ration free. A blitzed sweet shop man who escaped with his life received a consignment of chocolate and biscuits the next day so he made them up into equal parcels and sold from a table in the street. Ice cream people appeared who were very welcome. Fortts[7] were made to open their reserves of tins and serve lunches, which they put out on plates on trestle tables.

All drinking water and milk had to be boiled which made a

bit of a problem as there were few who had anything on which to boil it. The Bath Gas Co. is the best and cheapest in England but had been almost exterminated. However there were lorries going round with large tanks of drinking water, I suppose brought from outside, from which people could fill jugs. The electricity never failed, and the telephone only locally.

There was too much sightseeing with people saying they would love to help but it wasn't their job, or having to be told what to do rather than finding something and getting on with it. Against this, there were countless stories of bravery and people surviving after being buried for days. One dear old railway man, who had chronic glaucoma and who had lost both arms in a railway accident years ago, came saying he was afraid his eyes weren't quite so good as they might be. As he had been buried for an hour he had unfortunately lost his drops, and didn't like to bother us before!

A good many people had broken or lost their glasses, but strangely enough there has not been one perforating injury in spite of all the glass about. As always, many were fussing about nothing, while the ones with something really serious did not bother us or apologised for giving trouble.

I finished OPs in good time and should have been home in time for lunch for the first time for months if I had not had to pick up Elizabeth from the Colleys where I had left her to milk goats. I found that the wretch had gone off for miles on a bicycle with Peter Colley to look at anti-aircraft guns and had to be pursued. Was full up with appointments in pm so the delay meant no decent time for lunch. Quite unreasonably irritated about this.

Saturday 2 and Sunday 3 May
A quiet weekend of odd jobs and garden. All this Bath business seems to have completely removed any desire to earn a living or do anything more than the immediate job under one's nose. Planning or arranging anything ahead seems just silly. Even when making an appointment I feel like saying 'If any of us are here then.'

Mac was at the Chippenham hospital in pm[8] and Mary came with him and stopped off here. She looked dreadfully tired and ten years older and was jumpy of aeroplanes and bangs and was nervously restless. Part of the area behind the Circus is still evacuated owing to an unexploded bomb in the road. (I've only just realised that an unexploded bomb is quite different from a time bomb.) It has gone down more than 30ft, and digging for it they are finding more Roman remains. Apparently one bomb exploded in the grass patch in the middle of the Circus but strangely did not put any house flat, only removing roofs, windows and odd bits. Another in Kindersley's area exploded and did practically no damage (his wife had gone to Taunton suffering from nervous shock after first having her photo taken sitting on the bomb!). By far the worst mess was at the back where the remains of the Regina Hotel have been thrown into the back rooms of this block of the Circus.

Mac had to climb in at the back to salvage his electrocardiograph, which was his one idea. He took it off to the RUH leaving Mary to collect some clothes. While he was gone a policeman saw Mary and forcibly ejected her. She had not made another rendez-vous to meet Mac, and waited 3 hours on the corner below the Eye Hospital. She would have sold her soul for a cup of tea in my car. It was on the Monday when I was there and trying to find her or someone similar with my thermoses and I never knew. I begged her to have our flat for the duration of the war and she thought it would be heaven. But Mac said it was too far out, and they must be nearer the hospital. They are at Freshford at the moment but want to get in even nearer. Mary wouldn't borrow anything although she is almost as big as I am and is one of the few people who could have done so. Both were grateful out of proportion for our small offer. They did not seem to realise that we were hurt because they hadn't just arrived or assumed we should have them. Both are windy about another raid tonight as Exeter had it a third time last night, and Bath followed Exeter before.

Colley rang up to ask if he could dump the three children on us for the night but not themselves so had to say yes and conceal my conviction that other people's children are just about the last straw. Broke the news to Elizabeth who took it reasonably well though she had said before 'All these Colleys are too much for me.' I know exactly what she meant as all five of the family tear round everywhere and never stop talking, whereas one alone is really very nice and interesting. I must have concealed my real feelings from Colley as he thinks I am a good-natured person who doesn't mind the house being filled up at a moment's notice, as of course I don't when the visitors are adults.

Tuesday 5 May
Beginnings of normality in Bath. OPs of course very dark due to sort of tarred felt windows and I cannot see KP[9] (always a bête noire of mine), I must really make an effort about a fresh battery for torch.

Wednesday 6 May
Clinic at Devizes Mental Hospital. Discovered a very melancholic old thing with a chronic glaucoma missed for many years. What to do with her? She is too mental to go into Eye Hospital for operation and Colley would never operate at Devizes. I temporised with Pilocarpine[10] drops till next time, but got thoroughly ticked off by him, though he has often done the same himself and I think he would have done in this case, but I can never do the right thing.

Thursday 7 May
Saw a sandpiper by van[11] on the riverbank in pm. It is incredible that we have lived here 18 years and never found this place before. It would be perfect if not for Chippenham's small boys who swarm around, but considering it is so near and so attractive that is not surprising. The woodpecker went to his hole and a kingfisher almost hit my car. Water rat has eaten the moorhen's eggs. The phone went 8 times between 12 and 4.30 when we got off, and endless people rolled up with minor ailments when Eric wasn't in, including a bloody scalp wound just at lunchtime. They always seem to arrive at that time and always make me feel sick. After

having spent some time nearly vomiting as I cut off matted hair and blood, I found the wretched girl was someone else's patient after all, and could quite well have gone to her own doctor as it was not serious. I was furious.

In the afternoon I wrote to Tangye, turning down his latest plea for more school medical inspections, also to the headmistress of a private, evacuated school that wanted the same. I think I must be getting really old to turn down good remunerative work like that, but felt I just could not face having every minute of every day filled up with a definite pre-arranged programme, and no flexibility for contingencies or emergencies. At the moment it seems more important to be able to give some help to my friends when bombed out, or take over holiday work for Colley if required, or leap into any breech that arises, than to sweat on the routine of school inspections for £3.3s per day, though I once jumped at this. Anyway I loathe the work so intensely and feel it is so useless and a waste of a doctor's time. An intelligent nurse or mother could sort out any problems and send the child to their own GP with much better results. What can possibly be the good of counting up the number of tonsils or adenoids only as opposed to both together and with or without glands in the neck? Going through the damned cards 8 or 9 times, never getting the wretched statistics right – and feeling I am too old now to do it any more just for the money. Anyway the Chancellor of the Exchequer will get half if I do much more extra work as it will take us over the super-tax line. I always said if we ever got to that point I wouldn't begrudge the tax, but now we are nearly there the difference between being only normally tired at the end of the day and being done in with never five minutes to spare and with no energy left for an emergency, is too great to be worth the little extra money involved.

It has been such bliss this winter with an assistant to help with surgery for the first time, and only occasionally other people's work besides my own. Not to feel chronically tired, and not too done in the evenings so that sometimes I can to do a little something – like this bit of writing or sticking in a 20 year accumulation of photos.

The writing has been rather like the photos, a thing I have always meant to do when I had the time, which was never. The accumulation of back stuff was always discouraged until Eric said, 'Start a new book with this year's and gradually fill in the back ones as you can.' A brilliant idea as otherwise one never catches up, and in the case of writing never catches the emotion fresh. How one does forget emotions, and can look back completely dispassionately on incidents which have roused one to frenzy one way or the other in the past. Though with my wretched writing I can never get the emotion I mean on paper and the result is incredibly dull, clumsy and lifeless. I gave up attempting to write after my miserable failures ten years ago, and decided that I was a doctor and not a journalist, but the Bath blitz has shaken it out of me.

We seem to be living in such extraordinary times and doing such extraordinary things that the random jottings of the doings of an ordinary middle class family might be of interest, if only to one's children in the future. Or someone who can write might be capable of editing it. Actually any medical practice could provide interesting incident for many books, but medical memoirs are usually dull because so tactfully expurgated. I am determined not to do this here, or to moderate what language seems appropriate to the occasion!

The temptation to digress into the past will be extreme and probably acceded to during spells of nothing but the daily round and common task, but must be resisted strongly if it means getting behind with the current issue. I'm sorry I didn't get the emotion down before. Probably the most interesting part of my life was before I was 40 yrs when I was building a career and family. After 40 yrs one tends to live on the fruits of one's labours and become laissez-faire about everything, Before that, when one could have been interesting, the lack of time was too acute, especially for such as I who must sleep eight hours to have any brain or temper at all. However it is no good crying over spilt past intentions or missed opportunities, and anyway what does it matter? It will all be burnt out in the Chippenham blitz anyway. And if not, my whole craze may die out when life becomes normal again.

2

. . . AND AFTERWARDS

8–19 May 1942

Friday 8 May 1942

Charles Kindersley rang up to know if he could bring Peg with him and leave her here while he was at the hospital and have lunch first. Fortunately for once I did not have many appointments in pm. They arrived before I got back from Bath. Peg horrified me even more than Mary Mac. She looked a complete wreck. They had been sleeping in different places almost every night. Charles spent several nights at the RUH, and again would not stay with us because too far out. Peg had got practically no clothes out, but Charles had salvaged his fishing rods! The psychology of what these people have got out when they could only get a few things is, though pathetic, intensely interesting. Bastow got things from his consulting room, Mrs Colley her jewellery, Mac his electrocardiograph and clothes for Mary, Miss Brabazon[1] some china ornaments while her sister grabbed tinned food. Poor Peg had no clothes or sanitary towels (though Charles did get her a whole case later, so that she swam in them and nothing else).

The Kindersleys had finally fetched up in the Kersleys' house on the opposite side of the Circus. Mrs Kersley had left it, and Peg was trying to cook for 8 on one oil stove and one electric fire turned upside down. Four doctors were trying to practise from the house and she didn't know where anything was in another person's house, so she had reason to be a bit shattered. I put her on the chesterfield in the sun after lunch and besought her to sleep while I saw patients, but she was at the stage when she couldn't, and would fuss round mending her stockings and doing letters. I did persuade her to take two pairs of shoes (she could wear mine, to my great surprise) and a blouse, but would not hear of anything else. They were both quite inordinately grateful for the interlude.

These blitzed people seem to have a special psychological reaction. Charles recognised it and called it 'Plymouth Pride'. Apparently in the Plymouth blitzes the city was so determined to manage with its own resources that it would not call in fire or medical help from outside when needed, to the city's detriment.

In Bath the National Fire Service saved that happening by sending help automatically. Charles is keen enough on medical efficiency to see that it didn't happen medically. Bristol sent teams of surgeons and resuscitators, but the Pride seems to have taken hold of individuals. They won't ask for help, or say what they would like done to help them, and if they get it are almost too gushingly grateful about any slight service rendered, which is embarrassing and makes them difficult to deal with.

Eric would take them out to look at the wisteria and pears, which seemed to me dreadful, drawing attention to one's own good fortune as opposed to their woes, but Eric said it was a good thing to take their minds off it. They are completely oblivious to any outside news, have seen no paper and heard no wireless for days, had not heard of the Battle of the Coral Sea[2] which I suppose is the biggest naval action since the war began. After we had told them about it they said later that Eric 'seemed to be interested in something about a ship'!

Audrey Holt-Wilson looked in with one of the few existing copies of *German Spies at Bay*,[3] which is the genuine authentic story of all the chief spies in the last war and how they were caught. Her husband was the head of the whole organisation and vouches for its correctness, as opposed to most of the rubbish of the usual spy story that one reads. She is worried about her children who went to Torquay by pre-arrangement the day after the third Exeter blitz, and the trains were crowded and disorganised, but she had heard that they had arrived eventually at 10pm.

Saturday 9 May
Basil Fletcher blew in during the middle of morning surgery on his way from Bristol to Romsey. It was like a breath of fresh air to talk to a really sane person again who had not been in Bath. He was cheerful and very optimistic about how things were going and could discuss world events, which no one here has been able to do in the last fortnight. It is perfectly understandable and I am sure we should be the same under similar circumstances if our loves and our property were destroyed or in danger, but all the same it's a joy to see someone from outside it all.

The foregoing all sounds as if morale in Bath had collapsed and everyone had given way but the case is completely the opposite. Everyone just carries on with their work, if not in exactly the same way the nearest to it that they can. All the stories of individual bravery and heroism are true, but I suppose that being doctors we get a bit deeper than the facade of normality, and tend to hear about the things that have gone wrong and need assistance.

At lunchtime Peg rang up to say that the Circus bomb had been removed (after digging down 30ft) and that they had got back to their house and were starting on the mess. We said we would go down and help so I threw some tea and supper into baskets and we got off in half an hour. Poor Bertha's face was the epitome of tragedy. Seeing us with our oldest clothes and picnic baskets she immediately jumped to the conclusion we were going to the van and was jubilant, and when we said no it was heartrending to see her face fall. I have never known a dog able to put so much tragedy into its brown eyes, and that is saying a good deal.

We took enough tea and supper for the Macs as well; but unfortunately got so involved with the Kindersleys that we didn't get to No.16 till 4 o'clock when we organised a tea break. By this time the Macs had left, completely exhausted and with no tea and would have been thankful for some, I subsequently learnt. I always seem to just miss the bus when I try to help them.

When we arrived, Eric and I flew into No.18, not tired and full of bright ideas from outside. We went to the consulting room where the windows were intact. 'Well,' said Eric brightly, 'This room is not too bad. We could easily make this habitable for you. Let's start here.' 'Oh,' replied Peg 'We have just done this room!' And that was what it was like. First removal of broken glass, bits of stone and plaster, stuff from down the chimney, splintered wood and debris from window frames or bits of the Regina Hotel. These were taken up in dustpans, emptied into buckets, which were subsequently emptied onto piles of rubbish in the road outside the front door of the beautiful and usually immaculate Circus. 2nd stage was to hoover, then 3rd stage ordinary sweeping and dusting, and then Rep. Mist.[4] ad infinitum. As fast as one layer was removed more blew in from the back windows with most of the powdered stone from the Regina. Looking at it from a detached point of view afterwards, I think the bits did get smaller each time, though at the time they did not seem to do so. It was discouraging to say the least, to find a room on which one had spent much time and labour smothered with dense, white dust again in a few minutes.

Eric and Charles went up to the roof and shovelled the Regina into buckets which they organised on a pulley with the van rope and tackle, and were quite happy doing this for hours, emptying into the back garden. Charles says he will then request the Regina to come and remove their property!

The two Hoffmans were helping, a charming pair of whom I had heard but not met before. He is a budding physician now in the Navy, but home on leave, and handy with a broom, and she had brought two vacuum cleaners. We could have done with ours too. Eric had an interlude when he dashed back to Chippenham to deliver a baby, but returned.

At 4 o'clock we knocked off, pushed the K's into chairs and poured tea and bread and jam down them, dirty as we all were. We dare not wash as there was very little water, and we did not know if the drains were clear, so washing up a cup became a major problem and we used one knife and cut and spread the bread on a piece of brown paper.

Mrs Kersley reappeared from her holiday, a dream of loveliness with perfect make up and platinum blond hair, but rather too exaggerated to be true. However she did take the cups to wash, and produced hot supper for us all at her house later in a lovely silk shirt and exotic rust-coloured slacks, so deserves a good mark for this.

We went on again till 7.30pm, fed and got home about 10pm, pretty beat from the unwonted (for us) exercise. Found Elizabeth having a tantrum, probably because she had been left at a moment's notice and felt deserted and out of things. She carried on till after midnight when she suddenly pulled herself together and came into my bed where we all drank lime juice and ate biscuits. Just got off to sleep when the darned phone went, and it was the police wanting Eric for a 'drunk in charge'. He pushed them onto Hirst so there is some advantage in having an assistant, though by this time we were thoroughly disturbed again.

Sunday 10 May
Woke up feeling a bit battered, but determined to help the Macs today if possible. Got them by phone at Freshford and arranged to meet them at their house in the pm with tea and supper. Thought we would go back to the Kindersleys meanwhile but found that today we were not welcome and everything was wrong. Boys had arrived from Cambridge, 6–8 builders were in house doing roof and windows and Peg only wanted to be alone. Anyway it seemed hopeless to continue cleaning while the men were trampling about, but may be more worthwhile when the windows are blocked and a certain amount stopped blowing in. They are using a sort of waterproof linen material for this. It makes it all very dark and gloomy but does keep out a certain amount of mess. We gave the boys rather a choice meal of slices of spam on bread and butter with cold sliced potatoes on top and the whole wrapped round with a lettuce leaf, and fruit salad drunk out of our picnic drinking mugs which we could take home and wash. Total washing up there was one knife, which was actually wiped on paper instead.

The Macs decided not to come into their house eventually as

their doors wouldn't open (the Kindersleys' wouldn't shut) and they were afraid of structural damage so decided to have it vetted by builders before starting to cope. We came home with a vacuum unused, whereas yesterday it would have been invaluable. It is difficult to know exactly what is wanted each day as it changes so quickly, but hot tea and coffee seem to be the great things, in any amount at any time.

Really very glad to get home and get a bit of a sit as it is our fire watching night. At 9pm we listened to Churchill's two years in office speech. I have never heard him so optimistic. He was almost rollicking and made us rock with laughter. A great relief as any highfalutin' stuff would not have gone down well in our state of fatigue.

Monday 11 May

Oh for a shampoo and wave. My hair is in the last stages of filth and awfulness although I tied it up. No prospect of getting it done till there is gas unless I do it myself which means foregoing the wave, and as there is no vestige of perm left this is a grim prospect. The Pounds' shop where I always go is OK but they do everything on gas, and their home crashed about them and they were bruised, shocked and buried but not seriously injured. They have not reopened yet as are helpless without gas. Thought of lending them my mother's old spirit tong heater! Have now found a home for all my other odd electric and spirit things.

Eric on the warpath about Nurse England's petrol. They have been cutting her down and down and she has now run out, and the fool clerks at County Offices talk glibly about using a bicycle. Little do they realise what 24 hrs a day duty means year after year, when they arrive at 9.30am (or later) and take at least an hour's break for lunch, and shut up shop at 5pm. Nurse England does about three people's work on the district and is one of the few remaining fanatical people with a mission, no other aim or object in life than to do her work well. She never stops and is nearly at breaking point as it is. She is damned well going to get as much petrol as she wants if we have to write to the Times or our MP about it. There will be a public stink made by us about people getting it for church or shopping if difficulties are made about hers.

The worst of it is that being a nurse she is inclined to accept the decision of authority and try to carry on instead of saying she can't and won't. We have had no trouble about ours as we made it clear early on that we must have it or would shut up shop, when there would soon be an uproar. We will make a fuss for her and if publicity is necessary it will be easier to do for her than for ourselves.

Mary Mac rang me up after lunch rather depressed having just got into her house. I had three patients to see here but was determined to get to her somehow, so polished them off as quickly as I could and set off with tea and the Electrolux. I cannot seem to manage to take the right thing on the right day. Their house was considerably worse than the Kindersleys'. Large boulders had been flung into their back rooms. A piano was in small bits and all their lovely drawing room covered inches deep in glass and stone, both powdered and in larger bits. The wall between the drawing room and their bedroom was down and much more plaster, ceiling and door damage. Several lovely Heppelwhite dining room chairs pulped and great chunks gorged out of the sideboard by flying stone. They had no one extra to help them apart from her maid (who is a treasure), but I can't see Mac organising ropes and buckets and getting black all over in his shirtsleeves as Charles did. They need Eric's help badly but he is busy this week having rather pushed things off from Sat and Sun. He has twins in the offing and is full up with appointments tomorrow. Altogether a very awkward moment, but should like to help them a bit as no one seems to be doing so. There house was always so perfect, too perfect for our taste with everything to period and never a speck of dust or anything out of place. Having no children and no animals Mary lavished all her energy and what affection she was not giving to Mac on her things, and was very down about it all. She said she would never be able to live there again, though on the whole she was less neurotic about it than some of the other wives.

Rain at last just in time to save next winter's food for us, but I fear it will find many leaky roofs in Bath.

Picked up an RAF man who complimented me on my driving. Felt this was a very great honour from the RAF as I never feel I am a real driver. Also an airborne man who might have known Miles if I had thought to ask him. Also a traffic control military policeman who had been doing a lot of work in Bath. He was very sore because the Army had to take over all traffic control for a fortnight except for two hours when the King and Queen were driving through when the Civil Police took over.

Tuesday 12 May
OPs in the morning, becoming more normal. Took sandwiches and ate them in Matron's room, then went straight to the Macs with tea for them, and the vacuum which today was of great use though it kept getting choked and having to be emptied and shaken every 10 minutes or so. Shall become quite a good housemaid at this rate.

Wednesday 13 May
Biz's birthday (she is nine). We managed to raise her a tent from salvage stock, though not obviously damaged and she had several other parcels despite the war.

Saw several patients after surgery and then set out for Bath with Eric at about midday. The Macs need a strong and handy man very badly. Decided to embark on getting the stair carpet up (a lovely deep red pile) which was getting completely ruined by the squad of first aid men filling in windows who were treading all the muck in. Got very intrigued as the colour gradually became visible. Thought Eric would do the taking up, but he got involved clearing an outside shed where electrocardiograms are developed, so tackled it myself. All the half landings were professionally fitted and nailed down with extreme efficiency (not so nice to undo). I don't believe I have ever taken up a carpet before, but one lives and learns. Poor Mac is very upset in case the same happens to us in Chippenham and he will feel he will have to return the aid in kind! Of course we should never expect this of him. After all, he did spend most of last Easter Sunday deciding about Elizabeth's appendix, and the Communist ideal 'From each according to his ability . . . ' etc could be applied here. We seem to have the ability to jump in and cope with a mess, and provide food at the right moment, whereas if it had been a question of going to their funerals, nothing would have induced us to do so!

Mac insisted on taking us out to lunch at Fortts. I think he felt it was the least he could do. We didn't feel exactly like going to Fortts in the stage of dirt and shabbiness that we were, Eric in his very oldest 'Sunday' trousers, though to be consistent with my communist ideas I should have enjoyed it. But being me of course I did not enjoy being seen in public looking a sight and with my hair ghastly. Worked again at the stairs till four when we pushed some tea down them and rushed home. Unfortunately Eric's five o'clock patient was on the doorstep, and he just had to change and clean up before becoming a doctor again, but we explained what we had been doing and all was well.

'The Gondoliers' on the wireless in the evening and we were so physically tired we were just about fit to listen to it and nothing else. Elizabeth was taken to 'The Pirates of Penzance' done by the Chippenham girls club. She was thrilled to the marrow, perhaps as much as anything at going to an evening performance. Sorry her first Gilbert and Sullivan should have been quite so amateur and a poor amateur at that, but she enjoyed it *tout de même*.

Thursday 14 May
Devizes school clinic in morning. Went to Bath in afternoon till 6.30pm, cutting hospital committee as we felt it was too theoretical to sit through such a thing in our present mood. Tackled Mary's bedroom, which hadn't been touched. This only leaves the drawing room completely untouched and everyone has funked this, and it is difficult to get in and out with the partition all hanging down in front of the door.

Saw the Bastows for the first time since the Blitz. They were remarkably cheerful, having lost everything except a little out of the consulting room and downstairs. They said they were so jolly thankful to be alive at all they weren't worrying about anything else, and indeed it is extraordinary that they are, as he saw the bomb fall on the Regina. The mental strain seems to have been greatest on the people who were kept out of their homes for a fortnight not knowing if they were going up in smoke and flames or not, and then having all the mess to cope with.

Came home and had a bath before going to supper with Holt-Wilsons. Felt much cleaner except for hair about which I can do nothing. It is too ghastly for words. Looking at it in the glass I thought 'Mon Dieu, am I really as grey as that?' Probably a certain amount will come out in the wash. We now have gas in Chippenham relayed direct from Bristol, but not in Bath yet, though there is frequently a strong smell in the road, as if they were trying it out to see which pipes still want sealing off.

Eric has now finished the spy book he was reading and I am half way through it. It isn't actually very exciting to read as it is merely the office files of each case with no embroidery or added colour, but is the actual facts. We got Sir Eric Holt-Wilson going on various unpublished and unprintable cases, which were more interesting. As with medicine or anything else it is the unprintable stories that are by far the most interesting.

Friday 15 May
Eyes all day so no time for salvage operations. Eric had a baby before breakfast and another before tea so was late and rushed for both surgeries, with patients waiting before he got in. Even so, it felt like quite a slack day in the evening not having done any hard manual work.

Saturday 16 May
Went to Macs again immediately after lunch and actually got Mac into shirtsleeves! He had a beautiful navy pin stripe suit on and

apparently couldn't produce any 'Sunday' trousers, so Mary tied one of her white aprons round him with the result that he looked exactly like a grocer carving cheese. He did fill a few buckets with glass but would not empty them out of the front door himself, and carefully put on his coat again before coming to see us off. Eric, with his help, managed to get the partition which had come down between their bedroom and drawing room back and nailed roughly into place, so that it at any rate prevents a lot of stuff blowing through from one to the other. We also moved the remnants of the piano off the carpet with a view to taking up the latter but did not get near this as had wasted a lot of time on the partition, and Eric had to be back for 5 o'clock appointments. We were very sorry to have to go so soon, just when we felt energetic enough to tackle the drawing room, which was enough to appal the most stout-hearted.

They decided not to work on the Sunday but to come to us to rest instead. A pity to miss the opportunity when we could have helped them for longer, but it will give me a chance to catch up a bit with odd jobs which have all got left, to say nothing of the garden where weeds are swamping everything.

Sunday 17 May

Paid books[5] and did a good bit of arrears of writing. It is heaven to have a slack day. Rained on and off all day, so that in between showers dashed out and tried to weed, getting in a frightful muddy mess and doing more harm than good. However the rain is doing an immense amount of good and should be getting down to potatoes and fruit by now.

The whole household wakened in the middle of the night by an idiot who put his finger on the bell and hardly took it off till Eric had got down (never a very rapid process). One would have thought there was at least a femoral artery spurting on the doorstep, but he found that it was only a request to visit some woman who had been 'sick in the night'. Really some people are the limit. He went nevertheless.

Macs came in pm and Mary went to bed and to sleep after tea. We had put Elizabeth's birthday tent up to see what it was like, but it rained so much we couldn't get it down again, so it had to stay up for several days. The Macs would love to have the flat but still feel that it is too far away from Bath.

Monday 18 May
Leech-Wilkinson at hospital in pm and came back for tea. First time we had seen him since the Blitz. He had a pretty bad time apparently with a good bit of damage and the place where they had been standing a minute before swept away. Seems to have cleared his own mess with a minimum of fuss. I always rather liked him but felt he was a bit 'soft' and almost too sympathetic and human with his patients, but his behaviour seems to have been far from soft. He is quite sure that he and his wife were saved literally 'by the grace of God'. Strange that I can get on with or like anyone who feels like that, but I can, and he is so honest and genuine and also has a brain which makes him quite interesting intellectually as well. He was certainly one of the least neurotic post-Blitz people that I have seen. Is it because he and his wife are as one, or because he has a religion? Certainly the latter must lead to great security of mind just like a child has if it gets on with its parents, but I cannot see how anyone with any education at all could really contemplate such beliefs, though I know some do.

Tuesday 19 May
A shampoo at last in the dinner hour after OPs. Blissful to have a clean head again. Heard all Mrs Pound's experiences of 5 storeys of house having fallen on top of her which were some of the worst yet. She said the time lag was so awful, hearing one crash on top of another. I had always been told that one didn't hear the bomb that hit you, but suppose that does not apply to a crashing house. Can't think how they were not all killed, but they managed to climb out, up fallen walls that they would not have thought possible in the daytime. They had a very miserable few days, filthy and with no

clothes. The ones they had on were torn to ribbons. If only I had found them they would have been overjoyed at my thermoses, or to come out here and be lent things to carry on with.

Their shop is all right, which is something, but they have been able to do very little because of lack of gas. The house where they had their flat is to be demolished but is at present considered unsafe to fetch anything out of, though one man did go in and found Mrs Pound a coat. They will have to wait until it is demolished and then pick what they can out of the ruins – a grim and filthy task. All over Bath now are bits of smashed furniture and filthy and torn clothes being picked out from the debris, and people going through the rubbish like old rag and bone men to salvage some of their precious belongings.

Couldn't keep away from the Macs altogether so went up to see how they were getting on and eat my sandwiches with them (forgot to do so under the drier) at 3.15pm. They had not got much further with their drawing room.

3

LIFE GOES ON

20 May–11 June 1942

Wednesday 20 May 1942

The question of voluntary work is a very difficult one. The better Tories of the old feudal type all say that one should give service to the community in the form of public work of all sorts, and many of them do it very well and have time and private means enough to do so. On the other hand a great deal of the work is very badly done, or not done at all if inconvenient. The Left tend to say that the principal of voluntary work is all wrong, and would be better if done by properly trained and appointed people as a paid job. Personally I think there is a frightful lot of snobbishness about it. I have been talking to Mrs S who gave up her job after many years in the clerical department at Westinghouse to live as a lady of very small means. She has been slaving away at the British Restaurant[1] for many weeks. I said that I thought that after having once been started these were to be run by paid staff at prices which would make them independent but not profit making. She was horrified at the idea, saying that if there was a question of paid help she would cease immediately, that it would never do to mix paid and voluntary help. I am sure that she does this work because she gets a social kick out of meeting other women whom she considers socially superior, and not from any sense of community. I cannot see the argument that the same work can be perfectly genteel and ladylike if undertaken as a charity, but beneath contempt if paid for and done as a proper job. I should not feel insulted if offered a salary for my Eye Hospital work, in fact I think it is a scandal that hospital work should still be unpaid and that doctors have been exploited by the public and the big insurance companies for far too long.

Certainly the argument that voluntary work is badly done does not apply to doctors working in hospitals. That always come first, and if it is a case of holidays or sickness when something has to be missed it is always the private and remunerative work that must be given up first. Duty and loyalty to the hospital come before anything else – at least that is so with all reputable members of the profession, certainly all our friends. We have occasionally come across consultants who have said 'Oh, a hospital patient' when rung up about a case, but very seldom, and those individuals have never been sent a case again by us, hospital or private.[2]

Thursday 21 May
Devizes school clinic in the morning but I had to see a well-to-do patient and her son first. She is very hurt because having his T's and A's out has not immediately cured his cough, and also because he has some impetiginous patches on his ears which she looks upon as a personal insult in some way. She now wants him to have short-wave therapy in London and not Bristol. She is a person of the 'something must be done immediately' type, and thinks that every symptom should have its appropriate treatment or injection and be immediately cured. She is one of the loveliest things I have ever seen, with natural platinum blond hair, very little make-up, and perfect taste in tweeds and cashmeres. Her husband is the loose-limbed, tweed jacket, old flannel bagged, rolling-on-the-lawn-with-puppies type of Hon. Admiral, with no 'side' and a much easier and more charming manner than a similarly placed general or army magnate would probably have had. But oh such neurotics, both of them. Always so careful and protective, trying to do the right thing about their children and themselves, completely defeating their own object with their search for security, and having produced two weaklings who are nanny and mother ridden, full of asthma, hay fever and susceptibility to infections of all sorts.

Colley looked in after his clinic in pm, to see a case I have been looking after for him in the Chippenham hospital. Gave him five newts in a bucket to take home (the swimming pool is being emptied).[3] He had to go via Melksham to see another patient and the bucket slopped all over the car, which annoyed him very much. He stayed to tea and I told him about a conversation I had recently with Biz on the subject of virgins. She wanted to know what one was exactly and after going into the matter in some detail she said 'Yes, I see. Was J.F. a virgin?' As she was the only one of our very pure and proper governesses who might not have been, this was a bit of a poser, but I had to give her the benefit of the doubt and say 'Yes, of course.' Colley said that none of his boys (eldest aged 12) had thought about the male side of it at all, although they have masses of animals with young – goats, dogs, chickens, cats – but apparently no obvious mating has been done on the premises. I can't help thinking that there must be a hitch-up in many parents' minds about this, even though they may be quite modern and progressive and full of explanations about the female side of birth.

Certainly none of my family has suffered from ignorance. With Jimmy and Gerda carrying on all over the garden nothing was hidden, causing Ruth to remark 'Poor Jimmy, I hope I don't ever treat my husband like that and walk away at the critical moment.' Years before this both Ruth and Arthur were in the habit of discussing Mima's matrimonial affairs and offspring with the chimney sweep. I don't know why it always was the sweep but somehow it was and I can remember several distinct occasions. I suppose the sweep is an interesting person whom children make a point of talking to, and he generally comes in the spring at a time when a cat party is likely to be in progress outside the back door or down the surgery path.

Friday 22–Monday 25 May (Whit weekend)
Worked very hard all day Friday till tea when we threw some things into suitcases and set out for Swanage about 6pm. Only the second

time since we were married that we had been away for the whole weekend at Whitsun, and thought we must seize the opportunity while there was still a bit of basic petrol about. The weather had seemed to be improving and with recollections of former heat at Whitsun I snatched up some cotton frocks. Alas, would that I had laid hands on winter coats and fur linings instead. I have seldom been so cold in my life except occasionally when we have been to the school for Xmas. It started to blow up a real south west gale as we arrived and never stopped blowing hurricanes and raining cats and dogs at intervals all the weekend. The central heating had been put off and the house had no other form of heating, so I lived in outer tweed coat and cardigan underneath.

It was lovely to see them again, and Granny is, at 80, still mentally stimulating and enjoying an argument or discussion. I put my voluntary work problem to her as she has always been in favour of it. She was inclined to be hurt, thinking I was accusing her of socially climbing by this means, which of course was very far from the case. She has always had the strong old Quaker ideals of service given to the community together with a great and genuine interest in the work. I think also in her case a certain love of power and the pleasure in attending a committee of the hospital or grammar school and completely dominating it.

She also gets a tremendous kick out of many and long disputes with the Army about Oldfeld. She usually wins. It is marvellous that she minds so little seeing the wreck of her whole life's work. Of her it might be said with truth

And watch the things you give your life to, broken,
And stoop, and build 'em up again with worn-out tools.[4]

She is concentrating on keeping things all right for Arthur H.[5] to come back to, though we all doubt if Oldfeld as a private school will ever be a feasible proposition again, and if it becomes a government take-over all its originality will disappear.

She is also coaching a boy of 17 for a university scholarship as well as ordinary teaching of the nucleus of her few remaining pupils. All of this with a heart that compels her to stay in bed half the day, and not move or exert herself physically in any way.

We went to see the school housekeeper, Tan, whose house is so shining and clean that Eric hardly dared to smoke a cigarette, but whose mind seems to be closing up so that conversation was limited to what mutual friends were doing. I wonder if it is impossible to have both a clean house and any mind at all. There is Barton, Granny's house, which is filthy and a thoroughly untidy mess, though Jo works harder than anyone I know from 6am till nearly midnight without stopping, but in that house there are ideas, and one can discuss things about the world and almost any subject in it. I am rather worried about this as I can't help liking a clean and tidy house and I hope this preference is not a sign of approaching mental sterility.

To return to Jo. She has her two invalids to look after, all the cooking, all her garden where she is trying to grow vegetables and fruit not only for themselves but to sell, hens and 33 rabbits, 3 poodles, 2 cats and 4 kittens. In addition to her teaching, and just during the 9 o'clock news on a few evenings, she painted for me the most marvellous lampshade with deer on it. Every day she goes out with a bicycle and a billhook collecting two large sacks of rabbit food, battling against the wind and rain so that she can hardly push her bike up the hill. This made me determined never to keep rabbits. In addition she makes her own bread. No wonder the house is dirty.

Biz spent much time milking cows at the farm. On Sunday night there was quite a nasty raid, and although only a few bombs fell on the downs, it sounded like many aeroplanes swooping low overhead, perhaps looking for a convoy at Poole. They were very noisy and we had a most disturbed night. On Monday it rained and blew worse than ever and we came home in the evening frozen stiff and tired out. However some good came of the weekend as we managed to pinch two canoes which will be of priceless value to us at the van.

Tuesday 26 May

My 43rd birthday. Alas the grey hairs did not come out in the wash and are now more prolific and both sides of my parting. No one remembered what day it was except Mummy but her greetings telegram arrived while I was in Bath and lay on the hall table for several hours, thus reminding everyone in the house.

The may trees on the Sutton road have only just come out. Everything is so late this year that all sorts of things are out together that aren't usually. The rain has made the country incredibly lovely, keeping all the green fresh, but the gales have dashed our wisteria, which has been lovelier than it has ever been. It has scented the whole sitting room, so that people coming in and not seeing it outside the window have said 'What is this marvellous smell?'

Friday 29 May

At the Eye Hospital Colley told me that six more doctors are to be called up from Bath which is causing much heartburn and agony. The local war committee says they cannot be spared, but on the basis of one doctor to 3000 population, which is the centrally recognised amount, six can go. The result is that the ones with busy panel practices are being called. They are all over 40 but there are no under-40 general practitioners left, and the NHI[6] ones are foaming at the mouth and wondering how they can possibly manage. The high class private doctors can't be called up as they are all over 55, and can't be made to do NHI work, so it is going to be very hard on those left.

They have not had a meeting of consultants yet, but Colley says an eye man is definitely wanted, who should be Tizzard, which will mean I shall practically have to live in Bath. Thank goodness I did turn down the County Council's pleadings. It looks as if my little break of semi-leisure is coming to an end. It has been such bliss to have Hirst to assist Eric this winter so that I have been relieved of the endless grind of surgery 9–10am and 6–7pm and longer every day without a respite. I thought I would miss giving it up after 18 years, but the relief has been heaven. Not always to feel dead tired and cross has benefited the family and the whole domestic establishment as well. I have been able to read to Biz while she has her supper and take her to the dentist, to our mutual advantage.

When I do go into surgery and see some very old-standing patient we fall on each other's neck and are intensely pleased to see each other. It has surprised Simmy. She arrived originally when we were tired out and as Lawrence neatly puts it 'allergic to patients'. She is of enormous use on the phone and elsewhere, shielding me from the attentions of unwanted fussy patients. When she watches me suddenly meet some funny old man or woman in the waiting room and talk to them as if they were my dearest old friends she gets quite a shock.

Daisy has gone on holiday for a week so I am determined to cook. I am much hampered in this ambition by Mrs B who comes in the morning to 'help out' while Daisy is away, and Mrs Gillard, who is always full of helping everybody. I think they are anxious to prove that they can do as well as Daisy, but I am anxious as always to prove that I can do better and produce some really decent food out of nothing. I feel rather strongly that if a woman can't cook in her own kitchen, where can she cook? The answer I suppose in my case is in the caravan. Certainly it is difficult to cook in one's own kitchen if there is a super-efficient staff like mine, and though they irk me at moments like these, I know I am really the luckiest woman in the world to have them at all. Very few people seem to have any domestic help at all nowadays except the odd daily, but it does definitely enable me to keep on a pretty full time job.

Finished patients at 4pm and cooked till supper as only Mrs Gillard was in then. Made some delectable cream of spinach soup, an egg cheese and rice thing for supper, a pie with the remains of mince and all the left-over vegetables for tomorrow's lunch, and a bean roast for Sunday night. Lucy actually enjoyed my supper, thought it was 'lovely'. Mrs Gillard is very conservative and refuses to taste anything new, but likes it in her heart of hearts if encouraged to do so. I was tasting something and said 'Well it's all right, but not what I would call exciting,' and she looked at me very seriously and said 'Now I wonder what you mean exactly by exciting?' The idea that food could be interesting or exciting had simply never occurred to her.

Saturday 30 May
D arrived to see a bungalow opposite that we were considering as a possible surgery so that we could keep this house just for appointments. It worries me that Eric's Tuesday afternoon antenatal patients aren't comfortable enough. The waiting room is really quite inadequate for the numbers we have now, often overflowing onto the wall outside. D came willingly but didn't like the property. It is funny how he will always come over for anything to do with business even if completely unremunerative, but can never manage to come over just to see me.

It is a pity he didn't like the bungalow as it would make an ideal and very attractive central surgery. Of course it would make the practice less personal, but I am afraid that is inevitable when it gets to the size of ours. The choice seems to be between limiting it strictly, which is very difficult, or expanding the premises in the direction of centralisation. Even if a State Medical Service does come I can't believe that it will be for many years.

Tuesday 3 June
Colley in a flap in case he has to go in the Army instead of Tizzard. Frantic about plans as to how to arrange work, but I say 'sufficient unto the day'. Anyway I don't see why he should have to go as Tizzard is much younger.

Went to see Frankie on the way back as I had a great urge to talk to someone I had known for more than 20 years, and who talked my language and would dump herself and family on me in an air raid without being asked. Discussed what we meant by 'one of us' and 'talking the some language'. It is very intangible as it is so indefinite, but I am afraid that none of the Bath people do really. It isn't only St Felix or before, though having been school friends does make a difference and we both agreed we had made few friends since. It isn't social status or position, as one can get it with anybody; it isn't even similarity of tastes, as one of the things about the feeling is that one can disagree violently and it does not matter. Helen or Frankie (I forget which) once put it that 'one could always arrive on you about to have an illegitimate baby and say "I've come".' Which is near the root I think, but not everything. It is also never having to be polite or pretend to be what you are not.

I suppose with Bath the trouble is I see so much more of their husbands than the women, and would really much rather talk to the men. I don't mind talking domesticities or clothes for a little but it bores me unutterably to do so for long, and having Mummy that I can really discuss these things with is enough, and I don't want to go on and on about them to everybody else. I suppose that is why females on the whole bore me so excruciatingly. There seem to be so few who can discuss anything outside, or any abstract ideas. Thank goodness Eric's mother is one of the few. I really have been lucky to have a mother-in-law like that and not a society female who goes out to tea.

Started to cook a curry at 11pm. I was determined to do it after Lucy had gone to bed and she wouldn't go. As it was, darkness loomed and the blackout doesn't work in the kitchen, so I had to repair to the dispensary.

We have started a series of the most tremendous air raids over Germany, 1000 bombers over Cologne. When I think what 50 did to Bath it is ghastly, and yet it seems the only language the Germans will ever understand. Every book about them I have read lately, by people who have lived there for many years, seems to say that they are quite unable to see that cruelty anywhere or to anyone is foul. As long as it is they who are meting it out, any beastliness or terror or barbarism must be all right, but if it is done back to them it is another story. One of the worst things about the war is how it can change even those people who are super-pacifists and anti-killing of any sort, into people like I am now, thinking that such horrors are a regrettable necessity.

Thursday 4 June

Daisy returned so no more cooking. She is a damn good sort really but with no imagination and never will try anything new, always saying that we haven't got enough of something or gets out of it somehow. She says you can't make soup out of nothing, while I maintain that you can. I managed soup every night while she was away and we had run out of all carrots and there was only a bit of bone for stock once. She does not approve of my vague messes, and likes to know exactly what is in her food, and the idea of a dish as a creative work of art is entirely beyond her comprehension.

It was so hot that the thought of stereotyped tea and bread and butter filled me with nausea so I suggested to Eric that we should give it a miss and have an iced lime juice and supper early, but this idea did not go down well. He must have his proper tea. A pity, as it is the only meal I really dislike. I would much rather have lime juice in summer and coffee in winter with a plate of buns or biscuits on a side table so that everyone could come in and grab when they felt like it and take it to eat while they read their books. I loathe the idea of the gracious hostess presiding over a groaning cake stand. Perhaps it is all part of my hate of social trivia, as I don't mind a cup with a visiting surgeon when he blows in after operating. But the idea of asking anyone to TEA in advance and arranging a special one fills me with horror. A perfect dinner party with hostess in becoming long dinner gown would be another matter, though not indulged in very often even before the war, and never now.

Friday 5 June

Colley still agitated in case he should be called up. Did I think I could do his private work? I said no, that I could try but could never hold it, that I could have done it better five years ago when I had more patience to make myself pleasant to wealthy, tiresome, fussy old ladies. He said that was all nonsense and that I didn't know anything then but I did know a bit now which was all that mattered. I disagreed, and we had a violent argument about how to be a success. I said I should have to buy a new tailor-made coat and skirt but could not as I hadn't got the coupons. He couldn't see why, least of all that it was more to bolster my own inferiority complex than anything else. I told him it was all due to his influence that I could not do with high class patients any more, because he had been leading me more and more to the Left. He said that was a natural evolution and development of my own common sense and not him at all. However we both agreed that we would much rather do hospital work only, if it was paid and there was no necessity to earn a living or educate one's children.

Desperately hot in the consulting room while seeing patients in the afternoon with the curtains drawn. Daisy produced a cup of iced coffee for me as a surprise at tea. It was heaven, really she is a treasure though I do rail at her frequently.

Sunday 7 June
Went to the van and brought our luggage down in the donkey cart because of the hay, so I have learnt a completely new thing this weekend – to harness a cart! I am very proud of this and also felt it was very grand and real to have dealings with a donkey. We tethered her to the cart and she never brayed once, being very sweet though as lazy as possible. Elizabeth enjoyed having her very much. A heron came and settled just opposite us, but the woodpecker tree has fallen down. Mrs Self pressed butter and real cream as well as milk on us so we did well.

Monday 8 June
Eric had to see one of the Italian prisoners working on the farm. I tried him with '*Buon giorno*' and Eric says he tackled him with some Italian, but that he did not seem to understand. We hope that it was because his Italian was too much of a local dialect but fear it was because ours was too bad to be understood.

Eric went to a meeting in the evening about United Nations Day on June 14th. He has just begun to have a conscience about our having avoided any sort of meeting or local activity for 18 years, and feels that as a senior doctor in the town he ought to take a little interest in town affairs. I said he should suggest that they had something out of doors apart from religious services in order to give an opportunity for the non-religious of the town to join in. An interdenominational thing would not meet the case of the many who are not in any way religious, but too inarticulate and lethargic to say so. But of course he didn't. However even the clergy apparently admitted that they would get more people if they had a ceremony in the park and not in a church, which is a concession on their part.

There was a movement to get as many nations present as possible, and some merriment was caused by the suggestion that the Italian prisoners should be counted as allied nations since they are blissfully happy on their farms and the last thing they want to do is to return to Italy and fight. Eric says the Germans would not see that sort of joke.

Thursday 11 June
My nearly new summer covers are on the sitting room furniture, and with the two new rugs, Jo's lampshade and the tapestry chair seat I have worked the sitting room looks quite attractive. We only need a new floor, the boards of which are appalling. It seems rather dreadful to have had new mats and be thinking about the appearance of one's sitting room at such times but it is very hard to draw the line about what to get and what not to get. Necessity is such a relative term. Really, no floor covering is a 'necessity'. If rugs wear right through they can be thrown away and one can exist with bare boards; many people in Russia would be only too thankful to have these. Yet the prudent housewife in me says 'Keep up household replacements while you can, so that there will not be too much to do after the war when stocks will be scarce and expensive for a long time.' I would always go without anything in the house rather than pay a fancy price for it but having found some pre-war stock of Persian rugs at my price and colourings I am afraid I fell for them.

With clothes the problem is easier. Having a definite rationing scheme one feels justified in having one's ration, though really there again there is no 'necessity' to have anything new while one has a pair of shoes and a skirt that hang together at all. The same is true with food. People grumble and grumble and say they don't know what we are coming to, but scientifically there has been an adequacy of everything except Vitamin C, and we must be by far the best fed nation in Europe.

Is it Britain's strength or weakness that it must go on with life as normally as possible to the last gasp? When France was falling and I was working terribly hard with Spong's practice on top of everything else, I remember being horrified at passing a crowd of people going to a fete in aid of 'Warships Week'. It seemed so dreadful for people to dress up in their best clothes and go for an outing when all those awful things were happening across the Channel. Then I thought that perhaps my animosity towards their going to a fete was due to the fact that it was the sort of function I would cheerfully walk ten miles to avoid, and that if it had been some occupation that would have made me personally happy I might have called it 'justifiable relaxation'. Anyway it may be that the refusal of a small market town like Chippenham to be put off its pre-arranged Saturday afternoon fun, just because Paris happened to be falling, typifies the British spirit in fighting a losing battle. We have more staying power and resistance than those who panic and fly off the handle easily. Certainly one cannot keep at a high emotional pitch for ever, either of fear, grief, depression or anything else. We must have our comic relief and relaxation even in the midst of horror.

4

PATIENTS AND PETROL

15 June–12 July 1942

Monday 15 June 1942

Simmy has started on her annual fortnight holiday. This means I shall have to go into surgery more, and take on testing all the urines, a job I relinquished very willingly when she first came. We shall now discover how much we rely on her, for besides being secretary-dispenser she knits jumpers for the children, shops, mows the lawn, does up all parcels, interviews all commercial travellers and many other people who ask to see the doctor but can be fended off by anyone intelligent. For instance someone asked for me the other day saying she had come from the Reverend Mr F. I asked Daisy what he wanted and said at any rate I was not going to have any clergyman sleeping with me! I did not think what I had said till afterwards, but it was just when many people were seeking accommodation after the Bath blitz and I somehow thought it was someone wanting a spare room. I was determined I would not have a clergyman at any rate. However I told Daisy that Simmy was the person for clergymen, not me, and in she went finding that it was really about a Mrs P who had a gynaecological complaint, and thought it would be nice to see a lady. Simmy promptly switched her onto Eric and gave her an appointment, so I did not have to explain personally that I wasn't in the least interested in her female ailments. If I once started that sort of work I should be inundated with it, and I really could not bear living in women's vaginas all day, let alone the neuroses attached to them, so I leave it all to Eric who doesn't seem to mind so much.

Simmy also sees all the odd people who call for subscriptions or to sell stockings and tells them I am busy with a patient, and shall be for hours and hours. Altogether she is an invaluable person. We had not realised before we embarked on a full-time secretary how much she could save us in wear and tear.

Tuesday 16 June
Had my annual perm after the Eye Hospital so missed both lunch and tea except for the odd sandwich. A most uncomfortable, not to say painful proceeding but worth it. Makes one look ten years younger after the first few days when it is too set and awful.

I am tired of picking up people on the road, soldiers, WAAFs[1] and others whose conversational opening remark is always 'I suppose your greatest difficulty is petrol', or 'You won't be getting any more petrol next month.' When I reply that I have plenty thanks and am not likely to be short they are nonplussed and don't know what to say next, and often one can see them thinking 'Taint fair. Why should SHE get it for joy-rides?' Of course I can explain but I get very tired of doing so. I have my 'Doctor' notice tucked up inside the windscreen so they should be able to see this except that it is generally covered with other notices saying 'Local' or 'Full up'. I never drive with my Doctor down except on occasions such as just after the raid when I wanted to get through. I have noticed that it is mostly people with inferiority feelings who keep their notices of entitlement showing, and a good many of the women doctors do so. John Bastow is a male exception, and we ragged him about it one day. He said he used it because the police were less likely to stop you for speeding if you could look as if you were dashing to an urgent case.

Eric has been to see the Italian prisoner again and managed to get in a few words of Italian which were understood. It will be an excellent excuse for taking the car to the van if these prisoners need occasional visits.

Wednesday 17 June

Great to-doings about our scythe which Harlow had taken to be ground and been told they were short of labour and could not do it for weeks. Asked if he had said it was Dr Hickson's scythe he said no, so we sent him back to say so with the result that it will be done tomorrow. Eric says this is black-marketing, as Martin at the forge got something in his eye on a Sunday morning a few weeks ago and I ministered to him. I suppose in a way it is unfair to take advantage of the fact that one has lived in a place for 18 years and made friends with skilled artisans in most trades, but I haven't a very bad conscience about it. I think these people genuinely feel that in the past we have helped them over a difficult time and that now they are only too pleased to do something for us. Certainly we have had no difficulty in getting odd things that we have wanted – a bit of roofing felt from the builder or odd bits of wood (I had given him some tomato plants a few weeks before). Also chocolate at cost from various Nestlé employees (strictly illegal) and plumbing at a moment's notice whenever we want it. The chocolate people said they were so pleased to do this for the doctor as they had never forgotten what he did for their mother years ago. Actually the mother had died of carcinoma of stomach and Eric had done nothing except visit her occasionally. One always gets gratitude where it is least deserved, while a really good bit of work from a medical point of view goes without thanks and generally unpaid!

Quite a change to help Eric with surgery, though I am rather self-conscious about my hair, which is still a bit too crimped. Old E came in, who used to come down regularly every Saturday evening, nearly at the end of surgery, for a bottle of medicine for his asthma. We always knew when the end of the week's work was near, 'Thank goodness, there is Old E.' He is one of the first patients I remember in Chippenham nearly 18 years ago. Now he has given up work at the Westinghouse factory and retired on a pension, and sends one of his grandchildren down for medicine, except when the weather is very favourable and he fancies an outing, like tonight. He looks an old man now, as do so many of the patients that we have known all the time and seen regularly. But having been out of surgery for a bit and then going back they suddenly look even older.

These old original patients produce a spontaneous but warm feeling of friendliness when I see them, quite a different feeling from that felt for the hoards of newcomers, though these are of all sorts, some nice some horrid. Would we still have this feeling under a State Medical Service I wonder, and if not would it matter to medicine? A very difficult question.

One of the consultants came out to the hospital on Sunday and horrified me by saying that he disliked the Bristol working man with his aim of 'I'm as good as you are.' We have never found that in the least, or indeed thought about it in that way; perhaps that is why we have never met it. Some patients we like immensely, some we hate on sight, but it is quite irrespective of class, politics, education or even cleanliness, though we do prefer them clean. It is not uncommon for one of us to say, 'I do like the so and so family although they are filthy and their house is a pigsty.' Anyway, if one can generalise I infinitely prefer the good artisan to the fussy, wealthy, old lady with not enough to do.

Thursday 18 June
Nasty and cold in pm and not conducive to the van so decided we would have a red-letter day and go out to dinner for one of the last times there would be any petrol to do this. Went to the Cross Hands and had quite a nice dainty meal, though not much of it. Afterwards called in to see the Eastes at Marshfield. Decided we did no work at all. They have two practices to run four miles apart. She does all the surgeries in their own house, which is old and rambling and inconvenient. She only has a bit of daily help, does all the gardening which is not inconsiderable, has about 40 rabbits, ducks, two goats and two kids that have to have bottles and were very sweet but most demanding children. Found out several points about how to grow melons. Altogether quite an outing and very pleasant to get into nice clothes again and take trouble with the details of one's appearance.

Friday 19 June
News bad. We seem to have retired right back onto the Egyptian frontier[2] again and to have had a distinct reverse. Each time the Libyan battle flares up it's said in high quarters, 'Now at last we can meet them on equal terms of numbers and equipment.' Then a few weeks later when we have not apparently done very well, the tune changes to 'The enemy was superior in air support, numbers and equipment.' Apparently through all these campaigns we have been about a year behind the Germans in tank armour and anti-tank guns, and now again they have outstripped us. It is very good that the Free French were able to make such a stand at Bir Hakeim.[3] It will be such a psychological fillip for them and they only retired in the end because told to do so. It very much looks as if Sevastopol[4] will fall too, though if it destroys enough Germans in the taking it will probably have achieved its object.

Saturday 20 June
Definitely an epoch in our history. We launched a canoe on our own Chippenham river. It didn't sink though a certain amount of water came in, and it will definitely not take more than two with very little luggage. No dog possible, and it is very tippy and would submerge with the greatest of ease. Nevertheless if we can get two in it will be enough to have fun with, and prevent the feeling of 'No basic petrol, no holiday!'

Sunday 21 June
Down to see Ruth as the last time there will be any petrol for joy-riding. A lovely day and we had lunch by a pleasant stream with woods all round. She looked very well, but feeling her feelings and her adolescence a bit. Squibs also down for the weekend. She is just the same type and looks as she always was. '*Plus ça change, plus c'est la même chose*', or is it just that when we are with people we knew when we were young, we resort to being ourselves? I am struck with the fact that most headmistresses of girls' schools nowadays are utterly ordinary, conventional and uninspiring and not people

of great and individual character. I think that when I grew up it was the height of the 'New Freedom for Women' movement and it took much more character and ability for a woman to get to a high position, so that only the ones of the very greatest character did so, often in the face of many difficulties. Most of the famous headmistresses of that time and indeed most of the famous women one heard of were 'queer' to a large extent. Nowadays when anyone can be anything they want (they rarely seem to want to be much), there are many more utterly ordinary and dull women in high places rather to the disadvantage of their underlings. It has meant a loss of originality, which is so important in any big concern.

When we were at school we rather laughed at Miss Silcox and put her down as 'completely batty'. We thought her incapable because of her lack of practical organising ability, but I think that most of us, through the mists of the years, now think she was a really great woman who did things for St Felix which have endured and will count for far more in the long run than practicalities.

Certainly things seem to have retrogressed now, at any rate along the freedom path. There seem to be more rules and regulations, and the prefects and office holders do not seem to do so much of the organising, which even if it was a bad thing for the organised, was probably good for the organisers. There are stricter rules about going out and who is allowed to take walks. One would have thought that in 25 years the path of freedom would have progressed not retrogressed – but no. Of course there has been the growth of the 'Free Progressive School' such as Dora Russells, A.S. Neill and the Beltane but these remain rather extreme, and though they would slay me for saying so, partly exist to assuage the juvenile psychological disappointments of their staff. My children are all very interested in this type of school and do not oppose them, especially Biz who tried the Beltane for a term, but though she liked the staff immensely as friends, she could not bear the lack of organisation and the general unpleasantness of the other children en bloc.

It has been extraordinary how on the whole women have not

wanted or taken advantage of the freedom won so hardly for them thirty years ago, and how many of them, at any rate in this part of the world, remained just daughters at home until they married. Or, if they had some dud little career of some sort, they dropped it like a hot coal on marriage. *Je ne comprends pas.*

Monday 22 June

Tobruk[5] has fallen. A serious and unexpected blow. Only yesterday all the papers were saying that the Libyan reverse was not so great because Tobruk was and would be held as it was last year, and could menace Rommel's[6] communications, and now it has gone in two days. One always wonders what is behind these spectacular defeats (if anything other than sheer incompetence). The best we can hope for this time is that we have deliberately withheld adequate supplies from Libya in order to open a second front in the West – but I wonder?

Only a week or so before Singapore fell we were told that this was one place that would never be allowed to fall, and it seemed to go like a house of cards.

A year ago today Hitler attacked Russia. I shudder to think what would have happened to us if he had not made this fatal error. It is just impossible to realise what war on our own soil, or the Nazi regime, would be like. Perhaps it is just as well, or perhaps because we do not realise it, we still go in for luxuries and do not put the last ounce into the war effort.

Eric has induced[7] a very nervous, highly-strung and tiresome patient today. Hope she comes off soon as we want to go to Whitchurch while there is a bit of official basic petrol.

Tuesday 23 June

Nothing doing with his patient. I was made to feel a pig today in OPs by intense gratitude of a rather tiresome old man with cataract with whom I had been very impatient. Another woman had complained she could 'see nothing' after she had been working for about an hour. Her vision was 6/5 in both eyes, but on telling her that her eyes were all right and she did not need glasses she collapsed into tears. So many people who can't face life project it onto their eyes and would like to slide into invalidism. They are most difficult to deal with, especially in a crowded OPs where one cannot really go into why they are fed up with life in front of everybody else, and anyway it would be impossible with about 30 people waiting. The only course is to refer them back to their own doctor who probably knows nothing about psychology and has thankfully pushed every subjective symptom to do with the eyes onto 'an error of refraction' and can feel it is then none of his business. An unsatisfactory state of affairs.

Wednesday 24 June
Have been asked to give a lecture on 'Immediate First Aid' to housewives. Not exactly my subject but suppose I shall be able to struggle through. It is always so difficult in these very condensed lectures to find the language to use for people who have absolutely no anatomical or physiological knowledge, and not waste time on explanations.

We have the tamest flycatcher, which practically lives on Biz's high-jump posts, with occasional variations to the telephone wire. A pair of goldfinches are eating groundsel in the hen run. Terrible rumour that there will be no more hen food for backyard poultry keepers soon.

Thursday 25 June
Had a new patient, an Honourable and daughter at 10.30am (no Devizes today) and thought I really must give up my attitude of not bothering about trying to impress private patients and the better class of patients or we will have none left. I put on a new professional frock and my best manner. My God, these mothers who fuss over their children, 'wanting to do the very best for them' and making them complete neurotics, are just awful. She went on and on the whole while. 'Now darling, you won't be nervous will you – there's nothing to be frightened of. You know she is such a

nervous child. She won't be left a minute. Now do what the doctor tells you, won't you – she's not going to hurt. You will let Nanny put some stuff in your eyes, won't you, you must not mind if it stings – you know she's really very nervous.' I could have wrung the woman's neck. The child was a perfectly sensible one of 14 yrs or would have been if she hadn't been over-mothered all her life. However, I went down all right. It always beats me how these people don't see that my manner is all put on – but they don't seem to.

Into the garden to recover. It was full of vociferous young birds of all sorts, yelling for food, and their poor little mothers tearing about waiting on them. Birds seem so helpless for so long, and do not seem to be able to fend for themselves till they are quite as big as their parents.

Hirst has gone off for the day to his boy's school speech day, so we have to be in. It would have been blighting but Eric's midwifery case shows signs of starting so he has to be about anyhow. That woman is going to be a blasted nuisance. She won't go into labour properly or stay out of it, thinks the baby will be born at any minute when she has hardly started, and all her relations agitate.

Friday 26 June
Very long OPs at the eye infirmary, just because the Holt-Wilsons had come in with me for a lift and I had said I didn't think I should be long.

Enormous surgeries at home, I can't think why. It is so hot.

Saturday 27 June
Still big surgeries. News getting very bad. The Germans say they are in Matruk and they have an unhappy knack of being right, and we then acknowledge it a few days later.

Sunday 28 June
We went to Whitchurch although it was our Sunday on, but Hirst didn't want to go anywhere special and it seemed a pity to waste

the last Sunday of basic petrol. Lovely lunch in punt with Mummy and Scoot in just the right amount of heat.

Miles is now a captain and acting adjutant of the first Parachute Division ever formed in England. Scoot full of neuroses but refusing to see anyone about it.

Eric's 'Mrs Nuisance' came off yesterday after much song and dance, also one he was going to induce tomorrow, but there is another one niggling who we may have to leave to Hirst.

Monday 29 June
Was writing my lecture when I heard the loudspeaker van which often goes round saying that water will be turned off between certain hours, or gas masks will be fitted at . . . etc. Went out to see if it was anything that mattered and to my horror heard 'Mrs Hickson will give a lecture on Immediate First Aid at the Town Hall tomorrow at 7pm which we hope everyone will attend. Mrs Hickson . . .' I was overcome with confusion. When Eric came in at lunch he said it must be stopped at once as it might be considered advertising by the GMC.[8]

Tuesday 30 June
Picked up a wee laddie from Glagow (Army) going to Bath. He was very conversational, quite a change from the silent oafs I have had lately.

Got in a great stew about my lecture in the evening but actually it was a success and I had quite an ovation afterwards. When I got there the town hall was full. I thought my voice sounded awful and most forced and unnatural, but afterwards was congratulated on my delivery, so it must have been all right. Many people thanked me and one woman, who seemed to know me but I didn't know her, said her mother wanted to tell me that she had learnt more from me in one lecture than she had at a whole course of lectures in her village. There must have been well over 100 people there as I was almost mobbed for the little First Aid pamphlets I had to distribute.

Came back very hot for hurried supper and then a session at the bills[9] till 11pm. Then Eric had to go out again, and again at 6am, so that wasn't much of a day (or night) for him.

Wednesday 1 July
Clinic at mental hospital Devizes. A most depressing collection of cases. None could see 6/6 to start with and most were myopic with lens opacities, deeply depressed and melancholic. They wouldn't even try to see and were sure they never could. The only light note was an old boy of 77 who said his eyes were bad since they had put the 'internal combustion ray' on them! I couldn't find out whether he knew how to read or not but rather think not.

The woman with glaucoma that I am trying to treat with pilocarpine hadn't had any. They had simply forgotten to give it to her. My one case I have had since I have been there when it was really important. I have persuaded them to send her in to the Infirmary to see Colley about a trephine,[10] as I really don't like taking the responsibility, especially if the treatment I ordered is not carried out. It has obviously been going on for years and no one has spotted it. Meanwhile she has got into a state of depression. So should I, if I had glaucoma, but that is no reason to let her quietly go blind without attempting to do anything. Colley will curse me as no one will love having her at the Infirmary, but it can't be helped.

Bills again all afternoon. Finished the 2nd drawer, but still have the 'actives' to do. There seem to be many more 'account-rendered' than there used to be, due to all these fresh people in the town, and many 'here today and gone tomorrow' types.

Fire-watchers' meeting at 8pm. It is all being reorganised and we have to go on once a week with three people. Dear Mr Pineger from the cottage up the hill took the meeting and waffled on about who would like to do it with whom, and of course no one would say, but all giggled sheepishly. After half an hour of this we had to ask to be excused as Dr Royal had sent in an accident to the hospital from Castle Combe. Eric and I went up to the hospital and I gave an anaesthetic to a nice boy of 9 yrs with a nasty dirty road wound of his knee, which Eric excised, filled with sulphanilamide powder and plastered in the latest approved style. Took us till 10pm.

A short siren sounded at 2.45am for no apparent reason. Just settling off again when the bell goes; another baby for Eric. Was it accelerated by the siren?

Thursday 2 July
Should have been our half-day, but at lunchtime Eric was confronted with:
1.   Old Gullis who had nearly cut his foot off with some hay cutting instrument
2.   A woman with an antepartum haemorrhage
3.   A POP[11] at Foxham where the doctor needs his help
4.   Mitchell due at the hospital to see 4 cases at 4pm.

This does not seem to be a good week somehow, but I suppose a reaction from the slack weeks lately was bound to occur. Just managed to get to the van for supper and have a little trip up river in the canoe till we got stuck on the reeds.

Friday 3 July
Eric called up in the small hours for the third night running. It is really getting a bit thick.

Picked up several people going to Bath who only wanted short distances which was very annoying and delaying. I don't mind giving anybody a lift, but I do object to being a ruddy bus.

Quarrelled with Colley all morning, but I thought afterwards that I probably had been really rather annoying. The trouble is that now I am getting more self-confident in eye work I am apt to disagree with him violently, not on the actual ophthalmics but on general treatment of the patient. He was also not too pleased about my mental patient, which I knew would be the case, but I am forcing him to take an interest and he is correspondingly annoyed. He hates to be made to do anything he doesn't want, and nowadays I frequently insist on his doing something. However the great thing is that we can curse and swear at each other frequently. I could not work with anyone to whom I had to be polite.

News from Egypt a little better. They don't seem to have made a breakthrough yet, though have attacked in force. Each day they can be held means a day more for reinforcements to reach Auchinleck.[12] I think we must be sending large quantities out by air. Simmy had a letter from a friend in Cairo (airgraph) dated June 26th only, quicker than one has ever come before, and he said 'Don't worry, we are not losing.' Only hope he is right.

Saturday 4 July

Picked raspberries and redcurrants for jam and bottling. Quite a good crop, but have not had a strawberry, or to be more accurate, there were two but the birds had them. Also planted out Continuity lettuces in my rose beds.

Sunday 5 July

Weather improved a little so took Margaret Rudman to van for lunch and tea. Created an epoch in Chippenham history as Eric returned her to her own house by canoe amid much comment from all at the bathing place and in St Mary's St. I think she enjoyed it but it must have made her feel rather awful as Walter would have enjoyed it all so much, and they had talked of having a boat for so many years. The thought of Walter was there all the while even for me, so don't know what it must have been like for her. One could imagine him joining in everything so vividly.

Monday 6 July

Mummy arrived for a fleeting two-night visit. I had told her she really must make an effort to come at least every three months now there is no more basic petrol for me to go there. However busy she thinks she is, she really cannot deny that she has more time to waste in trains than I have. I have persuaded her this once, but I expect I shall have a fight next time.

Old Mr Carr chose today to have all the stair, hall and landing carpets up and put them down again so the tread wore more evenly. I gave him some lunch. The maids' faces when I ordered a place to be laid for him in the dining room were a sight to behold, also Simmy's when she burst in with a message. I told her not to look so critically at my boyfriends! The worst of having a perfect staff is that they are terribly interested in what you do, and so extremely critical and disapproving if I behave in what they consider an unorthodox manner. It infuriates me not to be able to ask who I like to what I like without comment.

Tuesday 7 July
Colley was quite good about my mental woman with glaucoma in the end, though he made a most frightful fuss about seeing her at all. He is going to take her in and trephine both eyes, so I foresee 'Happy days' for the whole hospital.

Had lunch with Mummy afterwards at the Old Red House. I don't think I had been there to a meal since before Arthur was born and he is now 17 yrs. Meant to take supper to the van to show her our river, but it poured with rain, so instead she pulled all my hats to bits. There was an awful old blue straw that we completely transformed and changed from a very dull hat with a brim into quite a chic little toque with a veil and quill at the back.

There seems to be a brief lull in Egypt, but both sides probably regrouping. Russian news bad. The Germans claim to have crossed the Don[13] in their much vaunted spring offensive. Now Sevastopol has gone, there will be vast reinforcements available, but at any rate its protracted resistance did delay them a bit.

Wednesday 8 July
I could not persuade Mummy to stay longer. Mima in labour. She haunted me all day, miaowing unless I would sit and hold her hand, and produced two black kittens at about 10pm. Fortunately the milk ration had been taken off, but I am afraid they are both females which will make them more difficult to dispose of, unless I can foist them off on somebody who doesn't like to ask.

Friday 10 July
Very busy with eyes all day. Life is very dull and uneventful at the moment, probably the quiet before the storm! Have rather a conscience that I am not doing enough for the war effort at the moment, as have really quite a lot of leisure, but if I take on anything more, such as County Council work, Tizzard is certain to be called up, and then we shall all be in a mess. Colley and I both think there is dirty work and string pulling going on. There is absolutely no reason why he shouldn't go into the Army, young, unattached bachelor as he is, but the local secretary of the Bath War Committee is a friend of his and has been to London to the Central War Committee to get the 6 GPs due to go reduced. These really can't be spared, as they are all the ones with busy panel practices, but we can see no reason why Tizzard shouldn't go as they are wanting ophthalmic surgeons badly, and a lot of the Bath work is pure luxury. The difficulty is that the work, which is really necessary to the community, is unpaid, and if it were not for the old ladies who fuss unnecessarily about their glasses none of us could live. The same old hospital question again.

Saturday 11 July
Decided to take up two hen-runs and dig them for winter greens. As we shall have to reduce the number in October it seemed a waste to have so much enclosed, and we are short of greens. Eric and I had to plunge into nettles higher than ourselves and cope with wire and posts. It is the sort of objectionable job that one has to do oneself if it is to be done properly.

We have had most marvellous food this week. Should like Hitler to know how well we eat in the third year of the war. On several evenings this week I said that if we were millionaires in peacetime we could not have had anything nicer for supper. Salmon mayonnaise with every sort of vegetable salad and strawberries and cream (top of the milk). Another night it was fricassee of chicken (old hen) and raspberries. The only thing not being home produced was the salmon, which Mummy had provided, and of course the milk. I am only putting these food notes in as they may be interesting in the future if it is chronicled that we were severely rationed and starving in 1942! Of course we who have gardens have a great advantage, *sans doute*.

Mr Carr arrived with bunch of sweet peas for me probably as a token of gratitude for giving him lunch on Monday. Very nice thought. Great merriment among staff at my boyfriend, and even Lucy laughed about it, and she is too proper for words.

Sunday 12 July
Delved through nettles to root up hen wire most of the day, and having got the way clear to the trees cut off a lot of lower internal and nearly dead branches to make a winding path through them, a thing I have been wanting to do for years.

5

A FAMILY FUNERAL

13 July–3 August 1942

Monday 13 July

Jo rang up at 8am to say that Granny had had a stroke and was unconscious. Eric was very philosophical and said he only hoped she didn't stay alive paralysed. He had just been making her 80th birthday present with Biz, a book rest with her initials, and was hurrying to get it finished. I am glad we went at Whitsun, though it was unfortunate that Biz left them in a rage due to a disturbed night.

Picking blackcurrants and raspberries hard. We have heroically saved almost 1lb of sugar out of our household ration every week for a year, so really have quite a nice lot saved for jam, and what we can't jam we shall bottle. It will be a godsend in the winter. Again I only mention the above, not because I am a good housewife, but because it might be interesting to know that by refraining from making more than one cake a week, it was possible in 1942 to save some sugar out of ration.

Forgot the most thrilling thing on Sunday. While we were coping with chicken wire and nettles there were a pair of goldcrests feeding their babies. They were extremely tame and took not the slightest notice of us, and were the most adorable things I have seen for a long while. They must have a nest in the garden, but we didn't find it.

Tuesday 14 July

Gundred rang up after we were in bed last night to say 'How

quick and what about details and arrangements?' Eric didn't even know his mother was dead, which was awkward. He had meant to ring Jo in the evening, but had a patient after supper and then thought it was too late, and that he would have heard if necessary. However Jo rang early today to say it was so, and we must go down tomorrow. Resisted the temptation to say I couldn't possibly cancel my clinics, as I think Eric really likes me to be about even though we say nothing and he knows I hate funerals and anything to do with the church.

Just the worst days of the week to be away. Poor Simmy had to start cancelling 10 appointments for Eric. County offices have to send out 15–18 telegrams to cancel my school clinic, and by this time the mothers will have started using atropine[1] and be cross and disgruntled. The only thing is that everyone is prepared to be helpful and accept anything to do with death or funerals as a justifiable excuse for cancelling things, though one would much rather say 'owing to pressure of work it was impossible to go . . .'

Told Elizabeth when she came back from school. She said 'Oh dear, poor Father.' Pretty good for nine years. She then retired upstairs to weep alone. She was fonder of Granny than either of my other children. They were always exchanging letters and literary efforts.

Wednesday 15 July
This would be a week when I had more patients than I have had for some time. Saw them all morning and afternoon, trying to pack them in at short intervals. Took the plum and pale blue quill off the blue hat Mummy had redone for Biz's sports and substituted a navy pad. As Eric said, none of the family would mind what I looked like but some of the old retainers might. Funny mixture the few times I wear a hat. My darkish blue professional summer dress and coat, which is four years old, will have to do. It is at any rate neat and fairly inconspicuous.

Picked up Uncle Conrad at Shaftesbury. Eric of course is the only person with any petrol. We filled the tank up to the brim and put two tins in a box at the back (quite illegally, but after all it can hardly be called pleasure driving). Fortunately Aunt Annie was not coming, but we accepted the offer of a cup of tea, which Eric needed badly, and this meant half an hour of her which was worse than ever I imagined she could be.

'Well dear, this is a terrible shock. Uncle Conrad is dreadfully upset. Now Eric dear, you sit there and talk to Uncle. Now Joan dear' (in a piercingly loud whisper in a small hotel bedroom) 'Tell me, is Eric dreadfully upset?'

For something to say I said 'He hasn't said so.'

'Ah, I understand, the Quaker reserve.'

I could have knocked her head off onto the floor. We had determined we would go to a hotel and not to Barton, so as not to put extra work onto Jo, but when it came to the point of fixing up anywhere, the idea filled us with such extreme distaste that we all decided to stay in the house after all.

It was a lovely evening and we collected roses from Vera's garden after supper. I had brought rather a mixed bunch of things from home, buddleia, prunus etc. Fortunately no one suggested that I should take them up myself or 'go in'. Jo holding up much better than we expected. We all thought she would go to pieces completely. We dished out sleeping tabs all round, but I don't think Jo or Pip took them. The lay[2] have such a horror of 'drugs' and such a passion for patent medicines that don't do anything.

There is to be a short service in Swanage at 10.15am taken by the man they always call 'Padre' who took all the school services for years. He is one of the few really satisfactory types of clergymen, grey flannels and out for practical good in the world more than God-bothering. After the service we go on to Bournemouth crematorium at 12 midday, but no processing, and only just the family there thank heavens. Being so early in the day at Swanage and petrol non-existent, no distant relatives or friends will be able to get here, so we shall be spared that, and anyway Granny is the last of her generation except for Conrad. There are some compensations for war.

75

Thursday 16 July

Thank goodness there is to be no waiting about all morning, and there is breakfast to be got and washed up. Early mist, but blowing finer and sunny with variegated clouds. Not very hot. Why the hell did I have fried potatoes and bacon for breakfast. I think I shall be sick, and Pip has emotional diarrhoea. I have also got frequency as I always do on these occasions. A run on the loo, but it doesn't make any difference. Masses of people arrive with masses of flowers, on the whole not too wreath-like. Jo asking me to make a list, then with the antennae of the emotional 'No, you would rather not go into her room, it doesn't matter.'

Damn you, can't you do that for Jo? I started to hunt for pencil and paper as slowly as possible but by the time I had found them Pip had coped. Felt guilty and shut myself in Jo's bedroom while there were noises off. Can't look out of East or West window, damn it where can I look. Hat – nearly forgot gloves. Pierre tied up downstairs and howling. Their cat Martha has disappeared since yesterday. She was about to have kittens and always had them on Granny's bed. I shouldn't be surprised if she wasn't shut up there – Eric calling me to come. The Swanage church is associated with all I hate most and that revolts me most in the whole world. Eric's father's funeral, Arthur's christening, Arthur and Vera's and Pip's weddings, and always awful parsons. Fortunately there is a side entrance to the church and only a short way to a seat. I will not be false to my beliefs and pretend to kneel and pray. Don't look – I must not faint or be sick or make a fool of myself – I must not – look at the clasp of your bag, you fool. The parson much more passable than the revolting old man who did all the others, quite a nice little address with not too much God or the hereafter in it and more about a lighted torch in this world. If anyone has been that and has eternal life she has. Thousands of children have been through her hands and got a little something from her character and outlook. Wonderful to have had so many interests in other people right to the end. Endless letters from old pupils saying they can never forget what Oldfeld has done for them.

Service over very quickly – must manage to get out – the hearse gets right away independently thank goodness, needn't see it if I don't look. House again for more loo and cup of tea for those who dare, but I don't.

Two blasted rabbits have got out and are under the car. They would be, but perhaps helped a difficult moment as we all try to catch them. On to Bournemouth. Pip and I are in the back of Eric's car and Uncle Conrad in the front. Crematorium on the top of a hill, very open, sunny and windy with clouds and heather, not yet too built up or too many appalling headstones, the least offensive of such places I have seen yet. Gundred was the only one of the party in black. Service only five minutes, don't look – clasp of your bag – bright spot – hypnotism – I must not faint or be sick. Out, brief episode of forced conversation before lunch in Bournemouth and train for Gundred. Don't think we had the burial of the dead service at all, which was some relief. It does make it better if there is a passable sort of parson. On the whole not so bad as I expected, considerably less drawn out and full of relations than Eric's father's, and on the whole less obscene than weddings and christenings. I am surprised, or am I getting more tolerant?

I am so fortunate to have had in-laws like that. They don't flout convention aggressively as I should want to do, but just set no store at all by outward things and keep things as simple as they can. Quaker ancestry I suppose. They have never expected from me anything that I could not give them. I have just managed to get through it for them, but definitely could not do it for anybody closer to me for anybody's sake. This was just about the limit.

I can't imagine what it would have been like to have had anyone ordinary for a mother-in-law. She was pretty marvellous with me. Although her dominant personality sometimes overpowered other people including her own children, she never interfered with me in any way or even made any suggestion, even if she knew I was going badly wrong. Even when Arthur was a baby and I was doing everything wrong and she could see it, she forbore to offer advice until I was in such a muddle I had to ask for it. I have often been extremely unpleasant, self-opinionated and intolerant and must have annoyed her to excruciation but she never said so. The whole family have always made me feel one of them right from the start, and I have never had the feeling that they were bearing with me for Eric's sake, but immediately let me and mine into their lives. Can only hope I shall be the same with Arthur's future wife but doubt it.

I can scarcely believe there was a day when I rather despised them all because they were not 'smart', but I think those few years after I left school were not really me, but a mixture of inferiority complex and reaction after feeling I had missed the post-school 'good time' because of the war.

Back to Barton for tea. What bliss it is not to have maids buzzing round with funeral faces trying to do the right thing and invariably doing the wrong one! Out after tea on an expedition for rabbit food. Bit of fresh air and exercise good for us. Tomorrow business must be tackled. I think the rabbits really help. Utterly fagged out with repressed emotion. Eric and I hardly spoke the whole day.

In the middle of the night a piercing wail – good gracious they must have a siren at the school or it must be a special one for an invasion. No, it is Pierre howling just outside the door. Why do poodles smell so, they are so sweet otherwise, but to my mind it makes them quite impossible. Just dropped off to sleep again when the real siren went, and again reawakened by the All Clear. What a curse these short pointless sirens are. Convoys at sea being attacked I suppose.

Friday 17 July
After supper last night we were all sitting round the dining room table talking, Uncle Conrad telling stories, some mending stockings, playing patience with Marcus, talking, laughing and discussing everything on earth.

> Of shoes and ships and sealing wax
> Of cabbages and kings.[3]

It seemed incredible that Granny should not come in as she

always did, seize the problem and plunge into the discussion with that radiant vitality which she always gave to anything. What real unity there is in the whole family despite differences of belief, opinion and tastes, but none of that seemed to matter and merely lends variety to any discussion. I think the unity comes from intellectual integrity, honesty of purpose or something.

Interviews with bank managers, estate agents, the Army about the school and many letters to deal with. She has kept all the letters written by her children, but they are in separate boxes, so Pip suggests we should each take our own to go through at leisure and destroy if we like. Home after tea in cold rain.

Saturday 18 July

I am entranced by some of Eric's old letters and rather regret that I was brought up to destroy everything immediately. There are some written when he was Elizabeth's age which have intrigued her greatly and another one I found after he had spent his first weekend with us at Underwood giving his candid opinion of my family. He said they made you feel at home but were rather noisy! Also all his letters from India in the last war, which should be interesting historically and are mostly typed, so shall save these up to read like a book on winter evenings.

Bertha looked decidedly fatter after having left her for two days. Hope she doesn't have 13 as everybody will shrink from drowning them and there is no proper food about for puppies.

Monday 20 July

A scrum to catch up appointments, and mostly difficult and complicated as always when one crams too many in.

I dreamt last night I was about to have a hysterectomy. Interesting symbol in exchange for a mother-in-law!

Tuesday 21 July

Had my hair done after OPs. A new style which has gone right up off my forehead which I have always thought would be quite impossible. I have got rid of the buns at the back and put plaits round my head for the first time ever without looking as if I was going to have a bath! Everyone says the result is becoming.

Wednesday 22 July
I am reading Tennyson Jesse's[4] letters to America, *While London Burns.* She has no opinion of Lord Halifax and his narrow-minded Christian piety. It was said of him while he was Viceroy of India that he used to spend several hours a day in a chapel communing with the Deity and seeking his advice. 'Then he must have been very ill-advised' was the comment. Rather nice. She is down on him chiefly because he will rub in his Christianity stunts as if they were the only people in the world who wanted peace and humanity or a decent way of life, to the exclusion of Buddhism, Confucianism or Mohammedism. Have always disliked him myself and think these old school Tory idealists one of the most dangerous reactionary types. They always rake up a certain following with their religious ramps.

Thursday 23 July
News from Egypt rather better. We seem to have made a stand and even to be attacking a little. Russian news bad, very serious position around Rostov which looks as if it would fall shortly. We don't seem to be doing much to help them.

Saturday 25 July
We start an all night 'Invasion exercise' tonight. I don't think we shall be 'playing' unless the casualties become very numerous, and rumour has it that the 'Enemy' will not arrive before dawn. I suppose these stunts do some good, though the British public is quite incapable of taking them seriously. Russian news gets worse and worse in the south, though at Voronesch, which was supposed to be a key point captured by the Germans three weeks ago, the Russians are still in possession and even taking the initiative.

Sunday 26 July

Very noisy planes in night. Are 'enemy parachutists' dropping in the invasion exercise? The *Observer* thinks the situation at Rostov is very serious and that the whole advance here is comparable to the break through at Sedan in 1940. I can't help thinking that Timoshenko[5] has something up his sleeve and will throw in vast fresh reinforcements at just the right moment when the Germans are getting exhausted. Probably this is only my blind faith in Russia, contrasted with the lack of faith of the right-wing papers and their continued surprise at any Russian success. However even the Russians now say that their resources are not inexhaustible and have asked for a 'second front' pretty plainly.

Annual meeting of BMA at Devizes Mental Hospital. Only about 20 doctors present out of 78 members of division. Pretty poor. Medical planning committee's interim report on future of medical practice to be discussed. We had already discussed each point separately at much length in the study groups in the winter, but most of the people present today had not attended those group meetings, so they wanted to start at the beginning again, which made it all very lengthy. It is remarkable how much the report has recommended the same conclusions that we had come to independently, viz:

1. Extension of NHI principle of capitation fee rather than a salaried service.
2. Extension of NHI to wives and dependants, which would then include 95% of the population.
3. Provision of pathology and consultant services.
4. Encouragement of group practice at health centres to facilitate domestic arrangements, off times and holidays.
5. Regionalisation of hospitals.

All sounds very nice, but probably under any state scheme we shall be worse off than at present, though conditions of service and leisure may be better. They could not very well be worse.

Monday 27 July
Rostov definitely in German hands and they seem to have forced crossings on the Don. Where are Timoshenko's reserves?

A great deal of attention in the papers lately on the subject of beating submarine attacks by using enormous fleets of large transport planes to fly cargo across the Atlantic. A revolutionary idea, that ships could become unnecessary, but even considering the thought is revolutionary enough.

Some Bath workers, and some from Corsham, are being moved, rumour says to build an enormous chain of aerodromes along the south coast, possibly for our airborn invasion of France. It seems a bit late in the day to be starting only now to build these, but you never know. A large stretch of land between Poole, Wareham and Studland has been requisitioned and is to be evacuated completely of civilians, ostensibly because the military are to practise there with live ammunition, but could it be to do with the above rumour?

The worst of it is we always seem to be too late for everything. If we wait till Russia is beaten and then let all the Huns come back west, it will just be playing into their hands as every other country in Europe has done.

Tuesday 28 July
Ruth returned from school, very grown up.

Tizzard is going up for his army medical.

Quotation from *While London Burns*:

> To me anyone who thinks that any place or system in the world will provide an infallible receipt for a golden life is a sufferer from infantilism.

Rather nice, but very much what the Socialists are apt to do. They think that everything in the garden will be lovely because there is socialism.

Wednesday 29 July
The papers have been hammering into us that we are today (because of the breakthrough on the Don) in as serious a position

militarily as after Dunkirk. The public certainly seems to be unduly complaisant about the situation. Last year, when Russia was first attacked, the large number of anti-Russian people thought that they would be smashed and not hold out long. Those who knew at first hand, or even from intelligent reading, had great faith in both the Red Army and the morale and staying power of the Russian people. This year the position seems to be somewhat reversed. People who never cared two hoots about Russia before and who were sceptical about her powers of resistance have now been converted by her marvellous winter campaign into thinking she is invincible. They seem to believe it is quite all right to let her continue to fight our battles for us, and that we are doing enough to help by spasmodic air raids on German towns. The people who had great faith in Russia last year are now shaking their heads and saying that the position is very serious and that if they have to retreat beyond the Volga they will not be able to feed or support themselves, as they will have lost most of their fertile land.

Thursday 30 July

Devizes again in am, then a marvellous trip up river in two canoes 'through primeval jungle, exploring unknown land where no foot of man has ever trod'.[6] Probably almost true as we forced a passage up a bit of river completely overgrown with reeds which nobody but fools like ourselves would attempt. Anyway the river is never used, and the few fishermen on the bank are amazed and very resentful that anyone should try to do so and disturb their fish. For the complete egotist the fisherman seems to take the palm. It was a marvellous expedition, three hours and completely perfect weather, not too hot. Had to take one of the canoes out and empty the water that had collected in the bottom, but it all added to the spirit of adventure, and coming home Biz said she was 'All singing inside'.

Friday 31 July

Ruth has been working regularly at the new Chippenham day

nursery, with success. I refused to tell them her age and they have decided that it is 15 or 16. I dare not confess she is not yet 13 or they might say she was not old enough to take any responsibility. It is good for her in many ways, as besides getting her out of the house and away from quarrelling with Daisy, it makes her practise nursery rhymes on the piano.

Saturday 1 August
Strings of eyes all morning. Hirst started for his holiday, but I doubt if he ever got there as the crowds at the station were immense and many people everywhere said to have been left behind. People were asked not to travel, but most works and shops are shutting for a full week, which seems too silly for words. If there are to be no extra trains and too much congestion is to be avoided, and if individual staggered holidays are too big a problem, why not arrange the holiday at a different time for different towns? It is asking too much of human nature to ask them not to go away if they are given a week's holiday. If it is essential that we should not use the railways, then why not forbid us to use them except with a permit for really necessary journeys? Sometimes I think we are not totalitarian enough, much though I loathe the totalitarian system.

Monday 3 August
As a bank holiday it was a distinct failure. Royal rang Eric at 3.30am and asked his help with a very sticky breech primipara[7] that had been passed by the consultant as a normal vertex a week before. After deciding that things were pretty grim they got that consultant out to clear up his own mess so to speak, and the baby was lost. Eric got back about 7am, too late to go back to bed or enjoy his extra hour.

Mac at hospital in pm for 16 patients. Bank holidays don't deter him as he never wants to do anything else (except go out with Mary about twice a year, and as she is in Cumbria at the moment this did not apply). Another baby in the evening just to finish up Eric's 'nice quiet day'.

I was not idle, as Broomhead (now a colonel) came over with a bit of hedge under his upper lid, and I had already had a very nervous child with something similar in the morning.

6

THE RIVER HOLIDAY

4 August–4 September 1942

Tuesday 4 August 1942

Quarrelled really badly with Colley for the first time over the holiday question. He went white with rage and I threatened to resign. He said he was not going to be dictated to by an assistant as to when he took his holiday and if he wanted the whole of August he should have it. I said I had asked him last December if it would suit him to have early August this year, and for me to go later in the month, as it had been the other way about last year, and he agreed. Now he has altered his mind at the last minute. He has right on his side I suppose and in a state medical system a senior could muck up his junior's holidays as much as he liked, but we have always run on equity and mutual arrangement more than rights.

If only he had said sooner that he wanted the last half it could easily have been arranged, but now Hirst and Wheeler and the maids are all fixed up and can't alter their plans at the last minute. It doesn't seem unreasonable for me to ask for a fortnight during the family's holidays, considering that for 9 years I have never asked for a day off to meet, see them off, or tend to them when they were ill, but have frequently done his work at inconvenience to myself and their detriment, while he had done things with his children. I have always put work first, and I think to some extent they have suffered for it, but now these camping holidays are the one thing they are all dead keen on doing with us. For the next ten years or so they must have them – it will make all the difference to their future psychology and relations with us. They will want to go off with their own friends soon enough, but we find it very flattering that they want to be with us at this time in their lives.

I don't quite know how I stand with Colley now. Though we have had lots of scraps, I have never made him angry quite like that before!

Wednesday 5 August
Another siren, and also several telephone calls for Eric, altogether a very disturbed night. An important fire official arrived to look at the swimming pool from the point of view of 'static water' and was thrilled by it. Says he will provide two men and a priority order for cement and sand and they will empty it out and mend the cracks properly. It is wonderful as it still leaks badly and if we can get this put right on free labour, and probably the paving stones at the end relaid, it will be well worth while.

Another baby at 6am and another at 11pm for which I gave an anaesthetic. Nasty case for Eric but ended OK though he was very tired. That is 4 in two days exclusive of a midwife's call for a stitch.[1] Fortunately other things are slack. We always seem to live on our babies in the summer. All Chippenham is on holiday this week and not thinking about their ills unless they are very real ones.

Friday 7 August
Wondered what sort of reception I should get from Colley after our quarrel last Tuesday, but all was well, though we were both a little more polite than usual, and holidays were not mentioned! Tizzard is said to have passed his medical but has not told anyone personally.

Daisy tried making tomato ketchup out of our own tomatoes as it is difficult to buy it now, and if we are to live on haricot beans all the winter a tomato flavour is a considerable help. Much tasting and household discussion.

Sunday 9 August
Morning news gave out that Gandhi, Nehru and most of the Indian

Congress[2] have been arrested on the eve of launching a non-violent civil disobedience campaign with the slogan 'British quit India.' Gandi electrified everyone by saying that if the British could be induced to leave, he would immediately start negotiations with Japan. The public have taken this to mean that he would let Japan into India without more ado. Of course he did not mean that at all, but is apparently so much of a visionary that he thought he could personally, by asking the Japanese, persuade them to get out of China and give it all up, as well as all their aspirations to India! Some hope! The *Observer* has a long leader comparing him to Christ and saying he is the most Christian thing that has happened for hundreds of years, although he is a Hindu to the marrow.

All the same I don't really see that we could practically do anything other than arrest them, as we really could not allow a wide civil disobedience movement at this moment, and Nehru himself has stated that we could not be expected to withdraw while directly threatened by Japan. It was stated on the wireless, but not I think emphatically or often enough, that the 'Government of India,'[3] who decided on the arrests, consisted of the Viceroy, one other Englishman and 11 Indians, so that for them to say that it is cruel and arbitrary action by the British is exaggeration to say the least of it.

Monday 10 August
Germans still being held in front of Stalingrad in bend of Don, but making progress in the south towards the Caucasus. Riots in India, but on the whole not as bad as many people expected, mostly in Bombay, and obviously a hooligan element to whom any excuse is good enough.

Friday 14 August
Colley still appearing at the Eye Hospital though he should have gone away today. We have compromised about next week. I have said I will do the 25th and not go away till after then, and he will do 28th.

Saturday 15 August

Daphne Bryant's wedding. There seemed no plausible excuse to get out of it, and the best we could do was to say we couldn't possibly be at the church by 2pm, and would go to the reception. I really couldn't give up my 18-year-old accomplishment of having never been inside the Chippenham church, even to look at the architecture.

Sunday 16 August

The first fine day for over a week, so we were able to go to the van for tea and supper and introduce Arthur to the canoes, which he had not seen and was much enamoured of. Elizabeth found Avice Rita Dickinson riding the Hales' pony, and was offered a ride, which she took. Afterwards Avice fetched the Selfs' pony Harlequin and the two went off together, Elizabeth trotting and galloping all over the place, though she has only ridden a few times. She managed to fall off without hurting herself, and get up at once which is a definite experience gained. I darned my trousers and rode Harlequin to the house to telephone and back and trotted without falling off which was an achievement for me as I have only been on a horse about three times since I left school. Ruth and I determined we would borrow the ponies again and have some rides together in the fields. A lovely day *en famille*.

Tuesday 18 August

Eric's birthday, which everyone except Biz forgot. A bit of enemy activity in the night. Many flares, a few bombs near Trowbridge and Swindon, and our fighters rather surprisingly dashing about with their lights on. Daisy and Lucy were fire-watching, and as it was the first time anything had happened when they were on, Eric and I got up and went out with them.

It is always a problem on these occasions whether to put on a very old and decrepit skirt and jumper (5–6 years old) in anticipation of doing dirty and messy work putting out fires. Or one's newest and most respectable (2–3 years old) in anticipation of one's whole house being burnt out and being left with nothing else but the clothes one has on one's back.

Ruth had her nursery school superintendent to supper, an interesting elderly Scotswoman, who knew her stuff and was quite interesting on the development of nursery schools and education generally, but talked too much. She says that being run by the Ministry of Health, everything is done for the physical health of the children, but nothing for their mental health and development, about which no one in charge knows anything. I can quite believe it. There are two excellent Great Ormond Street nurses at the top of our local school nursing service, but after all it is meant to be for well children, not ill ones, and trained nurses phenomenally know nothing and less than nothing about bringing up well children, or their psychological problems.

Wednesday 19 August
News today says that we are in the midst of making a large raid in the Dieppe area. We have broadcast to the French that it is a raid only, and not an invasion, and that they are not to join in and invite reprisals.

Friday 21 August
Not only raining but blowing a gale and whistling round the chimneys, so I lit a fire. Everyone very depressed about holiday prospects, even the family, while outsiders think we are quite mad anyway.

Stalingrad still holds, though things get gradually worse. Spitfires have gone back to Dieppe to deal with more gun emplacements. Are we perhaps going back there again, really to invade this time?

Sunday 23 August
Started experimental rolls of bedding etc. The result was far too big and heavy either to carry far or take on any bus. Eric had a brilliant idea and approached the manager of the Bulwark Transport Co. whose wife has just had a baby and he is going to arrange for the

luggage to go on one of his lorries, or a series of them. Consequently we have made the rolls even bigger and heavier, putting in 3 tents, 3 sleeping bags, 3 ground sheets and 10 blankets! Some bundle. A good bit of family quarrel and argument about how we were going to pack what and everybody's individual rights. Avoiding the use of petrol and car for our holiday is going to result in very much more total transport as an end result, viz:

1. Special cartage of punt on lorry from Oxford to Lechlade.
2. Taking bedding to Lechlade, possibly on lorry that happens to be passing, but which I suspect will have to go several miles out of its way.
3. Trunk and suitcase sent by rail to Whitchurch.
4. Five people by train to Swindon.
5. Five people from Swindon to Lechlade, either by train, bus or hitch-hiking.

It would have really been much simpler and infinitely cheaper to have fixed the van to the car in the ordinary way and used the petrol for the 40 odd miles there and back, but such are the strange regulations of this country. We shall at any rate have a holiday out of the ordinary and not devoid of adventure, and a change from telephones and appointments.

I have been utterly fed up lately with the whole well-run establishment and business I have built up round me, feeling quite claustrophobic about it as if it were throttling me and dragging me down intellectually. Especially with all the various retainers who have their own idea and picture of what I am and what I do and what I want, and will be so interested and helpful with everything. Oh, to get right away to a completely new milieu where no one has ever heard of Dr Joan Hickson of Chippenham and her charming and efficiently organised home. A holiday will help, even a wartime one, but shall we ever be able to take a car across the Channel again for a month and with no plans?

Monday 24 August
All the old chronic patients to be seen before going away and

endless things to settle about what is to be lent to whom, canoes to Rudmans, van to Hales, flowers and vegetables to go to Hirst, bathing invitations to all and sundry, maids to have friends to stay. Also housekeeping decisions, which jam and chutney to be made, who is to wash blankets and where, the sweep to call, fire-watching rota to be changed and endless people to tell that we shall be away.

The staff nearly driving me dotty about what we are going to do and how we will live. Daisy is always fussing about food and ration books and is quite sure we shall starve and repeating 'You don't realise how difficult things are.' Simmy will ask when we are going, train or bus, how we are getting to Lechlade, when we are aiming to get to Whitchurch. If I merely say that I don't know she shakes her head and thinks we are congenital idiots and a few minutes later asks if we have yet decided whatever it was. Even the children want to know when we are aiming to get to Oxford. No one seems to realise the attraction of having no aim and no plans and not to know where or how you are going or eating until you are doing it. I could knock all their heads together for being so interested and wanting to know so much. We haven't decided nor are likely to decide in advance, though I know it is only affectionate interest and anxiety for our welfare, and I ought to be grateful that anyone feels for us like that.

The Germans are over the Don at one place towards Stalingrad and things look very nasty.

Tuesday 25 August
Pouring with rain all day and everyone most pessimistic. I spent a long morning alone at Eye Hospital, then hair done in lunch hour, patients at Colley's rooms after that and home to trial-pack our rucksacks. Still pouring, so decide that as macs will certainly be worn their bulky space can be filled up. Do not pack any sun hats but masses of sweaters and jerseys of all sorts.

Wednesday 26 August

The day dawns. Everything dripping damp but not actually raining. 8 o'clock news says the Duke of Kent killed in air crash. Thank goodness it wasn't Churchill or anyone really effective. Those brothers are a pretty dissolute lot I should think and cost the state in income far more than they earn in service (what awful heresy). They all strangely seem to be worshipped by the general public, except the real Communists. I always thought Edward VIII the best of the lot. Though he did drink too much, he was the most socialist minded of the lot, and would have done a spot of good if he had been allowed to.

Weighed our rucksacks for interest. Eric's was 28lbs, mine 26lbs. I believe the infantryman's full kit is 60lb. It must need some training to carry that. I find mine is quite heavy enough. Two picnic baskets and equipment in addition, also saddlebags on Arthur's and Ruth's bikes. Difficult to prevent Daisy showering us with more food than we could carry.

Embarked from Chippenham station much to everyone's benevolent amusement. Thought what a thoroughly nice, clean English family we looked, though cleanliness will not be so marked after the first day. Was proud of them all and grateful to be a member of it.

Swindon a mass of damp fog, pavements greasy, damp and slippy. Arthur and Ruth start for Lechlade on bikes, and we arranged to meet them there. Having carried our packs for a bit we decide to wait for the 12.40pm bus through to Lechlade and not attempt to hitch-hike there first. I think this was a wise decision. The bus was full of nice family parties going for an afternoon's fishing on the river, most friendly and sympathetic about our luggage.

Weather improving every moment. Before we left Swindon the roads started to dry. Panicked for a bit thinking Ruth was certain to have an accident skidding on the greasy road but my fears soon wore off.

Both children safe and waiting on the bridge at Lechlade and the punt all ready, so off we set. It was a good old heavy camper, with very dirty, ugly cushions, but it took all our traps without a murmur. We are supposed to be travelling as light as possible, but with bedding, tents, cooking utensils and everything for 5 it was not so light.

Had our first lunch a mile down as it was then past two. Sun almost out and we sat on the bank and I thought what bliss and what more could anyone desire? Nothing seemed to matter any more and the war faded into perspective. The old Thames has seen many wars and gone rolling along just the same. It was bliss to me not to know where I was going to lay my head that night, and to feel it didn't matter.

Actually we progressed downstream only as far as Kelmscott[4] (Eric and Ruth on bikes), and found a nice little inn there, the Anchor, just what we wanted. This however would do nothing for us except mineral water, as their catering licence had been taken away because they did not have enough trade to make it worth while. They warned us that this was the case with most of the smaller inns, and that larger ones would mostly only serve their residents with food, so we must be self-supporting.

They let us camp in the adjoining meadow, so we engineered an excellent supper with packet soup and slices of Green Gables chicken and tomato on bread and butter, then apples and chocolate. Pitched two tents and Eric, Arthur and I slept in the punt. This was just opposite an adorable pair of water rats' home, and they kept popping in and out of their holes, washing their faces, doing their toilet and having breakfast on the bank, giving us endless joy.

It was a marvellous evening, the sun setting up river behind the trees which with their reflections made a black band with no horizon line visible and capped above and below with pink afterglow through blue to smoke grey. Gradually the light faded, taking the colour but leaving the black band until the moon came up.

I was thrilled to be so near Kelmscott and determined to fulfil a lifelong ambition to see the manor, but was frustrated. We went up to make enquiries but found a chilling notice saying that it was not open to the public, but that Mrs Gordon Snell[5] would show it to students and genuine Pre-Raphaelite enthusiasts if application was made by letter and a mutually convenient time arranged. I pondered whether I came into either of these two categories, and decided that though not exactly I would chance ringing the bell, and hope that the charm of my smile and the perfect (though restrained) taste of my Braemar heather mixture coat and skirt would melt her hard heart. As she did not even condescend to answer the bell this could not be put to the test, but when we were crossing the field again to the river she and a boyfriend were gazing at us quite unabashed through the fence at the bottom of the garden! If I had been my mother I should have turned back and tackled her, but had not the face to do so.

This part of the river has changed extraordinarily little in the 20 or so years since I saw it last. The only new note is that of a myriad of aeroplanes which might prove very trying to some. There must be a training aerodrome quite near as there are dozens of Harts, Tiger Moths etc every minute, also one Whitley[6] towing an enormous glider going round and round, I suppose practising for our airborne invasion of France. Although the noise does disturb the peace, I am glad, as it is an interest for Arthur other than the river, which might have bored him in the doses in which we are taking it, but he is perfectly happy observing and snapping different sorts of planes.

Thursday 27 August

Not a very good night. The first one never is. One cannot help missing the Vi-spring mattress! The water rats also kept waking us up by jumping into the water with a loud plop, and we were so intrigued by them that we had to open our eyes and watch them each time. A tern decided that the top of the awning was a suitable place for his early morning promenade. The day dawned warm but with an intense, damp mist, the sun slowly breaking through, as perfect a late summer day as one could hope to have, with not even the nip of early autumn in the air. We got away in good time,

Arthur and I on bikes for a shopping expedition to Farringdon as bread was short and not so much other food. This proved an excellent move, as we found a marvellous International[7] there with sausages and fish cakes (which we ate cold for lunch). I was also rather pleased with my bicycling ability after 18 years. Everybody told me that my legs would ache after a mile, but they didn't and I managed 6 miles on a bike about 4 times too small in comparative comfort, though I must have looked a funny sight.

Punt progressed very slowly against an upstream wind. Extraordinary how the wind on the river always seems to be in the opposite direction to the one in which one is going.

Tadpole Bridge gave us a drink and a lovely swim but told us the sad news that we were not allowed to camp for several miles because of the proximity of an aerodrome. Also they could not provide us with drinking water, so Ruth and Eric and Elizabeth sweated back to Rushey Lock in the punt for this, then rejoined us further down the river. About a mile further on the tow-path was blocked with a large notice saying 'No Admittance, Air Ministry'. This was another blow as Arthur and Ruth had to find a road again and go on to Shifford while the rest of us, rather tired, pushed the punt on. We had hoped to call a halt early and have a good cook, but it was not to be.

Eventually we found a marvellous campsite on the tongue of land between the cut to Shifford Lock and the old river, with willow trees, a weir and first class pull in with the punt. We joined up with the others and hurriedly pitched our tents and cooked supper, which we fell on like wolves.

The blackout is a bit of a nuisance as we can have no lights at all, and must be ready for bed by nine though it was no hardship last night as we were all dog tired.

Friday 28 August
Another marvellous sunrise over the river through mist which turned to heat. An easy few miles to New Bridge, where at the Rose Revived we had a lovely swim and lunch, the first proper

meal since we had left home. It was a typical riverside hotel of the down-river type, not cheap so that for five we could not do it often, but it was much appreciated as an exception. The children do not seem to have as much stamina for this sort of thing as I had thought and hoped. Their immediate feelings of heat, cold, hunger, thirst or repletion seem to take precedence over their spirit of adventure. At 17 yrs Arthur should be tough and hefty and able to carry on and endure minor discomforts, whereas he gets tired and done in sooner than I do. He shows extraordinarily little interest in anything other than aeroplanes. Ruth is perpetually too hot or has a headache or a blister on her heel, and Biz grumbles if the bread is too thick or too thin or the coffee too strong. I suppose we have brought them up too comfortably, yet have always made a point of their being independent and able to fend for themselves. This trip will be good for them though I doubt they are enjoying it as much as I am.

Saturday 29 August
Arthur and I bicycled to Oxford where we laid in masses of provisions for the weekend and had some lunch. We meet the others at Swinford Bridge. Again we determined to camp early, but a thunder shower, the first spot of rain we had had, held us up and frustrated my good resolutions to make Eric a real cup of tea which I had not done so far. We found a most attractive camp site with willow trees, and cooked a colossal supper on a real camp fire as the methylated spirits for the stove was nearly exhausted and completely unobtainable even for medical purposes. Just after we had finished our troubles began. The atmosphere grew more and more sultry and a dense black cloud appeared, moving rapidly in our direction. We told the girls to get to bed in their tents quickly, and they had just got their clothes and bedding thoroughly strewn about inside when the storm broke with sudden and violent fury. They did not like the idea of being alone, so we all got into the punt, thinking it would be a matter of half an hour or so. Seldom have I known such a storm. It vied with the one just after Biz was

born 9 years ago when umpteen people descended upon us who did not mix but had to be given tea and shelter. This one went on for nearly three hours, the lightening illuminating the whole sky, passing off a little then coming back, away and back again time after time. Rain poured down, pattering on the roof with such violence that we could hardly hear ourselves speak even when there was no thunder. (Afterwards we heard there had been 1½ inches of rain in those few hours.) Gradually it began to seep through the canvas cover and drip into the punt, though with macs on inside we kept fairly dry. We had to bale out once in the middle of the night when the floorboards showed signs of coming awash. No one dared go out to see if the tents were still standing, as it would have been impossible to do so without bringing much more mud and wet into the punt again. It seemed impossible that anything in them could be dry or fit for the children to sleep on, so we stayed where we were for the night in great discomfort.

The rain stopped eventually, but morning dawned reeking with damp and quite impossible to contemplate lighting a fire or attempting to get a meal We were all pretty exhausted and seized with sickness and dizziness. The woman at the lock let us have a kettle and some goats milk to make some tea which enabled Eric to carry on, though I promptly returned it, though felt better afterwards. We could none of us face the hunks of bread and general mess of a camp breakfast, so pushed on to Godstow very shakily, Arthur and I going ahead to try and arrange lunch. This was impossible. The inn had no staff or accommodation and were only interested in selling beer, but eventually promised us sandwiches, and produced some rather stodgy unappetising ham ones. Only Eric and Arthur could touch these when it came to the point, though I struggled through half of one. The girls were in a state of collapse and vomiting at intervals, and the weather still not looking too good.

Under the circumstances it seemed imperative to find indoor accommodation for the night, so again Arthur and I set off for Oxford. This left all the punting to Eric, but I seemed to be the only person who could manage Ruth's bike, though with loose handlebars, a constantly slipping three speed, a loose chain cover clanking continually, and myself feeling dizzy, sick, faint and exhausted, it was no easy matter. We got nearly desperate looking for rooms in Oxford, which seemed to be full to capacity. Tried 8 places, all full, and I was getting near the end of my tether and feeling I should sit on the pavement soon. Then Arthur found the Royal Hotel near the station, which had rooms and could take us in. Very modern and perfect and expensive but I was past caring about anything like that by this time. Met the others at Salter's boathouse and put the girls straight to bed where they slept till morning. We had a real tea, then a rest and a delicious dinner with soup and cold chicken, which much revived us. Bed very soon afterwards and I don't think I have ever appreciated a spring mattress and down pillows so much.

Monday 31 August
Still drizzly and grey so we decided to stay here another day and go on by launch to Whitchurch tomorrow. There is also a circus here tomorrow afternoon. We tried to get up Magdalen tower but failed as it is closed for the war (probably acting as an observer post). Instead we went to see the deer down Magdalen Water Walks. They were lying asleep in herds, fathers, mothers and children. We decided they were exactly like the real Oxford, beautiful, decorative and aristocratic, completely sure of themselves having lived there for hundreds of years unmolested, but a little aloof from the active world of strife. After watching them for a time we were rather bored by their immobility and thought we would like to see them move, so clapped our hands through the fence and said 'Shoo'. Not the slightest notice was taken. Again we clapped and made noises, and Biz even barked furiously. Would they move? No. In their familiar safety they would scarcely look at us mere trippers and would not so honour us as even to be alarmed by our presence and mad capers.

I feel I am getting to know Oxford a bit and am attracted to it.

I think I should like to live near, possibly on some of the strictly private and forbidden Nuneham woods, with some job three times a week at one of the Oxford hospitals, and perhaps married to an Oxford consultant of some sort. But I suppose I should not like it unless I was really 'in' the Oxford medical world, and it is too late now to dig up my roots with any prospect of taking root anywhere else.

The circus was a very wartime effort and pretty poor (or am I getting too old for circuses?), but Biz was in seventh heaven. What animals there were looked sleek and fat and well groomed, but there were few of them and the riding and clowning were poor.

Tuesday 1 September
Caught 'The Oxford', the 9.30 boat from Salters. Not a very nice day and I think we were right not to keep on the punt. Strong headwind which would have been foul to punt against. I enjoyed it more than I expected. Biz was thrilled to be on a steamer. Arthur and Ruth to my surprise did not enthuse, though recognised a useful method of getting 30 miles by river in one day. I thoroughly enjoyed seeing bits of the upper river again after 20 years. There are still white ducks by Clifton Hampden bridge even in wartime, who were obligingly swimming across for me just when the bridge hove into sight. Three herons were in a field nearby, and one kept circling round and round the launch.

We have seen lovely animals and birds on this trip, and as I suppose the two prevailing passions of my life have been animals and the river I have been in seventh heaven (except for Saturday night and Sunday). Couldn't resist pointing out a certain number of landmarks to the children though I expect it bored them, but they were pretty polite about it and Ruth does sometimes genuinely like to know about what I used to do. After Wallingford they began to recognise their own places. Mummy was waiting for us at Whitchurch lock with the punt, and we got up to Underwood for tea.

She had arranged a marvellous 'home' for us, bedroom in

lower garage which she had cleaned out and furnished (even the roof cleared and not full of old sacks and spiders which I had anticipated), and a kitchen/living room on the loggia. There was a cupboard full of marvellous stores, almost pre-war, which must have come from her own supplies. The loggia is the apple of her eye and she must loathe the idea of our mess on it all day, but she says she has 're-orientated her mind.'

D in a state of depression, apparently because Miles has a girlfriend, and he has gone all psychological about it as he did when I got married. It must be his own Oedipus coming out. All the same it must be very hard to adjust to one's children getting married, and quite inevitable to think that whoever they choose is not good enough for them, though Granny was pretty marvellous about me.

Wednesday 2 September
Back home after being away for just a week, and what a week of adventure and unusual happenings for us. Had a thoroughly domestic day cleaning our blackened saucepans and washing all our clothes etc. Also heard some news, which has rather gone by the board lately as it was difficult to get papers at odd hours on the trip. Stalingrad still holds, but things are very serious there and it looks as if it must fall.

Thursday 3 September
Woke up and looked outside the garage door to see an enchanting squirrel sitting up in the path. Afterwards he ran backwards and forwards for about half an hour, I am afraid taking our nuts to his winter store, but he was so adorable I could not grudge them to him. Another gusty, unsettled day, not nice enough for the river with a good deal of rain. I began to get rather bored with domesticities. One day I enjoy immensely, the second it palls a little but is just tolerable. By the third I begin to see that there are advantages in having good maids! There is also a little field mouse with his home on the path outside the loggia. We give him all our crumbs and he

seems to have put on weight since our arrival home.

Friday 4 September
Arthur and I went up to London on an early train and separated for mutual shopping. It was emptier than I expected, no undue crowds in the shops and traffic extraordinarily less congested than I can ever recall it. A surprising amount of things in the shops considering, though it is generally necessary to search for anything particular. Lovely sweets so as we had none of us had used up our ration (¼ lb each per week) we did rather well. Got theatre tickets for the whole family (ex Biz) for next week. There seem to be a lot of good plays on now, making it difficult to choose. Generally when I want to go there is nothing but revues, musical comedies or rubbish. Perhaps the difficulty of coupons and clothes has had the effect of more straight plays being produced of the type that people like us like. Arthur and I met for a rather bad two-shilling lunch at a Flemings restaurant and went to a film *The First of the Few*. It was about the evolution of the Spitfire (with a great deal of sentiment and pathos added).

It is terribly expensive taking the family about like this in London, Oxford or anywhere else, but I feel it must be done for their education. I, who hardly ever spend any cash, was horrified at the way my £1 notes simply melted away. I must try not to be so mingy about this, as I am sure it is necessary for them. But we have got into the way of spending nothing on holidays in England, having always had Whitchurch or Swanage to go to with the van and the car, and wanting to save for the sake of a holiday abroad every three or four years. It has been a lovely day just because we decided to go to London. Ruth did most of the chores at home, and prepared a lovely fish dish for our supper. She is really quite good if given her head, but cannot co-operate with the maids, and I don't altogether blame her.

7

BACK TO WORK

15 September–21 October 1942

Tuesday 15 September 1942
A hell of a day making me wonder why anyone ever goes away for holidays at all – or if they do, why not stay away for ever? It started before I got down to breakfast, with a parson's wife and daughter from a village 8 miles away who arrived to see me with a story I didn't understand, but on some arrangement that had been made in my absence without my knowledge. It turned out that a local Dr had told Simmy of a very urgent case I must see before I went to Bath, and Simmy thinking it was just a foreign body in the eye or something similar had weakly consented. It turned out that the doctor was afraid that the girl had a detached retina and had told them that I would examine her and if necessary take her into Bath. It was the sort of case I would have normally have messed about with for an hour, but as she didn't arrive till I was due to start for Bath, and her eye would have to be dilated anyhow, it was pretty impossible even to start. Anyway I wanted some breakfast. I couldn't take her and the mother with me as all three children were coming with me for dentist appointments and there was no room in the car. In the end I persuaded them to come into the Eye Hospital in their own car, with much humming and hawing, it was inconvenient and they did not have enough petrol etc. They are the sort of parson's family who make me see red, never dreaming of paying a doctor for anything, but thinking it should be sufficient privilege for him to tend those in the church for free. They have an extremely good living, one of the plums of the church as far

as they go. When I was doing Spong's practice (eight miles from home) they kept sending for me at all hours when I wasn't going in their direction at all, and then not paying for it. Not that it would have meant any extra for me as I was being paid a salary, but it would for Spong himself. It always used to annoy me then, and now when they came at an awkward hour and expected to be given a lift to Bath it was the last straw. However the girl cannot help her parents. She had an acute choroiditis,[1] so we admitted her which at any rate saved having to run out there for nothing in the future. OPs was seething and Colley was still chilly and pained with me. I had written him what I thought was a friendly, conciliatory letter but he had apparently taken offence at something I had said (I had by this time forgotten what I had said), and it was all very difficult and annoying on the first day back at work.

Wednesday 16 September
Tizzard's OPs which I always loathe doing. Can't read his writing or discover what is supposed to be wrong with his string of old patients. Did not finish till 1.45pm and had patients at home starting at 2.30pm. They culminated with Mrs R-H who is quite mental and nearly makes me so, throwing dozens of pairs of glasses and prescriptions at me and asking for cushions and the loo and how my children are or anything but giving a straight answer to what I am asking her. I was so weak with exhaustion that I finally consented to change her glasses. My one idea is usually to resist doing this. She is well over 70 yrs and thinks that a change about every 6 months will help her facial neuralgia. She brings out all her old bifocals which she has muddled and wants me to check and tell her which is what and which pair she keeps by her bed and which in the hall. She was followed by an old lady of 87 yrs with sudden loss of sight in one eye and tiny pupils. Couldn't see a thing, and would her pupil dilate? No. Eric champing for the room for his 5pm patients so I had to send her home with atropine as if she were a child.

Thursday 17 September

Fortunately no school clinic so kept on trying to catch up with appointments here. Time to pay a few bills and, very late in the day, to collect some of the children's clothes which really had to be cleaned. Spent the afternoon carting a load of stone that had been dumped while we were away. We had asked the builder to get some for us and also wangled two bags of cement out of him, so we now hope to finish the pillars of the steps to the tennis court from the point where it had been left off at the start of the war.

Fighting is now on the outskirts of Stalingrad, the defence of which will probably prove to be one of the greatest epics of the war. It must fall now it seems, yet by its resistance it has probably made it too late for another German offensive on Moscow before the winter. The city is the only place (except a bit in the Caucasus) where the Germans are really attacking. They have had to put all they had into the offensive for this one place, so that if it falls (which was previously said would lengthen the war for ten years) it may be an empty victory for them, like Moscow was for Napoleon.

Friday 18 September

A hectic day again with no time to breathe between patients either in Bath or back here in pm. After I was dropping with fatigue the Holt-Wilsons arrived *en famille* as they always do, just at tea-time, and wanted a consultation, an injection and a friendly chat all at once. I am fond of them but they are completely vague as to time, and though they always refuse tea they don't realise that if we don't have it on the dot, Eric's 5pm patients start arriving and he is on the go till 7.30pm with no food.

Saturday 19 September

Still pretty busy with Tizzard's OPs all morning and several patients here in pm. Eric had six casualties at the hospital from one lorry which was carrying workmen and a concrete mixer, and all went in the ditch. One is bad with a chest injury.

The garden is a perfect wilderness, plants overgrown and full of weeds. Have had no time to touch it since we got back, hardly to look at it, which is perhaps just as well as it is too depressing.

Sunday 20 September

Eric's patient with a chest injury is bad, so we decided to try to get hold of the government Emergency Medical Services (EMS) chest expert who is supposed to be available for transferred essential workers. After two hours of continuous and expensive telephoning we managed to speak to a 'Regional Hospital Officer' who said he could get a message through to the required man Belsey, and would let us know. Later in the afternoon we got Belsey himself on the telephone. He was at Taunton on a case and said he would be here later – but when?

The children had asked the whole Awdry family in for a family bridge contest in the evening, so it was most awkward as we didn't know whether to put them off or not, or whether Belsey would arrive in the middle. We decided to leave it and await events and it was well that we did. Soon after 8pm there was a telephone message from Taunton to say that he had just left there and would be with us at 11pm.

At 8.30pm Bristol rang up wanting him urgently, and thought perhaps he had already arrived here.

At 11.45pm his own hospital at Kewstoke, near Weston, rang to say he had arrived there from Taunton and left again to see the Bristol case.

At 1.15am Belsey himself rang to say 'What about it?' As the man was rather better they decided to leave it till next day when he said he could come in the afternoon and would let us know what time later. Not much of a last Sunday for Arthur.

Monday 21 September

Full up am and pm with many held-over appointments. In the intervals tried to do Arthur's packing, and stimulate him to do the really necessary things, such as fetching his blazer from the cleaners, arranging for his luggage in advance and finding out the time of his train. Always a trying day. I am inclined to fly off the deep end because this or that or the other hasn't been done till the last moment. Or I haven't been told that something wants mending or cleaning or washing till it is too late, and Arthur flies into a temper or an argument about nothing and resists strongly if hurried or harried. My one idea is to keep him from speaking to the maids if possible, as if he does they say he is rude, and that starts arguments. However we got through it not too badly somehow.

About 5.30pm Belsey rang up to say he would be with us at 8pm. At 8.30pm a message from Bristol said he had just left and would arrive at 9.15pm. Some hope we thought in blackout driving. Actually he arrived about 9.45pm and proved to be quite surprisingly charming and talking the same language as us. Young and dark with a rather 'arty' green suit, rather pansy, but I am regretfully coming to the conclusion that I like that type. They are at least intelligent and easier to talk to than the hearty ones. He is a complete enthusiast about his work, and runs a chest unit for the EMS at Kewstoke. This job enables him to do chest surgery only, collecting cases from the whole of S-W England, a super-specialisation that would be impossible in private practice, so government service suits him. He works tremendously hard dashing about all over the country to look at many accidents and emergencies. Later when they came back from the hospital we got off on caravans and birds etc. He said he had had dinner, but judging from the avidity with which he tucked into the tea and sandwiches I raked up I doubt it.

We sat up talking till after midnight, and Eric said he could see I had fallen for the young man he had produced, as it was so unusual for me to be awake at this hour! I think we shall see more of him. Curious how suddenly, out of the blue and unexpectedly, one meets someone who talks the same language. One may have complete diversity of tastes, opinions and beliefs but one gets on immediately, yet with hosts of other people, even many doctors, one can never really talk about anything, but can only exchange inane platitudes.

Tuesday 22 September
Arthur went to the station and was seen off by Ruth who has an extra week owing to polio in the neighbourhood of her school. Raining again. We shall never get our haricot beans and potatoes dried at this rate. The onions, a marvellous crop, are in fortunately.

Fighting in the streets of Stalingrad. Every street and house and every floor of every house is being defended. The blood and beastliness of it all doesn't bear thinking about. One feels it simply couldn't happen here, except just after a bad air raid or sudden moments of panic when one feels it might, and that it is awful for anyone to attempt any form of normal life. Yet I suppose it is part of our strength to try to keep up a normal civilised life to the end, but may also be much of our weakness too, and a cause of not giving enough help to Russia.

Eric had an invasion committee in the evening out of which he was called to a baby at the maternity home for which he was devoutly thankful. He says they are very boring (invasion committees, not delivering babies), and that the military commander (a retired general and local magnate) sits with his hand to his ear and hears nothing – so typical of England.

Wednesday 23 September
Elizabeth started school with much joy, though most of her favourite mistresses have left. The great objection to that school[2] is that they are always changing their staff, though when I murmured about it to the headmistress she hotly denied it, probably because she had a guilty conscience. I could quarrel with that woman very easily, but keep out of her way for Elizabeth's sake, as it does seem to suit her most surprisingly, and the amount of general knowledge she amasses from it is remarkable.

Thursday 24 September
Carted wood in the afternoon. A load had been dumped by the side of the garage completely blocking the way through. Both girls helped well. They will do jobs like that with us, but will not do

them alone. Extraordinary how psychologically satisfying a job like carting wood can be, especially with the feeling that it will keep us warm in the winter. There is a mad publicity campaign for voluntary fuel rationing, which will mean that the conscientious will save till they are ill and the people with no social conscience won't take any notice. I am afraid we are rather the latter. Though quite prepared not to be wasteful and leave things on in unused rooms, we are not prepared to shiver unless everybody else definitely has to too as well!

Friday 25 September
One of those days that are all muddled. I had a big OPs in am and then Charles was due here to see two private patients at 2pm. My eye appointments started at 2.30pm which should just have been all right. Of course Charles did not turn up and Eric, Hirst, Simmy and I all waited and waited, having undressed his first patient, an old lady with one leg, and got her on the consulting room couch. At 2.45pm two of my people had also arrived, the waiting room seemed full and everyone was champing but still no Charles. Finally I said I must get on with mine in the consulting room whatever happened, and they could see the others in the sitting room or my bedroom for all I cared. The old lady went home rather hurt, and the next one was led up to the hospital where Charles had already arrived having forgotten about the arrangement to come here first.

Eric called out after supper urgently to a lady who said she had a 'frightened stomach', and by another lady just after he had got to sleep who had been vomiting for some hours. There is a bit of an epidemic of D and V at the minute, and people's relations will pour all sorts of muck from brandy to magnesia down them and then send for the doctor. It never seems to occur to them to make them warm and comfortable and leave them alone. It is really touching the faith this country has in a 'bottle of medicine'. Even most reasonably intelligent people demand it or an equivalent, the magic of an injection or 'electrical treatment'.

Wednesday 30 September
An article in the *News Chronicle* about improved medical services after the war on the lines that only the rich get the best treatment at present. Such articles make me see red, or any that insinuate that doctors do good work only for fees. Actually in the large majority of cases the reverse is the case. There is no other profession in the world where money counts for less, or which is so much exploited by the public. There is nothing else where any necessary work is done first and the ability to pay discussed later, and the fee adjusted according to the means of the patient. It is absolutely untrue and libellous to suggest that medical staff scamp their work in voluntary hospitals in order to run off and see private patients. Quite the reverse is the case. Nearly all the consultants I know are much more interested in their hospital work than their private patients because the work is more interesting with less society small talk. Of course there are black sheep in every profession and many in Harley Street as we all know, but taking it all round I am convinced that doctors are exploited far more by the public than the public by the doctors.

The very rich are liable to get the worst not the best medical treatment. Being ready to pay for magic, and most of them are ignorant enough to demand it, they are ripe for falling into the hands of charlatans, quacks and anyone who has a stunt treatment, and may often be harmed by excessive and unnecessary treatment.

The voluntary hospitals and still more the county institutions could be vastly improved in the way of general comfort and amenities and less red tape and institutional regulations, but I think it would be difficult to better the actual medical treatment of serious cases. Much could be done in the way of home helps for minor cases at home, more possibilities of convalescence at the sea after illness, and housing, food and hygienic conditions of all sorts need to be improved.

Not that I am in favour of the voluntary hospitals continuing unaltered, far from it. I have always thought it very wrong that the medical staff should not be paid, but that is quite a different matter to having them all under bureaucratic red tape.

Thursday 1 October
School clinic once more at Devizes. I had not been there since early August and had almost forgotten what to take (which is everything, with every likelihood of forgetting something vital).

Finished the last but one pillar of the steps to the tennis court in the pm. An old panel patient with pernicious anaemia, a retired stonemason, came out to look at the steps and was kind enough not to laugh at them. He would come for odd hours, and not charge us too much, to get on with the wall if we could find some more stone. We should have to do all the digging out ourselves and navvy for him generally as could not expect him to do that, but it would be nice to progress a bit.

Saturday 2 October
Eric had two babies between supper and bed, fortunately both in the Corsham maternity home. I went over with him and went to see the Wheelers. They showed us their new baby and cooed at it and asked me if I wouldn't like to start all over again. I felt very awkward and ungracious as never could make baby talk. Whenever I see one now, instead of feeling envious as a proper woman should, I feel thankful I am through that stage, and that my own are now sensible human beings who can do things with us.

Tuesday 6 October
A medical meeting of the Chippenham hospital medical staff in the evening to consider a report in which various recommendations are made, one of which is that doctors in hospital should at any rate be offered remuneration. This seemed the moment for us to press our committee to offer a fee to our long-suffering consultants when they come out and do hours and hours of work at the hospital for nothing.

Wednesday 7 October
A hectic day. Devizes Mental Hospital all morning, and patients
at home in pm. Eric was hauled out of tea to Marshfield Road
maternity home for two patients who were apparently having a
race to deliver. One was a breech that had been haemorrhaging
a bit the last few days and worrying him, so he went along with
the anaesthetic bag while I held the fort here. I had to put on an
Unna's paste[3] at 5pm and then do an insurance accident report, but
I sent home two antenatal patients for him to see at another time.
Surgery was a manageable size – 5 girls from a timber camp with
streaming colds, a pregnant woman wanting clothing coupons for
the baby at only 3 months when the rule is 20 weeks, 2 diarrhoeas
and 1 vomiting, a few coughs etc. Thank goodness no obscure
lumps on feet which usually arrive when I am alone.

Eric got home rather exhausted about 8pm having had three
babies since tea. One face presentation with prolapsed arm and
cord, the second was twins and another needed forceps! Did we
ever go down the river in a boat?

Friday 9 October
Charles at hospital in pm. Came in to supper afterwards and was
quite overcome because we gave him two eggs and bacon. Stayed
till 11.30pm discussing future organisation of hospitals and the
remuneration of staff. He is very keen on it, but doesn't want to
push it just to get a bit extra income for himself.

Eric had an anencephalic baby with complete spina bifida in the
night. Fortunately it did not breathe and was not encouraged to do
so, though he has to be a bit careful about active discouragement
in these cases as the night nurse is a Roman Catholic who may feel
everything that can be done should be done.

Sunday 11 October
The Germans for the first time are showing signs of slackening
their attacks on Stalingrad. They say it is because there is nothing
left to attack and that they will finish off what is still standing with

heavy artillery. I fear this may be true. The Russians have admitted that right back in August three quarters of the city was destroyed in 1000 bomber raids. But even if true, its epic defence has frustrated the German plan of campaign for this year.

Towels are now to go on coupons and stockings to be three coupons for one pair. Oh dear, I shall hate going without stockings with my unsightly legs.

Thursday 15 October

Lina Wood arrived at 4.30, also Leigh at almost at the same moment to discuss county policy on tonsils and adenoids. Later he rang to ask advice about feeding and management of a grandchild. He seemed never to have heard of a test feed. He is coming on Saturday *en famille* so I shall have to try to raise some cake.

Saturday 17 October

After waiting tea for over half an hour the Leighs arrived having had it. The baby a straightforward feeding problem after my own heart. Having dealt with this and done a test feed I had no conscience about asking Leigh to look at Lina who has lumps in her mouth and swelling in her neck when she has a cold. He said the lumps were epulis[4] and should be removed, as occasionally they turn malignant. Leigh is terribly gruff, rough and argumentative but I think a good sort and honest at heart.

Sunday 18 October

Took Lina to Forbes Fraser[5] and afterwards went on to see Leighs at their house, which he said was like a gaol near the Plasticine factory. It is like a gaol outside and pretty colossal inside, an impossible sort of place to run without domestics, as the unfortunate Mrs Leigh is now doing. They used to have four indoor staff.

I do so loathe leaving friends in nursing homes. It seems to be one of our jobs in life and always gives me the pip. It is the third time we have done it to poor Lina. Whenever she comes to stay it is either to have an operation or convalesce from one. Though it is only for about 3 days this time there is that terrible feeling when you go, leaving the victim to fate and the awful red tape of nurses.

Tuesday 20 October
Dreadful morning at Eye Hospital, starting with two deaf patients who always put me in a bad mood, followed by a completely mental old man who is a bit of a chronic of ours. We have been trying to discourage him coming as his dizziness and symptoms are due to his heart and blood pressure, not his eyes. Today he arrived with a large packet tied up with brown paper and string, which he said were his testimonials for his inventions for raising sunken submarines (he is a miner of the most primitive type). He said he had been congratulated by the King six times and that the Admiralty had accepted his plans for raising the Thetis![6] He wanted to leave these for me to look at but I beseeched him to take them with him, and he finally left saying he would bring them again on Friday.

The next hitch-up was a nun, an educated woman with two expensive pairs of glasses. She had seen someone in London only last month, who said she had early cataract, but she thought she would like another opinion. This made me nearly gibber with rage, and of course Colley pushed her onto me as he dislikes giving charity to the Roman Catholic Church which must be one of the richest in the world. I believe in religious toleration in theory, but it is often hard to give it in practice. In fact I was so boiling about the whole incident that I realised it was unreasonable and that there must be some psychological reason for my intense anti-religious feelings, so I controlled myself. I should so hate the psychologists to say that my anti-religion was due to repressed religious feelings!

Found Lina very cheerful at the Forbes and saw Leigh who said the baby had put on 11½ lbs since yesterday, which was his way of expressing appreciation for my advice.

Wednesday 21 October
A great speech by Smuts[7] to both Houses of Parliament. He didn't

give much away, though suggested that we were passing from the defensive to the offensive phase. Also that the war might not be ended till 1944. That is the first time I have heard anybody put an end to it at all. Even though two years ahead it is better than no prospect of it ever ending until we are utterly exhausted.

8

THE TIDE BEGINS TO TURN

22 October–31 December 1942

Thursday 22 October 1942

Lina a bit upset by her sojourn in the Forbes. There had been a death in the night and it had brought the memory of her husband flooding back. She was also nearly overwhelmed by the general stuffiness, smells and lack of air. They did go out on the balconies but it was all the more noticeable going in again.

The age for joining up is to be lowered to 18 yrs from 18½ yrs. That will mean next summer for Arthur. Oh dear.

Friday 23 October

It seems to me that mild neuroses are increasing again. At the beginning of the war it was not so noticeable as so many people had jobs which diverted their interest from themselves for the time being. Now they are all getting sick of it and tired and unable to cope with the difficulties of ration books etc, and are collapsing again. There are also many people in Bath who have 'never felt the same since the Blitz'.

Saturday 24 October

Lecture at the Town Hall by Sir Bernard Pares[1] on Russia, which was intensely interesting. He is a realist with no party bias. He must have trodden on the toes of some of the Socialists present, saying that Marxism had proved entirely unsuitable for an agricultural country. Karl Marx himself had intended it for England or Germany or other highly industrialised countries. Now all his tenets had been given up in Russia they were a self-contained Socialist community, but not a Communist one. He had a tremendous admiration for Stalin who got the methods of real practical value going and got rid of all Trotsky's world revolution methods.

The 8th Army in Egypt has started an attack.

Sunday 25 October

After a fictitiously bright morning, nasty cold rain set in and got worse and worse. Very blighted as had wanted to garden, and also to go to van and see what havoc has been wrought by weather and cows.

Monday 26 October

Lecture on incendiary bombs in the evening. All previous orders for dealing with these were contradicted. We must now wait at least 7 minutes before attacking them except from behind a 4½ inch brick wall as Jerry puts a delayed explosive charge in some of them. Also, instead of avoiding spraying them with water, we are now to spray them to make them burn out more quickly. No putting a bit of sand on, or carting them in a scoop. There is also the phosphorous oil bomb, which sticks to everything and sounds highly unpleasant.

Wednesday 28 October

Our Egyptian attack continues. The papers are being very guarded about it, which is a good thing as they crowed too soon last time, but it is difficult to get at the truth about its scale or the chances of success. One thing seems pretty certain, that we have more planes to use than before, though whether enough is another story. Every speech by anyone high up seems to be more optimistic in tone. Today is the second anniversary of the Italian invasion of Greece, and Churchill said in a speech 'The day of liberation is now not far off.' It is also reported that the Germans asked for a four-day armistice at Stalingrad to pick up and bury their dead, and that the Russians consented on condition that it was all published for the

German nation to see. But the Germans refused, not wanting their own people to get a glimpse of their losses.

Thursday 29 October
Have heard from FM that Miles has gone off somewhere without an address. I had sent for this as I had managed to get a collapsible aluminium drinking cup that he had asked for. Now it is too late, and FM from her curtness sounded pretty desperate and as if he really had gone off for good.

There is no doubt that there are offensive schemes of some sort on the *tapis*, but where and what? Burma or Dakar now? France next spring? Some people say an offensive in France is possible in the winter, but I can't believe that is so with all the mud etc. Eric heard in the greatest secrecy that at Westinghouse they are making railway parts to the continental gauge, which is suggestive, though the workers themselves are said not to know what they are doing.

Reports in the papers today that there are 900 cases of typhus in Russian prison camps in Germany. May it spread to the Germans.

Friday 30 October
Eric had two emergencies for Charles who came to supper seeing one before and one after. One was interesting in the light of Arthur Guirdham's book *Disease and the Social System* that I have been reading. He suggests that mental, physical and neurotic disease are all responses to the 'strain of life', and that these are to a certain extent interchangeable according to psychological make-up. Mrs H has for many years had queer turns and faints, having to be carried upstairs by strong and handsome young men. Finally had a hysterectomy after continuous pressure that 'Something must be done' though rather inadequate physical signs. Was an invalid after this for many months and finally went back to her 'turns'. In the end Eric had a straight talk with her husband and said he really must not make such a fuss about them. Since then nobody has been quite so interested in them, so she has now bumped into a chair when rushing to the telephone and has torn her quadriceps.

Now she has a perfectly justifiable and definite physical reason to be removed from the stress of domestic worries etc.

Obviously her whole autonomic system is out of gear probably largely from unsatisfactory coitus. His parents were non-conformist missionaries and he is probably full of guilt complexes but will not discuss it with Eric. She may also feel guilty for wanting it and be punishing herself unconsciously by ill-health, or she may be a case of inability to relax or rest properly without the aid of satisfactory sexual relations.

Sunday 1 November
Eric had been asked to be Home Guard Medical Officer (MO) for Kington Langley and Kington St Michael. It will be a bit of a muddle as Eric is already a Tank Island[2] MO. If we are invaded, and become a tank island, he has to be in charge at the hospital, whereas at the same time he should be fighting the enemy, or rather picking up those who do, from his HQ unit for the villages. He can't be in two places at once but with any luck it won't happen like that.

News from all sources a little better. The endless stream of retreats and defeats on all fronts does seem to be halted and we are even advancing, if ever so little.

Thursday 5 November
On the 7am news the phrase 'break through' was used for the first time. I went to London on an early train with Eric. Found a printed silk blouse with flowers on it of every colour of every skirt I possess, which cheered me up a lot. Met Eric to look for somewhere foreign to lunch. It seemed the only way to deal with my claustrophobia and craving for 'abroad'. 1pm news said the enemy were retreating in disorder along the coast road from Alamein and we were in hot pursuit, bombing them frequently from the air. Can't help feeling sorry for them in spite of Dunkirk, Hong Kong, Singapore and all Europe, but expect I should feel different if I had personally suffered more at their hands. It must be so bad for our psychology to gloat

like this over doing these barbaric things to other people, and yet how natural to be a bit braced after our numberless defeats.

Saturday 7 November
The 25th Anniversary of the coming to Power of the Soviet Government. Great speech yesterday by Stalin. He was optimistic but didn't think much of our efforts in Egypt as a 'second front'. I put on the 1pm news to find the tail end of some sort of salute to Russia programme which ended with the playing of the *Internationale*.[3] It is the first time I have ever heard it on the wireless – up to the present the BBC have always balked at playing it.

I had a patient today whose only complaint was that he felt he wanted to close his eyes between 2.30 and 3pm. REALLY. Told him I often did too, but could seldom indulge the desire, and he was rather hurt. As a matter of fact he had astigmatism and marked heterophoria.[4]

The news seems to be holding itself in today, with padding about numbers of prisoners and guns captured. Somehow it gives the impression of quiet before the next spring.

Sunday 8 November
It was the quiet before the spring. The morning's news said the Americans have landed in French North and West Africa. Many broadcasts to the French including a personal one from Roosevelt saying they have come as friends and solely to remove the Germans and Italians from North Africa. To give this to the Americans is a good move as the French won't be so suspicious of their ultimate designs. No word yet as to whether the French are really going to resist or not.

It is the sort of day when one hangs on to the wireless and dare not miss a word, feeling intensely aggrieved if people interfere by bringing their petty ills. It doesn't seem right for anyone to fuss about headaches or feeling tired when such great things are happening all over the world.

General Giraud[5] has broadcast from Algiers saying he is head of the French forces there and on our side. Darlan[6] is also supposed to be in Algiers and certainly is not on our side. How can they both be there without one being arrested? All a mystery, but Vichy[7] has said the situation in Algiers is 'grave', which looks good for us.

Monday 9 November
Algiers has surrendered, so presumably Giraud will be put at the head of the French forces there and they will come over to us.

Tuesday 10 November
The Germans say Darlan is our prisoner so hope it is true. It seems too much to hope that he will come over to us with the French fleet after two years' collaboration with Germany, and after the bitterness felt following the things we had to do to his fleet in 1940. It would be marvellous if the Vichy government were overthrown and we could really be friends with the French again. The tragedy of France to those who love her has been one of the greatest of this war.

Wednesday 11 November
Hitler is going to occupy the whole of France to forestall occupation by the Allies, or so he says. Were we really going into France from the south coast instead of across the Channel as everyone expected? The morning papers are now out of date after the 7 and 8am news and one can hardly wait to turn on the news and hear the latest. Extraordinary how one's own daily doings fade into insignificance when such big things are happening in the world, or perhaps more extraordinary that they don't unless world shaking events are occurring.

Hitler has chosen Armistice Day 1918 to break his own armistice terms to France in 1940 and occupy the rest of the country.

Armistice Day 1918 I was in the physiology lab struggling with horrible electric wires, which I never understood. The maroons[8] – this is it – everyone downing tools and rushing out. Later I remembered two people who didn't, but went on working quietly

– Mrs Madders and Mrs Jones whose husbands had both been killed.

Out into the streets of London to find D, he will know what to do. Yes, as always he would come out and play with me. But there wasn't much play, only marvellous to have someone big and solid to hang on to in the greatest pack and jamb ever. We found some lunch at Simpsons[9] having drifted with the crowd. Why we ended up there I have no idea, except that it seemed to be the only place not packed out, and had windows onto a thoroughfare from which one could see the crowd. Tried to get to Buckingham Palace or Houses of Parliament. Quite impossible. Eventually reached our flat in FitzGeorge Ave. late in afternoon, tired and battered. Hugh Meredith was in London and had sent message that he would take me out in the evening to see life. However when the time came I was too tired for any more 'maficking' so went to bed tamely.

Other armistice days – the intense embarrassment of the two minutes' silence. The first time I was still at college, going out into the quad instinctively with the crowd. Next year – no I couldn't, so I stayed in the museum in the medical school looking at bits of meat in bottles, subsequently always trying to avoid the embarrassment of being in a crowd or public place but often forgetting and getting caught. Often at Morley House spending it kissing Eric, or out on a county road. What good does celebrating the armistice do anyway, it hasn't stopped the next war.

Friday 13 November
Colley has asked me to do a clinic at Warminster. He is gradually shoving the worst and most distant ones onto me which I suppose is all to the good and I must be ready to take them even if it does mean driving 20 miles. It is no good being an assistant who is not prepared to do all the dirty work. It will be a long time before Colley will give up Trowbridge, which has proper quarters with a back lamp and letters.[10] Or Chippenham where there is a good fire! Meanwhile I have to perish in bad surroundings with no waiting room or conveniences at Devizes and Warminster, but such is life.

Saturday 14 November

British troops preceded by parachutists (Miles?) marching into Tunisia. Montgomery has sent a congratulatory message to his troops on having cleared the enemy out of Egypt, and has wished them 'good hunting' through Libya. Can't help thinking it is a mistake to get war down to a sporting basis, or for Montgomery to have had one of the captured German generals to dinner and fought the battle over again with cruets and cutlery. But perhaps it would be impossible to get people to fight without this idea, at any rate the British.

I am getting rather frightened at the utter callousness descending on the whole population including myself. Twenty years ago any act of torture or sadism or outrage similar to those that have been going on in Europe during the last five years would have raised horrified protests. Now the public has been so soaked in horror that it no longer cares, shrugging its shoulders thinking 'It doesn't happen here.'

I am suddenly overcome with the beauty and warm comfort of our sitting room. It seems to me quite perfect, or at any rate I like it, with just the right degree of untidiness and five animals peacefully asleep and for once not clamouring to be let out. It seems wrong to have this when people in other parts of the world are being blasted to bits or cold or starving. In my wildest dreams I could imagine nothing more perfect than this as a home. Anything larger would need more staff and anything more finished and technically perfect would be dull. We are in the enviable position of being able to afford anything within reason that we really crave if we are prepared to wait for it, plan and go without something else to have it, but not so that we can get or spend anything without counting the cost. It all seems too perfect to last, and it may not do so if the war goes on long enough for Arthur to be killed. Possible Miles has been already, but there is some hope if he only has the French to deal with. One report said that an aerodrome was captured after three hours' arguing and gesticulating. Miles would be good at that if he has not forgotten his French. Better to capture an aerodrome by argument than by guns.

Sunday 15 November
An article on carrier pigeons in the paper. Apparently every bomber now carries one. I had no idea they were so useful and lifesaving. I had always thought pigeon fancying and racing were on a par with 'the dogs' or the Derby (how the latter would hate to be classed with the former), but shall now revise my opinion of pigeons.

Civil Defence Sunday with processions and church bells to celebrate victory in Egypt. All a bit silly and the sort of thing that makes me see red. Having told the maids they could go and see the processing I kept house and tried to concoct a letter to the *New Statesman* on the subject of compulsory religious education in schools, about which there has been a lot of correspondence lately, but no one raising their voice against it. Some months ago I had something dignified and restrained at the back of my mind with such phrases as 'Those of us to whom all doctrine and dogma is an anathema . . .'; today I have lost all that and can only be abusive. So I desisted.

Wednesday 18 November
Papers full of what our parachutists are doing getting airfields in Tunisia. Oh Miles. I just can't bear to think of Mummy. Told Colley yesterday he had better stop asking me about my brother each time or it might be very embarrassing for both of us if one day I had to say 'killed'.

Sunday 22 November
The Russians seem to be starting an offensive and trying to get a pincers movement going north and south of Stalingrad, and have also had success in the Caucasus. Hitler will find it difficult to reinforce them or spare enough Luftwaffe[11] to stop them and to stop our bid for Tunis at the same time.

Tuesday 24 November
The Russian offensive gaining momentum and they say they have trapped 30 divisions. Have heard the Germans make similar statements too often to believe it but it looks as if, at the very least, the Germans will have to go right back to the Don and do it quick or be annihilated. A tremendous moral defeat after Hitler's boasts about having as good as got Stalingrad.

I did up parcels (books) for the family in Canada with a fearful effort. It is always such a sweat to get them off in time, but perhaps this year will be the last.

Thursday 26 November
Went to see the film, *Young Mr Pitt* in the evening. If it is historically accurate it is extraordinarily like today, substituting Napoleon for Hitler. It was very gripping and realistic and has inspired me to read up some history. Yet I remember being bored stiff with Pitt and Fox's dry as dust policies at school thinking they were over and done with, and what did they matter now anyway. If there were more films like that to make history come alive it might be more interesting.

Have had a beastly cold all the week which is really a judgement on me as I am always slightly superior about people who have colds and reckon that I don't, or if I do get one I throw it off in a day or two. Serves me right for not being sympathetic enough with Eric about his!

Friday 27 November
In the small hours of this morning German troops entered Toulon, against their express word of under a fortnight ago. They were resisted by the French army until the ships in the harbour were all scuttled. Some of them tried to storm out but the exits had been mined by German planes dropping magnetic mines. There are said to have been many casualties, many crews going down with their ships. Seems a pity that they could not have made up their minds to get away a little sooner to join us, and if it was necessary to

die to do so fighting the enemy and not by what has amounted to suicide.

Saturday 28 November
Elizabeth and I to dentist. She is very involved with plates, but I tell her *'Il faut souffrir pour être belle'*, and she tries to believe me, at any rate with more success than I would have done at her age. The intense reasonableness of my children sometimes almost appals me.

Nothing very spectacular on the news. We can't expect fleets to be scuttled or sensational advances every day, though we do, our appetites having been whetted.

Monday 30 November
The Beveridge report[12] on Social Security published at last. It had been eagerly awaited for many months and was expected to be violently opposed by those whose 'vested interests' were attacked. The summary so far available sounds most mild and sensible.

Tuesday 1 December
Reception of Beveridge report good on almost all sides, thus showing how moderate it is. If it is mild enough for even the Conservatives not to dispute it can't go very far.

Thursday 3 December
Another outbreak of foot and mouth disease at Biddestone, in a farm that had it before and has evidently been allowed to restock too soon. Many curses because Xmas markets and other movement of animals have been stopped. I thought Devizes looked less crowded than usual but didn't realise why till later.

Friday 4 December
Eric up at 5am with a nasty POP.[13] Nearly didn't go to bed the night before as was expecting it at any minute, so it was a good thing he kept to his principle of always sleeping when he can, even if only

for an hour.

Colley thinks the Beveridge report begs the question and offers practically nothing. He is very doubtful if the Labour Party will accept it, and certainly thinks they ought not to do so.

Sunday 6 December

Anniversary of Japanese attack on Pearl Harbour. Americans say nearly all the damaged ships have been repaired. There were 86 of them, but very few completely lost.

Tuesday 8 December

Came back from Bath to find that Simmy's fiancée has been killed in Egypt. She was just expecting him to be sent home and given a good job in England, and he was well behind the lines on the Ground Staff so it seems a bit unnecessary. Why is it always the people who have nothing else that lose what they have? It can't be altogether psychological when it is a question of being killed in war.

Wednesday 9 December

Went to Westonbirt School, now evacuated to Corsham Court, to examine St John Home Nursing. Rather fun, as schools are always so keen, and generally far better than the average village detachment. These girls could all read thermometers, which the village women seem quite unable to do, but had little idea about invalid diet or cooking. On the whole they were very good and I doubt if I can fail any of them. One of the maids was also taking it and was pretty poor but I must try and push her through. It would be too awful for her to be the only one to fail.

Saturday 12 December

A postcard from FM saying Miles had been wounded in N. Africa but no details. If not too bad will at any rate get him out of it for a bit.

Rush to get finished for early lunch to catch the bus to Lacock for

Biz's school play. I wore my tailor-made wine coat for the first time and felt the height of suitableness. Biz did not approve, probably because a little smarter than usual, and said 'Must you wear that fur' when my grandmother's old but still respectable sable came out. Ruth I think would have appreciated the *tout ensemble*, but Biz is at the age when she affects to care nothing about clothes. I am rather glad actually, she is much more like I was than Ruth, and is the only one who is a tree climber.

Other event of the day has been that Biz managed to get six oranges from a little shop down Sheldon Rd this morning. Children under 15 are supposed to have them occasionally but we have only had one lot in two years, so the appreciation is intense.

Tuesday 15 December
Ruth home, grown again. We discussed the question of Xmas and I suggested sending both maids away. She jumped at it and said it would be bliss to have them out of the house, however much work we had to do ourselves. Now I have got to break it to them and I am dreading it and afraid they won't want to go. Has any woman ever before dreaded telling her maids they could have a holiday for Xmas, or wanted to get them out of the house? Most people round here have none and would give anything for one of mine. We will not be able to get rid of Mrs Gillard, our old evacuee who has nowhere to go, but she is so inoffensive it won't matter.

Wednesday 16 December
Forgot to put in a Limerick heard at the Holt-Wilsons last Saturday, all mixed up in a discussion about how there was a higher rate of crime among the Roman Catholics in the Military Special Police than among other religions.

A Lesbian girl from Khartoum
Took a boyfriend along to her room.
He said 'Now my dear,
Let's be perfectly clear –
Which does which, and with what, and to whom?'

Thursday 17 December
Montgomery's 8th Army have got behind the German panzers[14] (or what is left of them) on the coast road in Tripolitania[15] and cut them off. There has been practically no news from there for several days, so suppose they were keeping very quiet till something was accomplished, but hope it is as important as they believe.

Monday 21 December
Good news continues from both Russia and Tripolitania.

Tuesday 22 December
Stayed to lunch in Bath with Arthur whose pyjamas are in shreds. Could only get horrid cottony ones but found a quite nice tweed sports coat rather surprisingly. No warm stockings for Mrs Gillard's Xmas present, no dried eggs about, or anything in the way of sweets or cakes, but managed to get some biscuits.

Wednesday 23 December
Russians still advancing and making big captures both of prisoners and guns, as well as stores. It really looks as if Hitler were in for his first big defeat, but I dare not even think that yet as he has had so many eleventh hour escapes. Snow, blizzards, fog and wind said to be raging. It must be hell for all. I snuggle into my warm vi-spring mattress in real satin nightgown and think how dreadful that we can be so comfortable, yet not wishing to relinquish any of it.

Thursday 24 December
Maids finally got off at teatime and I made a cheese and vegetable thing for supper, which we all liked except Eric. Of course as always happens when there is hot cheese which he cannot digest when tired, there was an emergency, the usual Christmas one. Dr Royal rang and asked him to go out and help with a delivery in a cottage right out in the blue miles away and he didn't get back till after 10pm. Arthur and Ruth helped put the parcels out. There were several for everyone although this is the 4th Xmas of the war.

Delicious sense of freedom with no maids, and children very good tempered and sweet and helpful.

Friday 25 December (Xmas Day)
Woke at 7am and found Simmy asleep on the sitting room sofa where she had been since 1am. She was supposed to be on ARP duty[16] and was coming in to have a bath and breakfast anyway. There was a dance on in the Neald Hall and the loos were in such a filthy state that the ambulance drivers went on strike and refused to sleep there.

Left Arthur and Ruth to get lunch and take any messages and took Biz to the hospital to help with dinners there. Eric carved turkey very skilfully giving everyone ample and leaving plenty over for the nursing staff. Spent whole afternoon putting haricot beans through a sieve. Listened to King's speech while doing so, and wondered if anyone else in the world was doing the same. Possibly some chefs preparing their evening dinner, but probably no one doing anything as plebeian as putting beans through a sieve. Arthur made and decorated some very attractive strawberry creams.

Sunday 27 December
Simmy came to tea and we had some music. Eric had given Ruth a flute of her own for Xmas. He managed to find a second-hand one with some difficulty and great secrecy and didn't tell even me.
Russians have captured 300 German aeroplanes intact and a train containing 50 more. The signs that the German retreat is becoming disorderly are the most cheering possible.

Monday 28 December
Bad morning back into the swing with tiresome patients, maids cross, and Biz running a temperature since Boxing Day. Have written no thank-you letters. Altogether a hang over. Most of Chippenham flooded into our surgeries.

Wednesday 30 December
4 telephone calls before breakfast, wouldn't let us get dressed. Charles to operate in pm but kept ringing up to say he would be late, upsetting all Eric's 5pm appointments. While mending a drawer in my bureau Arthur found two secret drawers, which I had never discovered, though I got it in 1917! Great thrill though no hidden treasure recovered.

Thursday 31 December
Woke up to snow for the first time this winter. Spent all afternoon and early evening doing bills (the whole family) so that we could get clear to go to the Awdrys to supper. For 14 years Eric and I saw the New Year in over the bills and on the 15th we got demoralised and went to a dance instead.

It was fun going out with the family. Arthur took my arm to stop his poor old mother getting a Potts fracture[17] off the edge of the pavement, Eric took Ruth and we sallied forth. There were dozens of searchlights meeting and signalling which intrigued us vastly. They seem to be used mostly to guide our planes home. It is heartening to think they are used for this and not searching for Jerry, and to be able to scan the sky for a noise without thinking something may drop at any moment. A jolly evening with some bridge and some music. Drank to 1943 in lime juice and water (mostly water as there was not much lime juice.) All agreed that there was a much more cheerful prospect than at the beginning of 1942 when we were about at our lowest ebb and starting to lose things at Hong Kong and Singapore.

We all drank to the speedy downfall of Hitler.

9

LOVES AND HATES

1 January–13 March 1943

Friday 1 January 1943
Signposts now appearing on the main road to Bath, a welcome sign of the times and of the passing of the Invasion menace.

Saturday 2 January
A postcard from FM to say she has at last had a letter from Miles. He has been hit in the nose, also bullet in back of head, and four minor wounds. Looks certain he will be sent home and probably no more parachute jumping. FM worried about his looks, but better than being killed which would have been pretty inevitable otherwise.

Belgian doctor to tea, attached to Belgian troops who are quartered here. Very interesting, took a year to get here via France and Spain, was in prison camp in Spain and had NO opinion of Spaniards. Quite willing to recount his experiences, apparently not too painful. Was assistant surgeon at a hospital in Brussels, now only a regimental MO and very fed up because he gets no surgery and very little medicine to do. He would like to get a surgical job in a Czech hospital but his Colonel won't let him go. Played the piano beautifully, though out of practice and ours is unfortunately out of tune.

Heard from D that he has got tickets for *Flare Path* in London for Thursday and he will give us lunch and come with us. An unheard of record for him to come to a matinee. FM will not come as it is about the war. Hastily made a little fur-trimmed hat for

Ruth, who said she had never had a hat except her school one, and didn't feel right in London without one in the winter, so felt I must try to evolve something. I was told years ago that my children's passions were bound to be hats, trains and church, having been starved of all three.

Tuesday 5 January
Mrs Creighton came down from London to see Eric. She is an old Russian aristocrat, widow of an Englishman, with three sons. One is in the British Army, one in the Air Ministry and the third some sort of liaison officer in Moscow. She has never had a good word for the new regime in Russia but the last year has had to admit they have saved our lives. She was very pleased with herself as had consented to have two Bolshevik officers (friends of her sons) to dinner, and found they were really quite nice boys (no manners of course). What particularly amused her was that after talking and arguing with them for some time, one of them said to her in surprise, 'You know you are really quite intelligent.'

Wednesday 6 January
I am reading an extremely light novel about an affair between a secretary and a modern Chelsea young man. He said to her 'Tell me all about yourself, your loves, your hates, your telephone number.' Thinking it over there is a lot in this as a guide to getting to know someone.

My loves. My family in a broad sense, animals, the river, sunny days and lying in the sun after bathing, going for holidays in Europe with no plans, in a car with a nice man. Also the intellectual companionship of intelligent men in general.

Hates. The Church or anything connected with it or with any church, any sort of swank or hypocrisy including social climbers, particularly those who want to climb on me. Insincerity, people who fuss about minor ailments, cruelty in any shape or form, mental or physical – war and everything to do with it.

Thursday 7 January
Flare Path with D. A fine play, very dramatic, but too near the bone for those with anyone in the RAF (the three wives waiting to hear the planes come home after a raid), and I am glad Mummy didn't come. Home on the 6.30pm train, which was very late. Found a fine selection of mixed literature at Paddington – Beveridge explained, *Free Europe, Homes and Gardens, Cavalcade* and *Struwwel Hitler*.[1] I am a bit extravagant on this bookstall as can always put them in the waiting room which doesn't get much nowadays.

Russians within 75 miles of Rostov. Germans said to be withdrawing from the whole of the Caucasus area on to Rostov, but it is a bit late in the day and the Russians might get there first.

Friday 8 January
At supper made the loves and hates stunt into a game (three of each if possible) to get at the children's innermost feelings. Results:

Eric: Loves – mostly around him, but on pressure said in addition to his family, driving a motor car, playing the flute, heat, his profession.

           Hates – war or anything to do with it, the telephone at night.

Arthur: Loves – animals, Mum when she doesn't go to sleep when playing bridge with me, comfort.

           Hates – War, boredom, Mum fussing after my minor ailments, Latin.

Ruth: Loves – independence, beauty.

           Hates – any sort of quarrelling, from maids' trivialities to war.

Biz: Loves – my Mum and Father, Catty,[2] my dog, riding (or is that only a like?).

           Hates – Hitler, the war.

These seem a good guide to their characters. Words of the moment: Quisling,[3] rehabilitation, social security, priority, utility, liquidate.

Sunday 10 January

Did an unheard of thing in the afternoon and went for a walk. The last time I can remember doing that, really from door to door, was a Sunday soon after we were married when I dragged Eric out as we had not collected much in the way of chores, garden, children or cars. I have often been with Eric somewhere and walked part way home, or taken the car out to the white horse and had a walk there, but a walk from home to home on a Sunday afternoon – no.

Eric took Ruth to Corsham and I thought now I really am a proper mother, letting daughter go out with husband and not going myself. I never thought I should be able to do this like FM did for a whole Xmas holidays when she let me go abroad with D while she stayed with the younger ones, yet here I am doing it, only for an hour not 3–4 weeks, but a step on. I do feel the society and companionship of their fathers is of such inestimable value for girls that I must make an effort about it, and it is not at all the same for her if I go and she has to sit as a child in the back of the car instead of being his companion in the front.

Wednesday 13 January

Have been given a warrant as a Fire-guard to enter premises to extinguish fires and rescue personnel. As if one would have it on one or stop to produce it at the crucial moment! Another thing to lose. Audrey Holt-Wilson rang up to say she was nearly frantic having left her handbag on the bus where it was promptly (and naturally) pinched. It contained all her own and her family's numerous cards and coupons – identity, food, sweets, clothing, hen food. She is nearly demented having to apply to different authorities for replacement, who all ask her to produce one of the others as proof of identity. She is unlikely to get any clothing coupons replaced, as she has to give in a complete list of everyone's clothes before they will consider replacement. Once she has done this, the authorities will probably not consider any more are strictly necessary.

The suggestion was that we should have had the whole of N. Africa cleared by the end of 1942. This is far from the case. If we are to do a big offensive in 1943 in Europe, either France or Italy, they should start in March, which is only 6 weeks ahead. Not much time for clearing up Tunis and getting something else big going. The weather has been blamed, but it cannot be so bad as it is in Russia. Last minute announcement on the 9pm news that the Russians have captured Millerovo, a tremendously important railway town on the line to Rostov. This was the one place that Haw-Haw[4] has kept boasting that the Germans still held, and that while they still had it the Russians could claim no victory at all. What will he find to say now, I wonder? Probably only threats about the submarine menace which is his great stock in trade at the moment, and indeed seems our greatest danger. No shipping loses are published, but reading between the lines these have been pretty bad lately, and there is talk for the first time of rationing bread.

Berlin was bombed last night for the first time for over a year. We only lost one plane, which was pretty good. They must have begun to think themselves safe and taken some of the defences to the ports.

Monday 18 January
Marvellous news – good all day in a small way from Tripolitania and Russia, then on the 9pm a brief announcement that the siege of Leningrad had been raised and Schusselburg captured, thus freeing one of the chief railways to Leningrad which has been practically cut off except across the ice of Lake Ladoga since Sept 1941. This was quite sudden and unexpected, though there had been indications of some sort of coming offensive up there. The Russians seem to be striking where they like now, in many varied places. If we can mount any sort of offensive in the West to take a bit of the pressure off Russia there should be real hope of getting Germany down this year.

Postcard from Mummy to say she has heard from Miles that he would give anything for a loaf of bread. They only get army biscuits and tinned stuff. We wouldn't mind swapping one for some of his oranges!

Berlin was bombed again, this time with the loss of 22, so they were more on the spot. London has had a few smallish raids again. I suppose they will say that they have taken reprisals for Berlin, but their attacks have not been on anything like the scale of ours.

Tuesday 19 January
Montgomery is only 40 miles from Tripoli. Russians ecstatic about Leningrad and advancing fast. Kharkov is now being suggested as a distant objective and Odessa and Kiev mentioned in the *News Chronicle* as possible targets for a spring campaign. I am inspired to get a map and move flags about, as there is so much movement in all parts now. The worst of it is one really wants a map of the whole world and it would need to be on a tremendous scale to show all the little places that are mentioned.

Nurse England came in this afternoon and asked me to go and see a baby with a sticky eye. Eric was in the hall fortunately and heard the name and address, and it happened that the husband had been in to see him with an acute attack of gonorrhoea a few weeks back. He had refused to go to Bath for treatment, and had never said that his wife was pregnant. So we got on to County offices immediately and got the baby into the Eye Infirmary within a few hours, whereas if I had not known about the father I might easily have sat on it for several days.

Wednesday 20 January
John Bastow to supper as he had a job to do at the hospital with Eric afterwards. He told us that after he had been burned out he had gone back into the debris and found a metal container full of pickled eggs, which he had dug out with much joy and taken back to his wife. But on trying them they were hard-boiled! On thinking about it of course they would be, but somehow one never suspects it can happen to pickled eggs.

Day raid on SE England and London. Only about 24 planes, six reaching London and eleven brought down, but a school was hit killing about 40 children, so they can be nasty even in small numbers. No war maps to be had in Chippenham and have never had any with flags. Seemed surprised at the idea that we might make these ourselves.

Saturday 23 January

1pm news announced that some of the 8th Army had entered Tripoli. The Minister of War spoke afterwards and was very cock-a-hoop and rather blowing our trumpet. Perhaps it is the right moment for this. Whatever we have done or not done, we have transported an army, including all water, petrol and food for 1400 miles, along only one road, mined and trapped all the way, with no railway and against opposition. It is our first real military success of the war.

Lovely sunny spring day. There are more flowers out in the garden than ever before in Jan. Many iris stylosa, and primroses from Ruth's garden.

Rather a nice clerihew in *New Statesman*:
The Beveridge Plan
Gives Mr Everyman
An Inch – lest he should snatch from ruddy Hell
An Ell.

True, and I cannot see why the die-hards and 1922 Committee cannot see it. It is their one hope of continuing the status quo and patching up the old system, and if they brought it all in and produced it as their own idea they might prolong their period of office a bit.

Monday 25 January

Very restless and claustrophobic. Feel that after the war I must go to Europe at least for 3–6 months on some sort of medical relief stunt. Eric says it is merely my usual spring fever, which in non-war times takes the form of getting a map out and ranging all over Europe to decide where we might conceivably go for a holiday. I am green with envy of all these journalists whose books I read. They flit from Chunking to Moscow, Ankara, Cairo, Stockholm,

Finland etc as we might go into Bath, and the minute they arrive in a place they are asked out by all the interesting people who live there, political or otherwise, or at any rate meet lots of amusing journalistic friends. I never seem to meet anyone with a mind at all. They may have a brain and use it in one particular direction such as medicine or surgery, but no larger view or grasp of big problems.

Rumours that Churchill is in America or somewhere. He has not been mentioned as doing anything in England since he went to *Flare Path* some weeks ago.

Tuesday 26 January
A sunny day with spring in the air. I got rid of my claustrophobia by putting my foot on the accelerator and driving into Bath too quickly. Really I am very lucky and less tied down than most people, having these two trips to Bath each week when I can get my hair done or shop at the same time, and usually another trip on a different day in the opposite direction to Devizes.

Wednesday 27 January
Eric came up to bed last night (having stayed down to listen to the 10.45pm overseas news) saying that an important announcement was to be broadcast in 5 languages at 3am. He thought that such an announcement at this hour might be one to the French that we were about to invade and wanted their help. We searched for an alarm clock, but our only one turned out to be in Mrs Gillard's room and we hadn't the heart to wake her. We both determined to wake at 3am, but woke at almost every other hour during the night but not then, so we had to wait for the 7am news. It was not that we had invaded the Continent but that Churchill, Roosevelt and all the chief service people have been having a ten-day conference on a united strategy. They have affirmed their determination to fight on until they get 'unconditional surrender' from the enemy, and until the amoral governments, not the people, are completely destroyed. It is too early yet to say what they have achieved – if anything.

Thursday 28 January

The Read children are developing measles. I am quite glad to have some outside visits to do as Bertha does so enjoy the run down Jackson's Lane. She has had so little exercise lately. It is incredibly muddy down there and she jumps backwards and forwards in my car, sitting on my seat when I am not there, plastering everything with mud, but no matter. Found some pussy-willow, the first.

I have raised a large map of Russia and stuck in flags, and one of the world, but cannot get one showing all Europe and N. Africa in one.

Reply to last weeks clerihew:

The Beveridge report
I retort
In giving us an inch, makes it less hard
To take a yard.

Sunday 31 January

Pouring rain all day as it usually is on a Sunday when we might have had time to go in the garden. Amused ourselves making little flags for our maps. We got quite good at hammers and sickles, but the American stars and stripes on about ¼ inch was too much and we had to made do with one star and one stripe.

Sunday 7 February

Eric and I both reading books on Russia, he *The Great Offensive* by Max Werner, me *Josef Stalin*, both lent by Colley. We keep reading out bits to each other when they get thrilling. So many of the same places mentioned as in 1812, it all dovetails in. I can't help thinking how all knowledge does this, and how any little thing one reads or learns will often fit in with something else, years later perhaps, but will make that easier to comprehend and more interesting.

It has been such bliss the last year to have more leisure for reading. People like Simmy and Daisy think it is a waste of time and look at me disapprovingly if I sit down for a bit before tea if I finish early. They think it more profitable to knit jumpers furiously which I consider a waste of time unless driven by sheer necessity, or during the news or talking to people who have dropped in.

Friday 12 February
Project for building a new outpatient department discussed at the hospital committee yesterday and Eric has been put on a special committee to produce a plan, which will be fun for us both though a good bit of work. Charles to supper after his hospital operating list. He felt it would be a complete waste of time to have anything other than a temporary structure for our new outpatients as in any National Health scheme our whole hospital would be completely inadequate for the present size of the town and a new one would be needed. We decided the chief need was for cubicles. At the moment doctors waste so much time waiting for people to dress and undress.

Mima busy having kittens all evening. Charles very intrigued as had never officiated at the birth of an animal before! Always says he hates cats, but was most worried when one didn't breathe and thought we should do artificial respiration on it. We rather hoped it wouldn't as there were already three and the milk ration simply does not allow for three, and we cannot bear the agony of drowning one.

Sunday 14 February
A great to-do with our prize neurotic Mrs H. Having lain in the Forbes Fraser since Xmas till about a fortnight ago, she returned home and has been getting up for a little each day. Suddenly she 'seized up', and sent for Eric in a hurry saying she had had 6 enemas without effect and was sure she had a lump. Very tender and difficult to examine, but E finally thought she might have a tender, fluctuating lump in the pelvis. The awful thought arose that all her pains and symptoms might be due to a swab left in at her hysterectomy two years ago, and that we had been maligning her and misjudging her by calling her neurotic. However when examined under anaesthetic by Leech-Wilkinson he found only

hard faeces. What an anti-climax. Great problem of what to do with her as there is no psychologist nearer than London and she would probably refuse to see one anyway.

Tuesday 16 February
Went to lunch with the Leech-Wilkinsons. They have just bought a blitzed house cheap, which is still in quite a mess, but they have got three rooms habitable and don't mind. We had bread and cheese and coffee in the kitchen and she didn't even have to apologise for it. She is so charming and nice and different from the other consultants' wives who get in a fuss if things aren't perfect. Yet she isn't haphazard and all her furniture is 'period'. They were so pleased with this house and what they were going to do with it, just as we should be, though it was everything we should loathe about a house. Basement kitchen, stone floors, enormous larder, dingy scullery and china pantry, up and downstairs all miles from the dining room. No maid or prospect of one either, only a woman for two hours cleaning, and Joan Leech-Wilkinson goes out to work. They are very definitely active Christians but it seems to agree with them surprisingly, and they are not bigoted about it. In their case it does seem to make them very nice people, though this does not often seem to be so.

Thursday 18 February
After lunch we set off on a great expedition down the underground factories at Corsham, ostensibly to see what working conditions were like, really because we were interested, though we do constantly get asked for certificates not to work underground.

There are several factories there. The project is not yet completed but they took us to a very hush-hush part where their experimental designs were worked out. It didn't convey anything to me that I could tell Hitler, there were rows of machines producing queer shaped metal parts that might have been anything. But the general layout, lighting, air-conditioning and spaciousness was pretty marvellous. All sewage is apparently pumped to the surface and dealt with there.

However I decided I would not chose to work in a munitions factory if I had to change jobs. The noise was pretty bad and although conditions were about as perfect as possible the girls all looked white and tired under their make-up. Several only semi-skilled ones were earning £5–6 a week, but I felt I could sympathise with them wanting to spend it all on fur coats and luxurious living after standing eight or more hours putting one thing through one machine all day.

Sunday 21 February

Great celebrations and speeches all over the country on 25th anniversary of the Red Army. Eden spoke from the Albert Hall, and a message was read from Stalin, rather pointedly ending by saying he was looking forward to the day when we should take the offensive together, and go forth to complete victory.

The whole country is getting rather frustrated again about our inaction, but if we don't do something by next month at least – well, I don't believe we ever shall.

Eric and I worked at plans for new outpatients with some success, so that we were fired with the grandiose idea to start making plans for a completely new hospital. We know nothing about hospital administration, what sized kitchen or linen store is required for how many beds, but the whole thing is such a fantastic impossibility that those are mere details. It may keep us off planning caravans or country cottages for ourselves which we have no chance of having. We seem to be people who need to be planning something, so it is a good thing to let our imaginations run on something that would in the end be state produced!

Wednesday 24 February

A letter from FM saying that D has gone off to a course where he has marvellous food and gets mixed up in cubicles with girls. No mention of what course. The last time I heard he was prone with bronchitis, so don't know if this is a convalescent home, or whether he has joined the army in his old age, or a lunatic asylum or what. I have written for more information. It is a marvellous inheritance for our children that they should have grandparents on both sides of the family who at over 70 yrs have the mentalities that can dash off on courses of whatever nature.

Thursday 25 February
In the evening had an almost unique experience of going to a dance in Chippenham. It was given by the police in aid of the hospital so we thought we should go. When we got there we found we were some of the guests of honour. On the whole it was quite a pleasant experience. Had to go in my embossed velvet dress, which was grubby and nine years old. We had not been to a dance of any sort since New Year's Eve 1939.

Thursday 4 March
Bertha has a strange malady. She has started lactating although no signs of pregnancy. Added to that she has a maternal urge and keeps making nests everywhere. She would I think cuddle a kitten and let it suck but of course it wouldn't. It must be some hormone, but I hope it isn't an ovarian tumour.

Saturday 13 March
Decided to go to *Gone with the Wind* at the pictures. Eric was hauled out for a baby in the middle but fortunately it was at the nursing home almost next door and he was back within an hour – quick work. It was a marvellous film and didn't spoil the book at all. Can't help seeing many similes with my own life but they are quite impossible to write about even in a diary. I thought I was going to put down what I really thought and felt about things, but find that when anything touches me on the raw or gets near to my deepest private emotions it is quite impossible to put it on any sort of record.

10

COUNTRY PRACTICE

4 April–21 May 1943

Sunday 4 April 1943
A marvellous day like a perfect summer one that is not too hot, and we all got down to digging the bank away by the steps to the tennis court, where the stone wall is to come. If we do a yard a day we should get through to the swimming pool by the end of the Easter holidays.

Monday 5 April
Another lovely day. Eric had building subcommittee meeting and took another plan. The estimated cost is over £2000, of which we hope the EMS will pay 50–75%, but it is only a hope, and they will probably produce a plan of their own which will be quite different and not meet our special requirements.

Thursday 8 April
Eric put on another hospital committee to revise and redraft the hospital Rules and Regulations which date from 1896! He is becoming quite a committee man in his old age.

Our plans went round and everyone said 'Very nice' after one glance, which was no compliment as they couldn't have taken in the details or thought of how they would work in that time. If that is all the attention paid to hospital plans by interested parties, including doctors, no wonder hospital buildings are so inconvenient and unworkable. Extraordinary to leave it to architects, who never think of how the place is to be worked and probably doesn't know in the case of a hospital. As we discovered from building this house they have to be watched every inch of the way, over every door and light switch.

I took the children to *In Which We Serve*. It was grim, and I wished I hadn't gone. Not the least grim was the attitude of the audience, some of whom giggled when men were gasping for breathe on rafts etc. Have they no imagination? How anyone could enjoy such a film I cannot conceive, though I should think it would have good propaganda value in America. It was of course a marvellous film from the technical point of view, but far worse than *Mrs Miniver* for horrors.

Friday 9 April
Eric did not arrive back from the hospital till after surgery time and then in a bit of a state as they had had a death on the table, an old man having his second leg amputated for gangrene. Not a good risk for an anaesthetic. From the patient's point of view it was probably the best thing that could have happened to him as he was having a lot of pain and no prospect of improvement, but such episodes are always unpleasant for the doctors concerned.

Sunday 11 April
Had a marvellous afternoon digging in the garden *en famille*, collecting newts from the pool and putting them into the overflow etc. all completely happy and united. Thought how lucky we were to be doing things in our garden, until the thought of Europe and the Jews made me feel quite ill. One of the very worst things of this war seems to be the blunting of people's sensibility to cruelty. If it wasn't blunted I suppose no one could survive at all, but it does seem dreadful that we cannot even go so far as to offer immediate sanctuary to the few who could escape from Europe. What is the good of Parliament standing in silence in condemnation of mass massacres, of Eden going to America to discuss the matter and calling a conference for several months ahead, while every day thousands are being massacred in the most foul manner. Apparently

even if we gave an immediate guarantee to Switzerland and Turkey to receive those who could escape to them, the estimated number is not more than 10,000, but we cannot even modify our visa system to give unconditional refuge to these. If we are so frightened that one or two spies might be slipped in with them surely there is some island to which they could go until the end of the war. Even if we had to feed them for a time, and they were all psychological wrecks and incapable of producing anything or even running their own community for a time, it would gradually even out. It would be a small number to deal with, even compared to the Italian prisoners whom we seem to take on in hundreds of thousands and support without turning a hair. There does not seem to be much hope for the world, or that we are fighting for any of the things we think we are, if we cannot even do this.

Monday 12 April
Arthur and Ruth started out on bicycles for Swanage. Simmy and Daisy full of questions and exhortations and wanting to know what time they were starting, when coming home and how etc. I took a leaf out of Arthur's book and just told them I had no idea. I did so sympathise with the children for wanting to do it their own way, even if wrong, without everyone criticising and asking questions although they are so kindly meant. One of the things I look forward to most after the war is to set forth with Eric in a car and when asked where I am going to reply 'I've no idea.' Then I shall send a postcard from Timbuktu. I wouldn't even mind setting out on a bicycle with him at this moment.

Biz came in from a walk with over 20 different sorts of wild flowers and I have a marvellous bowl, kingcups and cowslips mostly, with a sprinkling of everything else. I drew the line at dandelions, as there are plenty of these in the garden.

Friday 16 April
A dear old Chinese lady washerwoman tried to slip me 2/6d in OPs. Didn't realise what was happening till she shoved it in my

pocket and I had to thrust it back into her hand and point her towards the donations box. I hope she didn't think me ungracious, but she took me unawares. She could speak hardly any English and nobody could make out what her complaint was or what she could see so it was more difficult. We are still getting colossal numbers so it simply wrecks the whole day if there is one hold up.

Saturday 17 April
Arthur and Ruth returned midday by train. They had enjoyed themselves but didn't fancy the long ride home. I think they were more tired by their 75 mile ride than they would admit.

I have finished reading *This Above All* by Eric Knight. Very vivid and tragic. The hero reminds me of FT[1] as does *Gone with the Wind*. Extraordinary how two such different things can remind one of the same.

Sunday 18 April
Another marvellous day though not quite so hot. Put 'settle nettle' on nettles and dug all day. Had left my letters to get out early thinking it would be too hot midday and then it was just right so stayed the entire day till Audrey Holt-Wilson arrived with an irritating eyelash at 6pm. E had his second greenstick forearm fracture[2] this week. He will be getting quite good at them at this rate.

A baby just as he was going to bed, and then called out again in the middle of the night to a girl of 15 yrs who had just had a living baby down the loo and tried to strangle it – at least there was a nightdress sleeve VERY tight round its neck. She had apparently been going out with one of our very pleasant Spanish labour corps for a year or so, but her parents vowed they knew nothing about it, or even that she was pregnant. Be that as it may they had nothing ready and no arrangements and no nurse, so poor Eric had a happy party! Not a very bright outlook for the poor infant. The father has a positive WR,[3] his sister has several illegitimate children all by different fathers and has been involved in various local scandals, and the grandfather blew a trumpet in the Salvation Army. So typical and shows what happens when heredity and environment are both bad.

Monday 19 April
Dr P rang me up and asked if I could take on her village practice for a week as she had retired to bed. Fortunately there is no Devizes this week and I haven't got to go to Bath on Good Friday. Went out there and found a goodly scrum waiting and chaos untold. I had not been there since she took over the practice and it was not improved. Consulting room not too bad, but dispensary in chaos and indescribably dirty. Of all the pigsties I had seen there over the years this was the worst. It rather amazed me as, though one expects that sort of thing with elderly male doctors, one does not expect it of a young female. She is reputed to be so keen on her work that she thinks of nothing else and even neglects her own child because of her devotion to medicine. This is probably a gross libel, but one would have thought she would have made at least some attempt to be clean up in the surgery and have some instruments and somewhere to put dirty dressings and boil things up. Apparently also she never writes anything down, so how she ever sends out any bills or gets any money in I can't imagine. It is very difficult when people bring their bottles in for Rep. Mists. There is no record and not even a name on the bottle, so one has to go into all their case again from the start, and then hope for the best and make excuses if it is not the same mixture.

Apart from these difficulties I enjoyed it and saw a lot of old friends whom I had treated when I did the practice in the first year of the war, who seemed genuinely pleased to see me, which always makes me feel good. I thoroughly enjoyed driving round the countryside, which with no basic petrol and practically no general practice at the moment is quite a treat. Did not get back from evening surgery till 8.30pm and was pretty tired.

Wednesday 21 April
A long country round of visits all over the place in opposite directions. Arthur drove me. Everything was a lovely spring green, the English countryside at its most beautiful. To be a GP with a few visits driving a car about in the country seemed the most ideal occupation in the world. Though in the depths of winter, on icy slippery roads in the blackout with the wind howling, trying to find a cottage one doesn't know across two muddy fields in the dark, with more work to do than can possibly be got through in one day, and worse tomorrow and tomorrow and tomorrow – that is quite a different matter!

Friday 23 April (Good Friday)
Eric up half the night with a baby, and the telephone didn't let us get bathed or dressed. Thought this was supposed to be a holiday or at least a day of prayer. I wish people would attend to their own devotions in the small hours of the morning instead of ringing up or coming to see the doctor about a few spots on the baby, and being hurt because he isn't bright and ready at 8.45am having been up half the night.

Another baby between breakfast and lunch. Should have been enough for one day, but the usual holiday emergency arose, an acute intestinal obstruction, so Charles was summoned. He brought Peg out, for a wonder, to have a nice quiet afternoon sitting in the sun in the garden, but it poured with rain. Good for the asparagus but bad for holidaymakers.

1st and 8th Army seem to be attacking at different points in Tunis, and gradually narrowing the bit held, but keep saying there is stiff resistance, and it will be very difficult to dislodge them. Will they be able to hang on long enough for it to be too late for a general attack in Europe this year? If so, I really do not see how the majority of people in Europe and Russia can actually survive. Mrs Creighton came from London to see E this week and her son just back from Russia told her the ordinary people get two salt herrings a week as their only protein, often with no fuel to cook them on, in the horrors of a Russian winter. Makes me wonder how they have the strength to turn out what they do from their factories.

The day ended and the next began with two sirens. It was so long since we had one that no one knew who should be fire-watching. Eric and Arthur went the first time and I made cocoa for which they came in when the All Clear went at about 11.30pm. Just as we had finished it and were dragging ourselves upstairs, dashed if the damned thing did not go again. This time I went out with Eric as Arthur was coughing. It was very unpleasant standing about in the rain. We did hear a distant plane which sounded as if there was something wrong with the engine, and saw some flickering lights over Lyneham[4] but that was all. Bed about 1.30pm. Some day.

Saturday 24 April
Hell of a hangover as if we had had a night of dissipation. Had to hurry off for surgery and all the visits I didn't do yesterday. Out again for evening surgery, which was packed with incident. The first patient could have had gonorrhoea, a new patient was very nervous and het up. As always the lack of facilities for washing or boiling things up appalled me, but I had to do something, so found a throat swab and poked about with it, and ultimately a microscope slide on which to make a film. When I went back to the dispensary to wash I saw, hanging on the hook I could have vowed I had just taken the towel off, a French letter! Really thought someone was trying to be funny and had slipped in out of the waiting room, but on mentioning it to Dr P she said quite airily that she had boiled it about a week ago and had put it there and forgotten about it.[5]

Two elastoplast support bandages to come off and two Unna pastes to go on, so surgery was prolonged. Nearly ruined my best scissors taking off the elastoplast as of course she hadn't got a special pair and ours were back here. Late home again. One of yesterday's calls has developed measles so that will mean visiting tomorrow and Monday, curse it.

Very tired to bed but fated again. First woken up by Arthur and Eric coming up to bed chatting about strategy, then the wind blew the blackout about noisily, and finally another siren. By this time I was too tired to sleep, so took a sleeping tablet and didn't even hear the All Clear.

Sunday 25 April (Easter Sunday)
Felt very reluctant to rise in spite of the extra hour. Out to see the measles, and had the two girls and Bertha in the car with baskets for cowslips so didn't look at all like a doctor going to see a patient. I was challenged by a policeman just outside the town, the first time I have ever been stopped on the road since the abolition of basic petrol. Told him I would much rather not be going to see a patient and we laughed about it and he didn't even bother to write me down.

Have really enjoyed this week of country GP, but I do wish these extras wouldn't always come in the holidays when the children are home and I want a little leisure to do things with them, or at any rate not be so tired in the evenings. I do get so tired when I have been on the go all day, and then I bite their heads off for nothing, and Arthur and Ruth are just at the age when they cannot have their heads bitten off for nothing.

Still felt so tired and reluctant to move after lunch I thought something must be done about it, so I took a benzedrine[6] with almost instantaneous and quite miraculous results. Gardened vigorously till tea time and again afterwards, all fatigue having completely disappeared. Marvellous drug.

Discovered from the local paper that there had been a meeting on Friday with the various parsons officiating to discuss the Jewish question, and they passed a resolution requesting the Government to take all steps possible to provide asylum for refugees. Wish I had discovered about it before as should like to have gone and added one more vote, and also to show that we could support and work with the churches on such a cause.

Church bells allowed to ring regularly today for the first time. I think it would have been more use to the community in general if instead of this the signposts on by-roads had been allowed back as they have on the main roads, but perhaps there is not enough traffic on the by-roads for it to be worth while.

A postscript after the news was given by Peter Scott, son of the explorer. I remember him as a small boy. His father had died in 1912. His family had rented a holiday home in Streatly the year we had one in Goring,[7] and he used to scull about in a dingy in a pair of shorts only, which was rather advanced in those days (1915 or so) when it was not usual to expose one's top in boats, or only in the early morning with no females about! His voice on the radio was nice.

Poor Eric is asleep and wants to go to bed really early tonight while I for once, being under the influence of benzedrine, am still awake. How humiliating it is to feel that one's whole personality is due to drugs or hormones. On the rare occasions that I feel amorous I can always trace it to an increase of oestrogen!

Monday 26 April
Ruth put cold water into a hot fatty frying pan, and when she wondered why she was in a greasy mess I expostulated very mildly and she retired weeping to her bed. Really she is supersensitive. She cannot bear a word of reproof or criticism of any sort.

It is just about a year since the Bath blitz and since I started this diary. Never thought I should keep it up for a year. It has been an incredibly dull one, and I have seldom done so little work, otherwise I suppose I should not have done this.

Tuesday 27 April
The Chinese woman turned up again in Bath saying 'Yellow wash see properly, no yellow wash no see properly.' I could not make out what she wanted but thought she must see yellow when she did the washing. Then she produced a note she had brought written in English saying that the yellow lotion she had made her see properly, but the white one was no good. On looking at her notes all she had ever had was albucid.[8] Finally she nudged me excitedly and pointed to my table saying 'Yes, yellow washing yellow washing.' I

looked and saw she was pointing to the fluorescein[9] bottle, which I suppose I had used for diagnostic purposes the first time she came. But she was so insistent that I had perforce to put a drop solemnly in each eye again, and she went off quite happy, and entirely convinced that she had a magic cure and could see much better than before.

Wednesday 28 April

Had a chat with Arthur about his future. He doesn't think he will get to Cambridge as to get a two year exemption he would practically have to promise to go into the Engineers and he is dead set against the Army, but would rather go straight into the Air Force as an instrument repairer. I suppose he will have to do what he wants, and he could always go to Cambridge afterwards – if there is an afterwards. He is pretty fed up with school and its petty restrictions and for two pins would run away and join the RAF if he could get in. Anyway he did tell me, which was something for him.

Friday 30 April

Arthur ordered to be in Bath for medical inspection at 8.45am which meant 7am breakfast. In the end he was keep waiting four hours and missed his train to Newquay so came home again. Apparently had not been tested for colour blindness at all and told them he wanted to be a fighter pilot. Oh dear, I did think the colour blindness had ruled that out at least, but it is no good saying anything at this age if he has made up his mind. With any luck they will catch him later, unless they are getting so short that they will take anyone.

Thursday 6 May

We seem to have started another major attack in Tunis. From all accounts enormous convoys of troops with landing barges have been going east from Gibraltar. Where will the next jump be? Sicily, Sardinia, Crete or even Italy? This according to all I have read would be a grievous mistake and Colley thinks almost madness as the miles involved, both to get to Germany and to get our equipment out, are incredibly more than straight across the Channel. Most people think the war must be won decisively on German soil itself.

Friday 7 May
The suspense of wondering where and when we shall attack next is almost unbearable, and difficult not to pool all one's little bits of information with other people, but there have been more public warnings that we really must not talk.

I was asked to judge a baby show next week but refused saying I was too busy. They always keep one waiting for hours and anyway it was in the evening when the babies should be in bed and not being dragged out to shows and fetes. Cannot understand the British passion for these activities.

This afternoon in Chippenham there was a 'Wings for Victory Week' procession in which Simmy as an ambulance driver was taking part. It blew and rained and rained and blew. Everyone got soaked as they stood about in the market place listening to speeches and singing hymns. REALLY, why religion should be dragged into buying War Saving Certificates I cannot conceive. Now there is bound to be a lot of lumbago, rheumatism and bronchitis next week from people getting wet, which will cause absence from work and may lose more for the war effort than will ever be collected from the Saving Certificates.

Thursday 13 May
Atlee has formally announced in Parliament the end of the N. African campaign and the complete liquidation of Axis forces there. One nice story was of our people when they got to Tunis finding a lot of cars and drums of petrol down by the docks, so they started rides along the shore for the civilians. Whereas Germans conquering a place would have immediately looked round for someone to shoot!

Biz's birthday and Daisy used her last bit of saved up icing sugar to make a pink iced cake (small). Biz wished to take this to school to share with her friends and several of the staff, also all the family, and the cake would not really stretch to both. So she wept, wanting to have her cake and eat it. However, we compromised, dividing it in half, one half to be eaten at home, and one taken to school and made to go as far is it will, thus proving my life-long contention that you can eat your cake and have it with a little care and attention to detail.

Friday 14 May
A thoroughly interesting day, filled with numerous discussions and arguments with various people. Colley very depressed and depressing about all the good news, and said we could not be on the verge of a general offensive or we should not have sent all our chief of staff out of the country (They are with Churchill in Washington conferring with Roosevelt.) Charles who came in the afternoon took quite the opposite view as was to be expected. He said we might have let the chiefs of staff out of the country to hoodwink the Germans. Then we got into an argument about home influence v. school influence until I found I was arguing on the opposite side to what I thought I was! Charles always affects me that way, but I enjoy it tremendously and we parted good friends.

Saturday 15 May
Elizabeth's beloved piano teacher Miss Enoch arrived at tea-time for the night, on a bicycle with rucksack and brown corduroy trousers and no change of clothes. She is an interesting personality of the artistic type. No wonder she left the school after a term. She has far too much character to get on with the headmistress.

Basil Fletcher also came for the night. He is like a breath of fresh air for us, bringing in ideas from a world outside medicine, and bringing us back again to the educational world. He seems to be making a mark at Bristol in his quiet funny way. He is so refreshing because he is completely uninterested in the annoying trivialities of everyday life in wartime, just ignores them even if he is affected by them, and doesn't want to keep discussing them or harping on about them. Lucy looked a bit scandalised at the mixture of Miss Enoch's trousers and Basil's open necked shirt at dinner as she is inclined to think we are not 'behaving like Ladies and Gentlemen'.

Tuesday 18 May
My old Chinese woman turned up again at the hospital, pushed her way to the front and clutched me by the arm saying 'Misee, misee – bier for you, whiskey no can get', and unpacked six large bottles of beer onto the floor. She then left saying 'I come for bottles Friday.' Complete collapse of all of us into giggles. Impossible to explain to her that she mustn't give us presents or that we don't drink beer. It was so kindly meant and we didn't want to hurt her feelings. As it was the damned bottles kept getting in our way and under our feet. Told matron who didn't know what to do with it. The obvious recipient would be the porter but he is a damn lazy fellow who drinks too much as it is, and she didn't want to give it to the nurses and felt it would not be good for the male patients.

Thursday 20 May
Colley looked in after his clinic and now thinks that if there is not a Western offensive by next month it will be because there are still many capitalists in this country who are afraid of helping Russia too much. He says that if we really take the pressure off them they will get through to Berlin before we do and dictate the peace terms. If we wait till next year both Germans and Russians will be further attenuated and we may have an easier passage to Berlin. But meanwhile the rest of Europe will be almost past saving from starvation.

Friday 21 May
The Chinese woman arrived again, this time with an interpreter. Apparently what really worried her was some small pterygiums[10]

which she has and which she thought were cataract. I explained, and put in some more fluorescein and she remained with her shut eyes cast to heaven for several minutes as though in prayer and thankfulness for the magic cure. The male patients have disposed of the beer.

11

FAMILY, FRIENDS AND DOMESTIC LIFE

22 May–4 August 1943

Saturday 22 May 1943

FM and D to stay to tell us the authentic story of our first Parachute Battalion in Tunisia last Nov. A friend of Miles has been invalided home and been to Whitchurch to tell them all about it. He was with Miles when he was wounded. They were dropped near Beja[1] on Nov 14th by American planes. They had to jump out of the sides instead of through a hole in the floor, which they hated. The pilots had never flown over that country before and knew nothing about it or where they were supposed to drop them. However, finding a suitable-looking valley, they dropped. Not a soul in sight. Patrol sent forward to find something out. French troops found. These said they were delighted to see them, but could not help them yet as had not had instructions on which side they were to fight! Told them of a German patrol at a certain place a few miles away. The 1st Parachute Battalion decided to wipe them out. Did so. Returned to Beja. By this time the French had been told they were on our side and made our people still more welcome. Gave the doctor part of a French civilian hospital. They stayed there for a few days, and then the French asked them to help take a certain pass. Did so. In the course of this Miles was sent back for some mortars. Some time during this little 'scrap' he was wounded by Italians. Dragged back to Beja concussed on boards fitted to a captured Italian motor bike, partly over railway tracks. (Mummy says that if anyone in

Whitchurch grumbles to her about the ambulance on the main road into Reading being bumpy she will just tell them what she thinks of them!)

Sunday 23 May
Jo here to discuss her financial position and that of Oldfeld with Eric and D. Did get a bit of estate business sorted out though Eric had to keep popping out for odd babies etc. FM always amazed by the speed at which Eric goes off to deliver a baby and comes back with it completed. To her it is an affair that should take all day or all night with the whole household upside down. She is also much tickled by my perfect service and the good food. Said it was dramatic irony that I should be saddled with two first class maids of the good old-fashioned type, quite against my temperament, and much more suitable for her. The food certainly was good considering it is wartime. We had killed two old hens as we are planning to reduce their number now. Daisy always annoys me, for if someone like FM, whom she likes, is coming to stay, nothing is too much trouble and she produces food from somewhere, whereas if it is anyone of whom she disapproves we always seem to be short of everything.

Wednesday 26 May
Off to Newquay to visit Arthur but had a moment of panic on saying goodbye to Biz. Air raids are definitely increasing again, though mostly on south coast towns, but I could not bear her to be in anything bad without me. Bertha's face fell more and more as the packing proceeded and she shivered pitifully, so that I could hardly bear it. We had the usual male/female argument, the male wanting to take nothing but what he stands up in and night things, the female wishing to be prepared for all contingencies and comfortable, with a slight idea of showing off her clothes in a decent hotel (never fulfilled).

Plymouth was a nasty mess, definitely the worst we have seen, with whole streets down. No signs of invasion preparations either there or in the Exe estuary. The hotel in Newquay was new, and therefore clean, but no staff at all and we were requested to make our own bed and only have one bath a week. Arthur came out for an hour after supper.

Images of other holidays appeared momentarily in my mind at intervals during the journey. When we were eating our lunch sandwiches (egg, to the envy of the other people in the carriage) a sudden picture of the Whitelock family going off down the river from Birmingham years before the last war. And the fresh cucumber and salmon sandwiches we used to have because Mummy said she couldn't fancy anything else in a train. She would not be so fussy now.

Thursday 27 May
Newquay is a foul place with hundreds of hotels of all sizes and thousands of every sort of hideous villa and boarding house, yet none of the amenities of a town such as Bournemouth or Torquay, and with none of the attractions of a little fishing village. Added to which there is always a wind blowing the sand into your eyes or your sandwich.

Had a chat with Newell[2] about Arthur's future and he suggested a course for aero-engineering in the Fleet Air Arm which gives six months at Edinburgh (or with luck Cambridge) and a year at Loughborough, a naval engineering college. It was decent of Newell to have us to supper. Mrs N has no domestic help at all, three children under fourteen, a mother of over eighty, and in addition does all the catering and housekeeping for the school of 200. It makes me feel rather guilty when I see how hard other people work.

Saturday 29 May
What they call here a 'nice fresh breeze' but what I would call a howling gale, but we managed to find some shelter on the shore in the morning. In the afternoon Arthur came out and we went sailing right across the main bay. I was not sick, which I thought

pretty good. Arthur would not bring a friend, I don't think because he was afraid of my disgracing him by being sick. It rather worries me, this never wanting to have his friends out, or even seeming to have any friends, yet Newell always says on his report that he gets on well with others.

Tuesday 1 June
One of the days mentioned for the 'Great Offensive' to start but it has not done so.

Monday 7 June
Still no news. Even the wireless says 'There is nothing to report that constitutes a headline.' The ominous quiet before the storm.

The tabby kitten is dead. We think Mima sat on it, which she often seems to do, but usually without permanent damage. Great weeping and gnashing of teeth as we were so bucked to have two such adorable ones.

Poor Biz remarked today 'Life is so dull. I would like to have some adventures.' She cannot appreciate that her home has been kept safe and almost as it was pre-war, and her education unhampered and unaffected in any way. If she got adventures now they would be in the nature of air raids, domestic upheavals and general loss of security and stability, which we have gone all-out to preserve for her. All the same I know what she means and often feel sick of the same old daily round without expeditions, trips to London or meeting interesting people. She would like adventures with ponies, having one sent to her as a present, meeting it at the station, coping with it at home and going off on camping trips with it.

Sunday 13 June
Arthur's 18th birthday, it doesn't seem possible. Also Whitsunday. So many memories of other Whitsundays on the river when it was a fetish to have lunch on the islands above the Moulsford railway bridge. We would set forth laden with mackintoshes and rugs and

much food and drink, sometimes getting to the Gatehampton railway bridge to shelter before the next shower and sometimes not. Those marvellous days on the river. I do hope the children have some to remember all their lives. I don't think I ever looked forward in those days or envisaged that I would enjoy days on the river with my family more than with odd young men. I was too much occupied with 'Having a Good Time', though could never make a party go without Mummy and D. Am afraid we shall not be able to do the same for our children in that respect.

Lampedusa[3] has surrendered. Now for Sicily which will be decidedly tougher.

Monday 14 June (Whit Monday)

Daisy and Mrs Gillard left by 11am. Had not had the house really to ourselves since Xmas so it was bliss. We have had a loud telephone bell put on the loggia so that we can hear it in the garden and don't have to stay in the house to listen if no one else is in. A notice on the surgery door tells people to come round to the garden if an answer is essential, and if they can't read it that is their look out.

The Awdrys came to supper. Fish cakes, rather choice creamed potatoes and young carrots, turnips and onions done together with plenty of parsley, followed by caramel cream, a Whitsuntide treat left by Daisy. Daphne has got the beginnings of exophthalmic goitre[4] and I have never known anyone change so much in a few months. She has of course been overdoing it since the war and has lost over 3 stone. As Mayoress of Chippenham for four years she has had a conscience about setting a good example to other people and has taken on much too much. She started the Citizen's Advice Bureau and went there every morning, did all the visiting for soldiers' and sailors' families, besides endless billeting of evacuees, settling refugees and other mayoral duties. She has very inadequate help in her big house and garden with pigs, goats, geese, hens etc. I suppose if people go on with too much for too long the weakest part of their anatomy ultimately cracks.

Heard from FM that Miles is home.

Wednesday 23 June

Still no news except increasing air raids by us especially on the Ruhr. Suggestion in today's paper that we are trying to wipe out the Ruhr so that German production is interfered with so much that they will not be able to replace their loses or eventually carry on at all. This has always been thought the wild dream of a few fans of aerial warfare up to the present, but the delay of the offensive rather suggests that we are trying it out. We have not attempted to take even Sicily yet. At this rate it doesn't seem possible for the war to be over this year.

Monday 5 July

Biz was discussing going to the Holt-Wilsons for the weekend and said they would probably take her to church, and that she didn't really mind for once as it was a good thing to do everything occasionally. Then she said 'But I don't like being preached at. You ought to be able to be good without being preached at. If you can't, I call it rather weak.' Pretty good for a ten-year-old.

Sikorski[5] has been killed in an air crash, and with him his aide-de-camp, Victor Cazalet.[6] This will mean a by-election for Chippenham. For one moment I had a wild vision of winning the seat for Labour, but only for a moment. It is very unlikely that the Labour party would have me as official candidate anyway. I should not be orthodox enough, or kow-tow to the party whip. Anyway I decided some years ago, when I turned the same grandiose delusions down, that my motives were not pure enough to apply. I wanted to do it really to get an interesting job in London where I should meet interesting people and be a member of the best club in the world i.e. the Houses of Parliament. I was not prepared to spend ten years apprenticeship working on the local town council agitating about whether an extra lavatory was put on the bridge or not, and it is people who have done this that the Labour party want.

Saturday 10 July

Invasion of Sicily begun at last. About time too. No mention of Sardinia or Crete. If each landing takes two months' preparation it will take till the end of the year to just win the Mediterranean.

I am studying the psychology of the kitten as being the only child. Mima has been keeping it under her motherly thumb, putting it in deep waste-paper baskets where it couldn't get out till later than usual etc. It is definitely mentally retarded though physically extremely fine and will be a most handsome cat. Being the only one it is so well fed from its mother that it won't make any attempt to lap, though five weeks old. All its physical reactions, like padding at a bit of paper on a string, are slower than if it was one of two. Altogether a typical only child and mother's darling.

We have seen in the papers that a Captain Johnson RAMC has been asked to stand as Independent Liberal candidate for Chippenham. We found out from the Medical Directory that he has had good appointments and is also a barrister so must have a bit of a brain. Eric and I drafted a letter saying that although we could not promise to support him politically we would be glad to put him up whenever he wanted to come to Chippenham.

Sunday 11 July

Not much further news about Sicily.

After tea Daisy and I put on old overalls, tied up our hair and went into the coal shed. We turned over about a ton of coal, separating the lumps from the small, shovelling up the latter and taking it to a separate place. Now we can take another ton before the winter. Not many maids would do this at all, let alone on a Sunday afternoon, and I really appreciated her for a change.

Wednesday 14 July

Went to Bath with Eric who had to go to the dentist, so it seemed an opportunity to go there for once when the shops were open and I was not exhausted from OPs. Was amazed at the windows stuffed with pretty things, not too expensive, fur coats, shoes and dresses. Food was patchy. Just happened to pass a fish shop with a lot of fish and not much of a queue, and managed to get a lovely hake, about 3lb for 2 shillings and ten pence, with a head for cats .Of course I had not taken any paper to wrap it in, and they only produced a very thin bag through which it leaked and smelt, so I had to rush back to the car with it and then retire to the dentist to wash the smell off.

Thursday 15 July
To Biz's sports day after Devizes clinic and lunch at Holt-Wilsons. Met various old friends, including Frankie, and I enjoyed myself enormously. The Greek dancing after the sports had to be indoors as it was raining, which was a pity as it is so pretty out of doors with the scanty clothing and bare feet. Biz distinguished herself. Several people remarked how gracefully she danced as indeed she did. Altogether she was one of the outstanding pupils, having won several of the races too, and my motherly heart swelled with pride.

Saturday 17 July
Colley was more cheerful yesterday than he has been for months. He thinks the German army will definitely be defeated by the Russians on the Eastern front, and that if we could mount a major diversion in the West soon it would take the pressure off Russia. But messing about with the Mediterranean islands is not a second front and is doing little to help.

Tuesday 20 July
Captain Johnson arrived about nine for the night. On the whole we were rather disappointed in him. He has little interest in medicine or organisation of medical services. He is much more the politician trying to catch votes with a fitting turn of words. It was difficult to put one's finger on what we did not like as he talked quite a lot of common sense. He is coming back with W.J. Brown (Independent member for Rugby) on Thursday and will bring him and another

MP in after a meeting in the town.

Thursday 22 July
A big fire guard practice in the evening which I was afraid would badly cramp Johnson's meeting. It lasted till 9.30pm when we hastily collected buckets and pumps and ran home to change before my MPs' party. Looked rather nice and so did the room and the flowers. Had whiskey, beer, sandwiches and cakes. At about 10.30pm they arrived, very elated and pleased with their meeting, and seemed glad to drop the onus of it and talk 'out of school'. They were frightfully hearty and full of anecdotes about the House. All very friendly, but it did not strike either of us that they were very deep thinkers in any way, they were too full of personal grudges and animosities about people in the House and criticised everything and everyone freely without offering anything constructive. We probably maligned them, as obviously in an election campaign the first thought must be for votes and how to attract people, but we were definitely disappointed that there did not seem to be more positive constructive ideas among them.

Saturday 24 July
Johnson for the night again. We accused him of not being interested in reconstruction and he referred us to the Liberal Party manifesto, which he is going to send us. We asked him questions on education, foreign affairs, the progress of the war, India, in fact as wide a diversity of subjects we could think of. We could not glean a spark of interest in any of them.

Had a heated argument with Lucy on the subject of vests. She brought me one of Eric's and one of mine saying they had gone too badly to mend any more. I agreed and told her to put them back in a drawer and we would go on wearing them till they dropped to bits. Her face changed and a look of horror spread over it, such as one might have expected if I had said we would walk up the town in them and nothing else.

'Oh, I wouldn't like to do that' she said.

'Why not?' says I, 'What does it matter?'

'Oh, but supposing you had an accident and were taken to hospital. I would not like them to see you like that.'

'Why would it matter if they were clean? One must wear one's clothes right out nowadays, and after a certain point it is a waste of time to mend them any more.'

Exit Lucy with what I can only describe as the 'funeral face' of the good old-fashioned maid, the one they only put on when there has been a major tragedy in the house. Later she comes back to me and says that she thinks she can back mine with some mosquito netting, and patch Eric's with the remains of one of her own! I shall find the netting scratchy in the extreme, but she must think it a personal affront to her own virtue for her employers to be going about wearing vests with holes.

Monday 26 July

Mussolini has resigned. If we had stayed up and put the 10.45pm overseas news on last night we should have heard it then. The King[7] has appointed Marshal Badoglio[8] to command the army and be Prime Minister. He says the war will continue, but will it? He is 72 yrs, and one sees a certain similarity with France when it was collapsing and old Pétain was put in power. He did not ask for an armistice immediately, but did after a few days. It looks as if events might move fast in the near future and the Chippenham by-election will be eclipsed by more world shaking events.

Tuesday 27 July

Colley went off at 11am and left me to finish it all. He went to meet his children and didn't reappear again. He always goes to meet his, who usually arrive the same day as mine, and I never do. Being a woman I don't like to ask for time off for any domestic reason, and the tendency is for him to say 'Married women are no good, they are always wanting to fuss with their families.' As it was, Biz was on the loose all morning in Bath, Ruth was due to arrive mid-morning with instructions to go straight to the dentist and then take Biz to have lunch and pick me up at the hairdresser's later, all of which they accomplished efficiently by themselves.

Friday 30 July
We came to Whitchurch yesterday for our holiday in the extreme heat by train, me travelling in hot wool London coat and skirt with wine hat with veil, carrying a bulky, shabby rucksack, which made my family hoot with mirth.

It is a marvellous day, and looks as if the weather were going to be set fair for our holiday. We went on the river in the punt. Weeds had been cut downstream for the army so we had a marvellous bathe and could all swim right across. Typical family conversation while sunning afterwards:

Biz: I've caught some minnows in my net – where can I put them?
Me: Well if you promise to wash it out after you can put them in one of the cups for the moment.
Biz: Then I shall have to put them back before we go home.
Me: Yes.
Ruth: You can easily catch some more another day.
Biz: But then I shall not know if they are the same ones.
Ruth: Does it matter?
Biz: Yes, because I shall have trained these to be intelligent. I am going to have a gymkhana with them.
Eric: What is the IQ of a minnow?
Me: Pretty low I should think.
Biz: Please explain what you are talking about. I don't understand.

Long dissertation on IQs in general and the amount it is possible to teach and train a minnow to the limits of its IQ. The relative importance of good and bad teaching and innate IQ in producing famous people of the world.

Sunday 1 August
D's 74th birthday, which we had all forgotten, so Biz hastily drew

a picture from the family. Showers on and off so did the chores all morning, sweeping the loggia for I regret to say the first time. Spent hours preparing masses of vegetables, which I hoped would last for several meals, but my voracious family practically finished them for lunch. Ruth and Eric reorganised hanging accommodation in the garage, and pitched Arthur's tent lest he should arrive suddenly. We miss him intensely and quite surprisingly. He is so quiet but so much one of us and has always been with us since we were the family as now constituted.

We hear the news when the very bad wireless permits, but no one seems to worry much. It is extraordinary how little anyone seems to bother about the war round here. People do vague Canteen or Home Guard duties at intervals, but all seem to have lots of leisure for doing other things too. One doesn't seem to have much discussion about the war, but still conversation about cricket and golf goes on. Nobody seems to work as we understand work. It is not Mummy, D or Miles that I mean. The former do a good bit for their age, and the latter in on sick leave, but all the people who live around.

Tuesday 4 August
Arthur turned up suddenly yesterday which was marvellous. We had a wonderful musical evening. Mummy, Ruth and Eric had been playing while the rest of us played bridge. They ended up with 'God save the King' with a flourish, but suddenly D woke up and produced 'I'll sing the songs of Araby' out of a drawer and we all started again on the old chestnuts. They even got me singing when they got to 'A Long Long Trail' which Eric and I can never resist, and we gave a special performance to our old UCH[9] words:

> Outs are growing very boring,
> Visits seem so long;
> All my wounds are going septic,
> All my signs are wrong.
> Bosses they are so exacting,

Wanting more of me;
Wanting till I think
I shall have to take to drink
And a bed in casualtee.

There's a long long time of waiting
Until you get your degree,
Till they grant you your diploma
If you pay your fee.
There's a long long time of waiting
Until you put up your plate,
Till the patients all come thronging
And you dare not get up late.

I have thought of that so often when we have dashed down to breakfast at two minutes to nine and the waiting room is already full, with people sitting on the wall outside and the telephone ringing without ceasing.

We went to the roof and got down D's old cello and tried to fix it up, or at any rate stimulated him so much that he promised to try and get some new strings in London tomorrow. I was suddenly filled with contentment and happiness and then with a dreadful horror that it can't be like this for always, and I want it to be.

12

WAITING FOR THE SECOND FRONT

21 August–30 December 1943

Saturday 21 August 1943

A quieter day at last, and able to get to my desk and pay some bills. Spoilt by a bevy of people bathing, mostly boys of fourteen, who threw crab apples about. I feel a pig for begrudging them the pool that I have not had time to use myself yet.

After supper a phone call from Mrs Eccles from the Angel asking me to go and see her, which I did. I had left a message for her at Conservative headquarters to say that we were not Conservatives but should be pleased to give them a meal any time. She was Sybil Dawson, daughter of Dawson of Penn, at St Felix with Scoot a year or two after me. I remember seeing her sitting in Clough[1] drawing room by the fireplace looking like a Rosetti picture. Now she is not so beautiful, but of course it was a bad moment, as she was obviously fagged out with electioneering. She was rather like Fleur Forsyte, hard and clear and fine drawn and decided. Obviously wanted her husband to be in Parliament but with a brain that really wanted to help him there. She was quite well informed and had read the Beveridge and Education reports which was more than Johnson had. I told her we had entertained Johnson as that seemed only fair, and that we were Left leaning, though didn't know if we would vote at all.

Eccles stands for the young progressive type of Conservative of the Quintin Hogg[2] sort and says he is very Left minded and wants much the same things that the Left do, but to get to them by different means. She said they would come in on Sunday if they didn't go back home. Johnson may also come in then – how ghastly if they meet in the swimming pool, murder will probably be done.

Sunday 22 August
A ban on visitors has been put on most of the south east coast towns of England. This would suggest that material is being collected there for a cross-channel invasion. On the other hand Miles has been told at a War Office conference that there were no invasion barges in this country except for a few trainers at the moment, which is directly contradictory. Ruth has a friend staying with her who says her father, who is a General, says that the Germans won't give up before 1945.

Tuesday 24 August
Election day in Chippenham. I did not vote. I did not feel Johnson knew enough about anything, and although Eccles seems much more knowledgeable and a reasonable, progressive type, I did not feel I could vote for anyone chosen by the Conservative committee only, however much he was shouting about being a candidate of National Unity.

Wednesday 25 August
Eccles is in by a majority of 195 only. A great surprise to everyone that Johnson has done so well. The Tories are shaken to the core and pale about the gills thinking about the election after the war.

Saturday 28 August
Reports of big air attacks on Germany and France so hope that this is the prelude to invasion. The news is so dull these days, yet one

dare not miss a bulletin for fear that very moment should be IT.

Sabotage and unrest seem to be starting in Denmark. The Danes have been very quiet ever since their occupation by Germany in 1940, and we had all rather thought they were co-operating and not protesting, but apparently this is not so and they have been merely biding their time. Something was said on the wireless about their waiting for a sign. Can it be that the invasion of Germany is to be through Denmark?

Thursday 2 September
We all went to London. I have the impression that things, especially woollen things, are not so scarce this year as last. Found just what I wanted in the way of a jumper for myself (blue), good wool dressing gown for Eric, and socks. *The Dancing Years* in the evening which the children had been longing to see. Home on the midnight train and bed at 3am. A very strenuous day but worth it.

All the London papers full of imminent invasion, suggesting a double pincer movement on France from the Marseilles region as well as the north west. May it be so.

Friday 3 September
Tired and jaded and Friday is a bad day to be so, with heavy OPs in Bath. Ruth managed to produce a hot roast and 2 vegetables, white sauce and gravy, and a hot pudding for lunch on her own with Arthur's help (Daisy is still away). Not a bad effort though not perfect.

It is the toe of Italy just across the straits of Messina where we have landed. A great disappointment after all the anticipation and expectation that it would be somewhere more important and exciting. It is the 8th Army again as always.

Saturday 4 September
Very strenuous day dashing from patients to cooking and back again. Children not too helpful today, feeling they did their share yesterday. They spent most of the day playing 'The Dancing Years'

on piano and flute. Sometimes with one finger only, till I nearly screamed as I dashed on my hectic way from kitchen to consulting room. Poor Eric was worse. He was up to a baby last night after the 3am stint the night before, and again tonight. Phone has gone about 5 times after we have been asleep both nights. What a life!

Wednesday 8 September
Italy has surrendered unconditionally and asked for an armistice. Now what? Russia announces the capture of Stalino which means all the Donetz basin.

Thursday 9 September
A day of rumours but we are told little authentic. There has been a large allied landing in the Naples area. The Italians have been asked to help up drive the Germans out of all Italy. A large-scale exercise said to have taken place in the Channel but the nature of it not disclosed.

Saturday 11 September
There seems to be a lot and increasing German resistance in Italy, and it looks like being a battlefield for some time.

Wednesday 15 September
Bath again to do Tizzard's OPs. Strings and strings of patients. He is going away for a month and the chairman of the committee is furious with him for making no arrangements about his OPs. I have been offered a County Council clinic rate of pay if I will do them to oblige so I suppose I shall. It is not enough for the work involved, as County Council clinics are limited to 8 new and 7 old patients in a maximum of two hours. At the Eye Infirmary we see 70 or 80. However better than nothing and it is a small step of principle to pay for some hospital work. This voluntary idea is just going beyond all bounds.

We had been driven back in Italy and the Germans have been saying that we are about to do another 'Dunkirk', but today the news is better, the counter attack is holding and the Navy are helping.

Tuesday 21 September
Arthur took the whole piano to bits and mended three notes. Extraordinary how he seems able to do this sort of thing.

Ruth back to school. She had gone when I got back from Bath. It was worse than it has ever been and I miss her more than I have ever done. Asked Arthur if he was glad not to be going too and he replied that he felt as bad as if he was.

Saturday 25 September
Eric had the first demand ever for super-tax. I always said we wouldn't mind paying it if we ever had enough income to have to pay it, but we do mind when it comes to the point, especially on top of 50% general income tax. However hard we work and however big an income we earn, and it is progressively bigger every year, we never seem to have more to spend. It all goes on expenses.

Friday 1 October
A classic case, but seldom seem.

A woman journalist, now working for the admiralty age 55 yrs, complaining that she had broken her reading glasses and couldn't manage her work without them. She found it very tiring working with so many girls in their twenties who would have all the windows shut. I had taken a quick look at her on Tuesday and seen some haemorrhages so had referred her back today for further investigation. She had advanced papilloedema[3] of both discs though her vision was 6/6 and she hasn't any incapacitating signs of cerebral tumour yet. But that is what she has got. It isn't once in years that this sort of thing happens. I have really got her on my mind, as she had no idea she had anything serious, was prepared to go on with her work and is a lone spinster living in digs. A grim outlook.

We are in Naples, or what is left of it. Will Rome be consistently sacked and burned by the Germans as they retire next?

About 8.45pm a strident ringing at the front door bell, curse I said, it must be an emergency for someone to ring like that. It was the police to say we had a bare light showing – and we had in the consulting room. It was full on with no blackout. Can't think how it happened, but the door was shut so no one saw it from the hall. It is the first time anyone has complained of our blackout, so I suppose we are better than some, but it will probably mean a summons or fine, and publicity, unless they let us go as first offenders.

Monday 4 October
Tried to collect things for Arthur to take to Cambridge in the intervals of patients, and eventually got his trunk shut filled with curtains, pictures, cushions, coffee, cocoa, sugar, jam and very few clothes. It was fun thinking of things he will want, but not fun to have wartime restrictions and not to be able to indulge him.

He was a bit 'last dayish' all suddenly, and very sweet to me in his own quiet way, sticking by me and trying to do whatever I was doing when I was not actually seeing patients. I was glad it was not a Bath day. I always try to have a job on hand that he can help with on these occasions, and this time it was shelling haricot beans. He soon had a patent contraption rigged up with the fireguard to sieve them through and a box underneath. Mima promptly said 'Oh, this is a little house, I can put my baby there' and got in. Bertha said 'What are you doing?' and knocked it over with her tail.

Tuesday 5 October
Arthur went off on the early train leaving me feeling awful. After all it is a bit of an epoch when one's son goes to university. Things didn't improve when the post came with a little parcel of things from Mrs Creighton who wanted me to sell them so she could send a food parcel to Russia. Apparently there are many deaths from starvation. Felt I must send her a cheque and some spam[4] and sardines from our store. Then a gruelling morning with over 70 OPs soon draining me of the luxury of emotional disturbances,

and I was so tired by the end of the day that I had long ceased to worry about my son having grown up or about the starving Russians. Nothing like grinding hard work for curing emotions! A pity more women do not do a bit.

Thursday 7 October
Came back from Warminster clinic to find a letter from Arthur. He has wangled a bed-sit to himself though it has an old fashioned washstand (Biz did not know what that was!) and sent for his wireless and various other things. Had a dreadful hunt in the blackout to try to find some wooden box or piece of luggage to take the wireless. The only thing was a wooden bottle crate, which was full of wet straw, slugs and wood lice.

Sunday 10 October
The Russians are over the Dnieper river above and below Kiev. Everyone thought they were stopping now because of the autumn rains and mud, but it looks as if they are going straight on. Our little attempts in Italy seem mere pinpricks in comparison. We are complaining that we are held up by mud and rain, but it doesn't seem to stop the Russians.

Tuesday 19 October
Biz has presented me with a story called 'The Remarkable Camel'. I suggested the subject for her free library, otherwise it is completely her own work, and all typed out by herself. It is so good I think I ought to send it to some children's competition.

General Smuts has made a great speech. He is a far-seeing and wide-minded old man and probably the only person whose advice Churchill takes. He stressed the need for speed in bringing things to a finish, before Europe was completely starved and anarchic, but said the all-out attack would not come till 1944. This time last year we were wondering how we could exist through another winter of blackouts and how save our faces for not invading in the West in 1942. Now we are apparently not even doing it in 1943. If we are war weary, who have had no hardships at all, except for the air raid victims, it is impossible to realise what the masses in Europe must be like having waited for us to come for over four years.

Sunday 31 October
Eric off at crack of dawn for a study day with the medical Home Guard at Bulford. He was not looking forward to it, but I think it will be good for him to have a man's day for a change. He is always so surrounded by women.

A slight domestic contretemps about lunch. Daisy had asked me what I would like and as Eric was going to be out I replied 'Curried lentils and save the joint till Monday'. This was not popular and every ruse, including saying Elizabeth would not like it, was used to make me change my mind, but I was adamant.

Then I tried to write my lecture on Anatomy, Physiology and Hygiene for the GTC[5] but it wouldn't come. I feel they expect 'What a young girl ought to know'. As I am a mother and a doctor they think I am a suitable person to diffuse this, but I am not at all suitable. My own family has assimilated it from the general atmosphere of the house where messages come in several times a day about people having babies. The cat has kittens three times a year and we stroll in and out of the bathroom naked at all times, including during menstruation, without thinking anything about it.

A great wave of revulsion for my respectable and secure way of life has swept over me, partly due to the above stupid lecture and the curried lentil episode, partly because I am left alone on Sunday in the rain, and partly because reading Gilbert Frankau's *World without End* has made me want to dash off to Paraguay or San Francisco, working my way as a deck hand if that was the only way. The comfortable secure home that I have built for the children seems so sterile.

Monday 1–Wednesday 10 November
I am getting slack about writing this, or perhaps merely busy. We

have been out three evenings this week – entertainments that we wish to go to always happen at once. Col Blimp at the pictures, local dramatic society play *Badgers Green,* and a Rules and Regulations hospital committee meeting.

Elizabeth got her half-term marks and gained a first in every subject. She definitely won't be able to stay at that school after the summer. She got in a muddle with proportion sums one night and wept. Wouldn't be helped because that wouldn't be fair on the people who did their prep at school. Finally I persuaded her to talk over the principles with Father which she did, without being helped with the individual sums. She went back to these before breakfast the next day and got them right. More and more I admire the way she sticks at her difficulties and fights her own way through them.

Called in on Frankie on way back from Bath. Talked very hard in turn, trying to get in everything we haven't said for the last year. It is extraordinary what a relief it is to see a real old friend, even if it is one whom I would quarrel with if I saw too much of her! We are about as intimate as two women could be but we could never work together daily – both too overbearing and fond of getting our own way.

Thursday 11 November
Letter from Ruth saying she was miserable and would do something drastic if I didn't remove her from school quick. No details given but think an emotional entanglement. Who would be an adolescent? Violent telephone calls to try and get a room nearby for the weekend. Finally got one at a road house two miles away and will have to pad back and forth on our feet. None of the trains fit and the journey will take four hours. Eric cannot come as he is hectic so I have got to tackle whatever situation there is alone. Oh dear.

Saturday 13 November
Borrowed a little dog from the pub (raining and blowing hard) and set out to walk to school, meeting Ruth half way. She was pleased

to see me but the great emotional storm had blown over. Discussed her work, what she should take in school certificate, taking 1st MB[6] from school etc and no more was said about leaving immediately. Tried to talk to the headmistress about unnecessary rules and regulations but she took the wind out of my sails by saying no one else found them so. Ruth said they had a new prayer that week not to ' chafe against discipline'. Especially for us?

Friday 19 November
Sir Oswold Mosley and wife are to be let out of prison where they have been since 1940, for medical reasons. Colley thinks it is very bad to let him out and that it will have an awful effect on the anti-Fascists in occupied Europe. I don't think he could do much harm now poor man. Three years in prison he must be utterly physically and psychologically broken, but I do see that to Europeans it might give a wrong impression to free the leader of the Fascist party. With the Gestapo methods to which they are used they could not see that we would be against keeping a person in confinement who is no longer a danger to the state, and utterly impotent to influence a large body of opinion in Britain.

Sunday 21 November
I have a streaming cold and spent the day reading André Maurois and little bits of Julian Huxley's *Evolution: The Modern Synthesis.* He seems to think man is progressing but not along predestined evolutionary lines, but determined by man himself. I particularly agreed with his point that 'Before progress can begin to be rapid, man must cease being afraid of his uniqueness, and must not continue to put the responsibilities that are really his onto the shoulders of mythical Gods or metaphysical absolutes.'

We have a sharp epidemic of 'flu with whole households going down at once. There is still no assistant at Corsham and it is very difficult to cope. Eric has been up two nights running with 'found deads', and will probably collapse himself soon, though Wheeler in Corsham will probably do so first. We are pushing Hirst over to help him as much as possible.

Monday 22 November
Eric has 28 visits. Thank goodness babies are fairly quiet at the minute.

I have been extremely interested in André Maurois' life *Call No Man Happy* as I remember his children when they came to Oldfeld for several summer holidays. Also Granny's description of going to see them in their Paris apartment. I do wish I could have given the book to her for Xmas and that she was still alive so we could discuss it.

Wednesday 24 November
Eric woke up with the prevailing infection and feeling rotten but struggled on. Fortunately I had not many eyes so was able to take a good part of his visiting list off him.

A short while ago I thought I would never do general practice again, that it was a dog's life, making quite unreasonable calls on one in every way. Today I thoroughly enjoyed it, the great pleasure of everyone when they saw 'the doctor' making me feel good. However by midnight after a large surgery and two late calls, I had decided that it was after all not an enviable job. Patients seemed like vampires, to be sucking one's vitality with all their demands, mostly futile and unreasonable. The way they go on yapping about nothing on the telephone at all hours and never expect to be charged for it is yet another unreasonable demand.

Thursday 25 November
Berlin has been getting very heavy bombing nearly every night this week. Can't help feeling sorry for them, though many people think it is the only way to bring home to the German people what war is. But are we just producing more hate and a desire for revenge in the future? Colley and I decided on Tuesday that the indicators are pointing once again to the opening of a real second front in the West, but they have pointed so many times before that we have all got sceptical about it ever happening.

Tuesday 30 November
All news is concentrated on the Pacific except for repeated nightly bombings of Berlin. Rumour that Churchill is off at a meeting.

I did another round of visits for Eric after getting back from Bath. It is extraordinary how dirty one village is as compared to another. In KL the nicest people are mostly old servants of Mrs G, the owner of most of the land, and their houses all shine with cleanliness, the paint is good and they have nice Chesterfields and easy chairs with loose covers. She rules them all with a rod of iron and is always popping in to see what they are doing and if she can help. Although they often don't want her interference it seems to be Feudalism at its best. In the next door village where the landlords are thoroughly bad, and rather dishonest people into the bargain, the cottages are in bad repair with plaster peeling off and all look dirty and uncared for, and in consequence they collect the worst type of family.

I went to see one woman with laryngitis and said 'You always get this when there is an infection going about, don't you?' She replied 'It was ten years ago when I had it last and you came to see me then.' How time does slip by without one noticing it.

Thursday 2 December
The secret is out. The conference is in Africa between Churchill, Roosevelt and Chiang-Kai-Shek, not Stalin. It has been mostly to do with the projected defeat of Japan. It is finished now and Churchill and Roosevelt have left for 'an unknown destination'. The inference is that they are now going to meet Stalin, either in Moscow or Teheran.

The 8th Army are attacking again in Italy but making haste slowly.

Friday 3 December
The Berezina river is in the news again. The Russians are rapidly pushing the Germans back to it. It was in 1941 that the latter crossed it in their first advance, and Miss Silcox found and read to

us at her party the following Kipling lines on Napoleon:

It is far from St. Helena to the Berezina Ice
A long road, a chill road, the ice begins to crack.
But not so far for gentlemen who never seek advice
When you can't go forward, you must e'en go back.

We hoped history would repeat itself that winter, but it has taken a little longer to do so.

Sunday 5–Saturday 17 December

The priority armament production for the USA up to the summer 1944 is landing barges. This depressed me hugely as I thought we would be done with them by then, till Eric pointed out that thousands will be needed for the recapture of the Pacific Islands, so I hope they are for this and not merely for the European offensive.

Continuing the weary round to try and find an assistant for Corsham. Poor old Wheeler is nearly at breaking point and if he gets 'flu I just can't conceive what is going to happen. We had 47 panel patients[7] in on Saturday, club and private patients uncounted. It is apparently true 'flu Virus A according to the BMJ. Eric is getting tired. Not just evening tired, but the sort of tired he was three years ago when his reactions to everything get slower and slower and he can't face up to outside problems.

The Ministry of Works have just woken up the fact that there is a 'flu epidemic sweeping the country. They are actually making arrangements for some of the out of work army doctors to help overworked doctors and we are going to apply for one at Corsham.

Saturday 18 December

Churchill has got pneumonia again, this time in Cairo. The second time within a year is not too nice at his age, even with plenty of M and B[8] and penicillin.

Trials of the first German war criminals have taken place at Kharkov. They had a proper trial with a lawyer to defend them.

Pleaded guilty to mass executions of men, women and children who were pushed into large vans into which gas was pumped. Also shootings of women, and children after they had seen their mothers shot. The criminals are to be hanged.

Sunday 19 December
Tried to write a few letters and get off the Whitchurch parcel, such as it is which is not much. Ruth and Biz hard at Xmas presents, weaving with odd bits of wool and making shopping bags out of coloured sacking. In the middle of the afternoon all the Swanage bookcases arrived unexpectedly by an odd lorry that happened to be coming this way, 18 shelves of them. We were short of book space, so said we would buy in any that were going, but 18 will take some filling.

Friday 24 December
Very few patients in Bath but no real feel of Xmas Eve, with no tree to decorate. I have simply not tried to provide presents except money and book tokens, and have been near no shops, feeling I cannot cope with Xmas. However, Eric did bring in a pheasant given him by some farmer patients – very welcome for our Xmas dinner as there are no turkeys or geese in the shops.

Announcement that Eisenhower is to be commander in chief of the 'Second Front', in those words. Last summer when there was talk of bringing Wavell[9] back to command the second front it seemed impossibly late in the day to make such an appointment. Now, six months later it is made and will probably take about three months to implement, making our attack in the West in March or April 1944. It really cannot be delayed much beyond this, though we have thought that before. What does seem a bit queer is that we are shouting about it to the Germans.

Saturday 25 December
Xmas Day. Not many parcels to open but a good few envelopes, mostly tokens. A quiet day, and dinner in the evening livened up

by champagne, some I was given 15 years ago before Ruth was born when I was being terribly sick. It seemed a pity to waste it in that way, and ever since we have been waiting for a really worthwhile occasion to open it which has never arisen, so it had gone very flat. We put it into a sparklet syphon and blew CO_2 through it and produced what we thought was a very good drink!

Contretemps with Biz. We said she had better have a taste and drink to the 'speedy destruction of Hitler'. She burst into tears – said she would not drink to the destruction of anything, she hated killings, and anyway hated the idea of drink at all. Finally retired sobbing, thus wrecking all our dinners. Later she collected herself and came downstairs and had supper with me alone, saying there was something she must tell me. It was all a religious crisis. She has not liked feeling she did not go to church like the others at school, and very much wants to go some times and has wanted to for two years, but has not dared to tell me so, as felt I should be so utterly disappointed in her if she did!

It made me feel ghastly to have been such a dragon, but though I vowed she could do just as she liked and I should only be disappointed if she were not honest about her feelings, or didn't tell me, we are too close for her not to know that I did mind really. We both went on minding till the emotional atmosphere was tense to the last degree. My heartstrings bled for her, it was so unexpected. Ruth was the one I was always afraid of going that way but has not done so. I LOATHE myself for minding, but cannot help myself, my antipathy for everything to do with the church is too great, though I know it to be unreasonable and with quite an undue amount of emotion attached. I think it is the only thing I hate.

I must now find someone to take her. I expect Lucy would love to do so, and perhaps if it has to compete with violin lessons and riding on Sunday mornings they may after a time prove more attractive. It may be a phase only, but Biz is such a strong and steadfast character that I am afraid.

Tuesday 28 December

Russians seem to have turned again to the attack on the Kiev salient as well as in the north. Everyone now believes a second front is coming at last within the next three months, and are also beginning to realise that it will mean casualties and hell, and are sobering up accordingly.

Family conversation at lunch:

Biz: Mum, when you crunch your celery you do it on a lower note than I do!

Eric: What note do I crunch on?

Biz: That's different again. You don't mind my noticing do you?

Me: I don't think it is rude to crunch or not to crunch celery in any particular way.

Arthur: Mum crunches on a lower note because she keeps her mouth shut more.

Biz: Oh. I think I shall do some research on it. Is it anything to do with William Pitt and the apple that fell on his head?

Me: You mean Sir Isaac Newton and gravity.

Biz: Yes. Does the moon have gravity equal to the earth?

Arthur: First half of question yes, second half no. The moon has a gravitational pull, but less than the earth because it is a smaller mass.

Me: You mean if I weighed this spoon on the moon it would weigh less?

Arthur: Depends if you weighed it on a weight balance or a spring balance.

Me: (After deep thought) Oooh, now I see. If it was weighed on a scales with weights the gravitational effect on these would be different to start with.

Biz: I don't understand what you are talking about.

Ruth: Pass up your plates please, I'm making a pile. Mima, here is a bit of gristle for you.

Thursday 30 December
Went to London with Arthur and Ruth to see *While the Sun Shines*. Very funny, but we missed Eric who was too busy to get off. It didn't seem a year since we had been to *Flare Path* with D. Bought three yards of decent knicker elastic off a man in the street at 1/- a yard. Was probably black market stuff but I couldn't resist it. Though I would not pay fancy prices for food (unless starving) I thought knickers coming down were really a different matter!

13

THE TENSION MOUNTS

1 January–30 April 1944

Saturday 1 January 1944

Everyone says that this year must be the end, but are at least starting to realise that it will probably mean big casualties and possible big air raid reprisals. Eric has heard from a lorry driver that the greatest number of bombs ever ordered are to go out from the Corsham underground stores during the week. Is this for the invasion or merely intensification of bombing offensive?

Tuesday 4 January

Pip arrived in the evening. Lovely to see her and we talked and talked about everything on earth. She did not look particularly tired considering how hard she works. She teaches any subject in which they are short staffed at the moment, is usually matron, no regular domestic help and 100 boarders and her own two children under 11! She takes it all in her stride and is one of those people in the world who just cope.

The prospect of civil war in all the Balkan countries looms larger as the war with Germany shows signs of finishing. The evacuated governments in London are all feudal and reactionary, and the people on the spot who have been doing valuable guerrilla work will want their own people's government. Some think that is when the real killing in Europe will start. Frightful prospect.

Eric and Pip made up a riddle:

'Why are members of the Civil Service like Roman Catholics?'

'Because they always refer to higher authority.'

Our telephone went on the blink yesterday and was still groggy today. Military operations starting, or have we got military operations on the brain?

Friday 14 January
Charles rang up at 8pm to ask for supper in half an hour. He came just before nine, having been at the hospital since 2pm without a break. Sat down in an exhausted condition, for him.

Monday 17 January
Iris stylosa in bloom in the sitting room. Quite an orgy.

Things in Bulgaria seem to be pretty chaotic. On the overseas news it said that only 50 doctors in the whole country were allowed any petrol for their cars. The whole transport system has been taken over by Germany, and Sofia is being evacuated following allied bombing raids.

Monday 17–Thursday 20 January
Days of petty irritations and annoyances. Eric has boils, which make him cross, Simmy has a bad cold, Lucy and Daisy suffering from diarrhoea and vomiting, so we are an ailing and irritable household.

Saturday 22 January
We shall burst if we don't get a weekend off soon, though it seems dreadful to even think of it with all the slaughter going on. It is the never getting away from work for a minute that is so wearing, never being able to pop off for a few hours in the car on a Sunday, and get right away from the practice and other people's ailments. Eric's boils have been making him feel rotten and disinclined to be sympathetic. He ordered a suspensory bandage a day or two ago, as one of his boils is right on the scrotum. It was sent up addressed to Dr J.F. Hickson. 'Well,' he said, 'That is the one sort of bandage that I don't think you could wear!'

Thursday 3 February

On the run the whole day with clinic in Devizes in am, then Trowbridge in pm and private patient here after that. Though a full day not unduly tiring, yet I earned over £9. If I could do that every day that would be £45 for a five-day week, say £2000 a year allowing for holidays. I could buy some decent clothes, a new van next year and make a hard tennis court the year after, with holidays with the whole family in addition. Yet the anomalies in medical pay are such that on other days when I see perhaps two or three times as many patients I earn exactly nothing.

Great news from Russia. They have advanced another 50 miles into Poland and are encircling nine German divisions in the bend of the Dnieper. Our invasion 'chiefs' seem to be mucking about going to the theatre and having lunch with the King. Why can't they stick to their work and get on with it?

Saturday 5 February

Distribution of oranges from Spain, 1lb for each ration book. Daisy came in with a basket of golden loveliness the like of which I had not seen for years. After some discussion we decided to use one from each book to make marmalade and eat the other two.

Tuesday 8 February

Emergency call last night leading to an operation at the hospital. Thought to be intestinal obstruction in woman of 65, possible carcinoma or volvulus.[1] It turned out to be an extremely mucky appendix with an abscess causing obstruction by two bands. Nevertheless Eric got eight hours' sleep subsequently which did him a lot of good.

Russians have captured Nikopol. Months ago it was said that the Germans must have the manganese mined there to carry on. However by now they probably have a big enough store to last 6–12 months. In that time we hope for an end from many other factors. There has been some depressing talk about 1945 lately whereas in 1943 our hopes were raised high.

Saturday 12 February
Lovely story yesterday from the *New Statesman* on the diverse duties of AMGOT (Allied Military Government for Occupied Territories) in Italy from a young British officer: 'Yesterday we went through something of a crisis, as a peasant woman had a baby in the outer office, causing my young Scots Lance-corporal and the American enlisted man the most acute embarrassment. However we got hold of a midwife and the office was shut down. It later turned out that the good woman believed that her child would be a British subject if born in my office. Cost of the midwife, which the woman could not pay, never having heard of such a luxury, I have entered in my books as "Reconstruction"!'

Lina Wood staying for a day or two and went up to London for an interview with YMCA headquarters. They are sending her to Northholt aerodrome which is a Fighter Command station and the head of the YMCA is there. She would much rather scrub floors and wash up as an underling than have to organise and be tactful, but doesn't seem able to avoid being put in charge. I tell her it is trying to hide her light under a bushel to avoid responsibility. Thirty-three years of being a parson's wife here made her too good at dealing with difficult people to be able to avoid it now.

Friday 18 February
We heard yesterday that the White Paper on Medical Services was out, and today received two copies from Eccles saying he thought we would like to see it at once and he would like our comments before he spoke in the house on it in three weeks' time. A unique opportunity to get our views direct to Parliament without going through endless committees. There is plenty to digest, plenty to criticise though the whole thing is only in the most general terms and goes into no detail. At present it looks a muddle still with too many authorities dealing with different things.

Saturday 19 February
We have read the White Paper from cover to cover. Very vague and

will perpetuate all the difficulties of the dual system. The public think it all sounds very nice as it is for everybody, but they may not like it when they get it. If we are to have our incomes halved and work as civil servants, then we must insist on conditions comparable with other civil servants. The work as work will doubtless be quite well done as far as the actual treatment of disease goes, but medicine is so much more than that. To be a good doctor at present, one's practice has to be one's hobby and one's religion, intimately bound up with one's whole life. If it is to be merely a 'job' with a salary, no one is going to stand the intrusion of the telephone e.g. when he is having intercourse with his wife. Perhaps taken over the whole country the standard of actual physical treatment of disease will be better, but if medicine is only to do this, there will need to be a vastly increased army of 'guides, philosophers and friends' recruited from somewhere else. The church should be able to do this, but won't, because it will insist on dragging theology into its good works.

A lovely present arrived from the ex-Sister of the Eye Infirmary, now married to an RAF man in Melksham. I had lent her the old nursery fireguard, and she has sent me three large cakes of Yardley soap, of a quality I have not seen in years. I was a little suspicious of the parcel. It was a long narrow one, marked Personal, and was reminiscent of one Eric received three weeks before Xmas one year before the war in a Carrington's jewel case. I wanted to put it away in the Xmas present cupboard, thinking that a grateful patient had really sent him a gold cigarette case or watch, but fortunately Eric thought this was too risky and insisted on having a squint. It was a bottle of urine from one of our few titled patients!

Saturday 26 February
Spent the whole afternoon writing a letter to the BMA about the White Paper. Eric saw it at teatime and approved of the letter but disliked the typing. After supper he redid it, but at 11.30pm we decided it was muddled and undignified and that we would not send it. However I suppose it worked off some of our anger. We

think the paper is completely hopeless from every point of view.

Sunday 27 February
Quite an outing for us both together, as we have two patients to visit in Bath. Simmy has a nasty infection of both ears and a little girl from the practice has diabetes. They are both in the Forbes Fraser hospital. This was an excellent excuse to then go on to the McKaigues in Limpley Stoke where they have a small furnished house. We wanted to 'consult' with them about a mutual patient. Unfortunately we met a police car at the top of Limpley Stoke hill, but he didn't stop us. We were going to say firmly that we were going to a medical consultation but it would have looked a bit thin at 4.30pm on a Sunday afternoon.

Saturday 11 March
Eric has resigned from the Home Guard. They have been badgering him to give a course of lectures on first aid for some time, which he has been trying to put off. He has done very little for them in the last year and the last straw was when they asked for a duplicate photograph in uniform and he hadn't got a uniform. As I had definitely turned down the GTC myself I didn't feel I could press him. If we had both taken these jobs we should never be in for the evening together at all. It is practically the only time we see each other. At breakfast we are too sleepy, lunch I don't get back till he has finished, Simmy is on top of us at tea and by supper we are too tired. Now that we are both on rather different lines of work and I am out of the surgery, it has meant a far less communal existence than when we started life doing everything together. For people like L in the old days this did not matter at all. He hated his wife and took no interest in his family and was glad of an excuse not to go back to them in the evenings. But with Eric doing so much night work already with his 3–4 babies a week it really is beyond a joke to take up anything else. I suppose the town think we are unsportsmanlike and unpatriotic. Perhaps we are in a way when you think of all the husbands and wives who are totally separated

at the moment and who haven't even their homes.

Thursday 16 March
Arthur arrived home two days ago and today we used the excuse of a visit to a very old patient of Eric's (before we were married vintage) who is in the Forbes, to stay in Bath and go to *Jane Eyre* at the Theatre Royal.. Pity Ruth is not at home as she would have liked it. Chippenham Secondary School is doing *Arms and the Man* on the 31st when Ruth will be home but Arthur will probably have gone again. The Shaw would have been so much more suitable for him and the Brontë for Ruth.

The Russians are rapidly destroying all the German forces in the Ukraine and we have broadcast a strong message to Rumania to get out of it while they can do so on good terms. Few of the general public seem to realise the colossal magnitude and significance of these operations.

Tuesday 21 March
A travel ban has been put on visitors to all coastal towns and for a band of 10 miles inland from the Wash to Lands End, said frankly to be for 'operational reasons'.

Vesuvius has started an eruption and lava is pouring down its sides and has already engulfed two villages and threatens a third. Seems an unnecessary extra hardship for the people of Italy and Naples who have had to put up with so much already.

Sunday 2 April
Biz has decided she is animal starved. How she can be in our house I don't quite know, as everyone else says we positively swarm, but she is so reduced that she has to tame spiders and woodlice. I besought her not to tame any of the new hens as it is too difficult when they get old and the time comes for them to be eaten, but most of the week she has been walking round the garden with one in her arms. When I protested she said 'Well, it insisted on taming itself.' Finally I suggested that if she really felt like that

she had better have a guinea pig, and since then she has thought of nothing else. The difficulty is to find one. She hunted Devizes market unsuccessfully while I was doing my clinic, but no guinea pigs only a myriad of rabbits, which I think are dull. Eric tackled Gibson (pathologist) at a lecture yesterday, thinking he would be sure to be able to oblige, but all his animals were destroyed in the Bath blitz when the Mineral Water Hospital got a direct hit. He said the part with the animal cages all went down under the rubble and it was assumed that they were all dead, but the next day many hungry little guinea pigs popped up among the ruins calling to the salvage workers for food. They were mostly picked up and taken home to their families! Perhaps a happier life for a guinea pig than being given tuberculosis. He gave us the name of someone from whom he gets them so there is still hope.

Thursday 4 April
A message to say a cream coloured sow would be arriving at Chippenham station at 10pm. I had asked for either a young female or a female in young, and this answer is non-committed.

Another meeting at the RUH to discuss the White Paper. Resistance seems to be stiffening against it, we were glad to see. The discussion was on principles only, no finance involved yet. It went on till nearly midnight, though we left at 11.30pm as I was dropping with fatigue. On the way back we called at the station for our 'sow' who was in a tight huddle in the corner of a wire-fronted birdcage in some hay. I really thought she was dead she was so still, and wondered how we could break it to Biz who had been in a state of complete thrill all evening. However we woke her up as promised and it wasn't dead, but very bright-eyed and frightened but quite adorable. We had to put it in her dolls' house as the real guinea pig house is not yet repainted and renovated. How stupid I am to get so thrilled about a little animal. Bed finally at 1am completely exhausted by the combination of very hard work on the future of our great profession, and guinea pigs!

Wednesday 5 April
Eric passed an epoch today. He had his first grandchild. I say we ought to give it a silver spoon and fork.

Audrey Holt-Wilson and her daughter to tea, partly on a running consultation with me and Eric indiscriminately, and partly friendly. So difficult as Eric was called away for his grandchild case in the middle and I nearly had to do surgery, but was just saved by his returning at the last moment.

Friday 7 April (Good Friday)
Thank heaven for a bit of extra time in bed. Double daylight saving started last Sunday and we can never get used to it for weeks. The second hour seems the last straw and as if we are getting up in the middle of the night. The cats didn't get so upset this year as last when they were persistently late for meals and wondered why. This year it has been pretty wet all the week so they have been in more and have heard the gong!

After working all morning Eric managed to get on with repairing the guinea pig's house in the afternoon and left it ready for redecoration which Biz can do herself.

Dr and Mrs G came in after supper with Simmy and he brought his violin. Biz joined in so we had two flutes, two violins and the piano. Quite an orchestra. Mrs G brought her sewing and I knitted, but we didn't listen to the music much as I found she had travelled a good deal and had been to lots of the places I had, including Oratava. Photos and things came out and we got well away. It is such a relief to find anyone in Chippenham who can talk about anywhere further off than Weston-super-Mare, or at most Weymouth. It was all most refreshing.

Saturday 8 April
Latest invasion rumours and gossip:
1. All army leave is being stopped next week.
2. The mass of army stuff being shifted on the railways is greater than ever before.

3. Isle of Wight is crammed with invasion barges.
4. Churchill is trying to get through on air bombing alone without a second front at all.
5. The Russians have not got far enough for the great blow from the West to be effective.
6. The Russians have got so far, that it won't be necessary for us to do anything!

On the whole the news seems to be the quiet before the storm again except for Russia who presses on as ever. Odessa is nearly surrounded.

Sunday 9 April

The Czechoslovak flag flies on the border of Czechoslovakia for the first time for five years. The Czechoslovak unit of the Russian Army waits with the latter to enter the country as liberators. The flag business is bound to have an immense moral effect in Europe. Word has been sent on all European broadcasts to the Czechs to rise up against the German oppressor – -to intensify sabotage and non co-operation in every way, and to take active action where they can. This is the first time that a definite message to strike has gone out to Europe.

Wednesday 12 April

Long letter from Arthur who at any rate seems to be getting fed well. Said they were told they got as much meat in a day as we get in a week. This and the drill and PT will really be very good for him if he can stick it. He says all leave for the Navy was stopped on April 6th. It really does seem as if things were going to happen soon, though it has been a question of crying wolf so often that we shan't believe it till it actually does happen.

Friday 14 April

Many rumours going round Bath about IT. Apparently all the Americans there have disappeared, also all the AA guns and crews. Many Dakotas towing gliders have been going over, carrying supplies?

Saturday 15 April
An article in the paper today says there is a shortage of flower seeds and a large demand for plants, which are soaring to greatly inflated prices. Apparently after five years of war and little to buy in the shops, and few outings or amusements, we feel we must have flowers and are prepared to pay for them.

The railway goods have stopped collecting returned empties and have refused to take our empty bottles, and the man told us there were thirty-five fish cases waiting at the fishmonger for removal.

Sunday 16 April
We are all just waiting for it to start. Russians have practically all the Crimea except Sebastopol.

St Georges Day is to be a day of National Prayer in anticipation of coming events. Oh lor. The two similar days in 1940 were followed immediately by great disasters. Why not try to get on with the work efficiently instead of relying on this 'unqualified assistance?' (That is a quote from somebody else offering up a prayer in the operating theatre.)

Tuesday 18 April
Scrum again in Bath, and a nun, which always puts me in a bad mood. The Government provides prison doctors and pays them for necessary medical work for their criminals, why can't the RC church do the same for its nuns?

Poster in the Bath evening papers: 'Invasion expected to start any day', then in very small print 'say Neutrals'. As they have been saying that for years there may not be anything in it. The wireless tells us daily that we shall get food supplies all right when it starts and are making arrangements for this that and the other to carry on, and are gradually working the public up to a state of hysteria about the whole thing. Why all this publicity now if not to warn the Germans?

Today all diplomatic privileges have been removed. No foreign diplomatic staff are to be allowed to leave the country and all diplomatic bags are to be censored. Jolly good thing too, probably a lot leaks through Spain and Argentina but it is an unprecedented thing for Britain to do, though for years before the war Germany was said to tap private telephones in embassies and look in diplomatic bags surreptitiously.

Thursday 20 April
School clinic at Warminster. I have never seen so little traffic on the road. A few jeeps from Salisbury Plain shopping in the town. Coming home I ran into a collection of guns near Lacock but that was all. They must have taken everything nearer to the coast. Eric says people in Bath have got invasion hysteria. Certainly the civilians there seem to have had more instructions than people in Chippenham, but the Government does seem to be trying to work up a definite scare about it. Perhaps it is to try to stop strikes of which there is an epidemic at the moment. I think people have got weary and sick of no second front happening for so long that they have given up bothering and think they may as well try to get some better conditions as nothing else seems to be happening. Some of the papers have pointed out that Dunkirk was now almost four years ago and a generation of apprentices has grown up with little memory of that time.

Saturday 22 April
Eric has heard that 'tonight is the night', but only from a report in a Madrid paper. I can't believe that it would not have been censored if this really were so.

A marvellous pre-summer day with blue sky and a few tiny white clouds. Got into the garden in pm. Biz went miles up chestnut tree with a boy friend till the men on top of the electric light posts in the road, who were mending the cable that a tank had knocked down, looked as if they were on the ground compared to her. She must have been 60–70 feet up. I couldn't bear it, but tried to as I thought of the time Mummy caught Polly and I coming in at the maids' bedroom window from the roof where we had been making a guinea-pig run. She said in tones of restrained fury 'I forbid you ever to go out there again.' We were so surprised, as she didn't generally talk like that and we couldn't think what she was making all the fuss about. Now I know.

Tuesday 25 April
Colley's horse's mouth tip this morning was that Zero hour was unfixed till the last moment but depended above all on the weather. 'Watch when the barometer reaches 30° he said. It is now 29.7°. The channel must be calm to take all those barges across and land them off beaches.

Wednesday 26 April
The barometer is now 30°. A lovely clear day with high cloud. Perhaps a trifle too much wind? It might be choppy in the straits. We hardly dare put the news on, though dare not put it on.

Friday 28 April
Colley said he had heard from a nurse in the Uxbridge area that all main roads round there were being closed to ordinary traffic from yesterday. Eric says perhaps only because of a time bomb, and nothing to do with the invasion. Weather colder and cloudy and the barometer only 29.7. Have they missed the boat?

All the Dominion Prime Ministers – Canada, Australia, New Zealand, and today Smuts from South Africa have arrived in this country for a conference. Let us hope it is not to make plans for the second front, but rather to witness it and the complete and sudden collapse of Germany. Perhaps they are discussing what Armistice terms to offer.

Saturday 29 April
Tremendous noise of bombers going out in the night, even more than usual. Eric wondered if we were doing an airborne invasion of Jersey preparatory to taking the Cherbourg peninsula, *mais je crois que non.*

Sunday 30 April

A heavenly summer day with all the spring green freshness, blossom, sun, forget-me-nots, lilac, wisteria. The garden seems never to have been so lovely or so freshly green, except perhaps in 1940 when we really were terrified to the very roots of our being that we might be invaded at any moment. Now again there is the feeling that each moment in this sunny English garden is almost too precious to bear, and that we ought not to be enjoying it so much on the eve of such frightful slaughter.

14

THE INVASION AT LAST

6 May–24 June 1944

Saturday 6 May 1944
The immediate expectations of invasion have passed off. We couldn't keep up that pitch of nerves for much longer when nothing happened. I suppose the shouting and propaganda is intended to have an effect on the Germans, and by shouting Wolf they will now relax.

Elizabeth had a thrill this morning. She appeared when I was in the bath with an apparently dead kitten, born yesterday and hideous. Eric and I both told her it was dead after cursory glances, but she was most anxious to resuscitate it so we told her she could try. With the aid of warmth and artificial respiration she got it alive again. She was tremendously braced and felt she had saved her first life. It could inspire her to do medicine in the future.

Monday 8 May
A relatively slack day so went up to see Daphne Awdry who is very fed up with life having got an attack of acute sciatica. Daniel was home for 24 hours' leave from Sandhurst. Last Saturday night twenty of the cadets were summoned to a dance at Windsor Castle and he was one. He enjoyed himself hugely and danced with Margaret Rose. I did not mind him enjoying himself but it made me see red to think of the petrol that must have been used. Why should the Princesses be able to have private dances with everyone arriving in cars when no one else can? I bet no one walked on their flat feet to Windsor Castle. Daniel said airily 'Oh, we had

an army truck.' It is such a bad example to the rest of us. Why the hell should we try to be honest about our petrol if the people who are supposed to be leading the country are so blatantly dishonest? Why can't the police stop some of those cars and make them state publicly in court what they were using their petrol for. It is not fair when they were down on a Bath man for running his children just outside the town during a siren, when they had been right through the Blitz and were terrified.

Leigh rang Eric up to ask if we were cancelling his list of tonsils and adenoids on Wednesday. The RUH have had instructions to take nothing in except extreme emergencies. We are letting his clinic stand, as have had no instructions to keep beds clear in Chippenham.

Wednesday 10 May
Anniversary (four years) of Hitler's opening attack on Belgium, Holland and Luxembourg. We have not celebrated by invading back, though they say that there were 4000 planes out over France yesterday. Everyone thinks the moon is too full at present.

Friday 12 May
Everyone in Chippenham and Bath (except Eric and I who slept like logs and never heard a sound) was kept awake by planes and gliders almost all night. Many thought it was the Invasion and got up and dressed though why they should do that I can't think except that many who were in the Bath blitz are so nervous that they get up and dress whenever there is much noise of planes.

Saturday 13 May
Biz's birthday. My mind went back 11 years to that date, also a Saturday, when I did my star turn of having a 10lb baby without missing a meal.

Daisy had a gruesome story today from a patient at the surgery door just back from holiday in Devon. He said that acres of moor had been taken over as a prospective war cemetery and that thousands of little crosses had already arrived. The story has fair given me the shivers.

Sunday 14 May

4 baby guinea pigs have arrived. As always I am smitten with their loveliness. Not having had any for about 8 years, even I had forgotten quite how lovely they were, or how large. No wonder mother was so colossal. No news – we still wait. America is said to be as much on edge as we are. May the Germans be more so.

Still no rain which we have been longing for, but hoping it would keep off if the invasion started, but as it has not we might just as well have had the rain that the garden needs so desperately.

Wednesday 17 May

Arthur is halfway through a two week course at Portsmouth and I got a letter yesterday but undated. I am told that Hitler said they bombed Portsmouth on Saturday night, such a tactful thing for anyone to tell me. Later today a large parcel arrived containing his suitcase and all his 'Civvies' including dirty vests. I think this parcel must have been sent off before he left Warrington, but there was no postmark or date. At any rate the label was in his handwriting, so it can't be just the authorities sending back the effects of the deceased. All the same it has given me the jimjams.

Saturday 20–Monday 22 May

FM rang up after supper to see if I could go over soon as she was worried about D. I promptly panicked but found there were trains on Sunday, and got over to find them fairly normal. It seems to have been a panic over Miles' latest girl. D developed a pain, which I think was probably emotional hyperchlorhydria.[1] I can quite understand how foul it must be for parents when their children want to get serious and there are ideas of marriage. They cannot take an impartial view so they are in a way the wrong people to offer advice.

I still remember how utterly at odds D and I got over my

wedding. As he appeared to mind about it I said that against all my convictions I would be married in church and perjure myself making the right replies, so long as it was at 8am and there was no party or visitors. I thought I had gone well over half way to meet him, but he still thought I was being pig-headed and obstructive and had made no concessions to him at all. There was complete deadlock, as we both went on being hurt with each other for many years. In fact even now after twenty years, and bringing all my reason onto it, I cannot think of it without emotion, or without feeling that they were terribly psychologically cruel, though I know they did not mean to be. It was all really that they could not bear me to marry at all.

Friday 26 May
Daisy went off to Dartmoor for her holiday yesterday. She says if there are no trains back she will ride a Dartmoor pony. That leaves me with no resident maid for the first time in my life except for the briefest times when Ruth has been here to help.

My 45th birthday today and all a bit of a rush. Up betimes to vacuum dining room and sitting room before breakfast. Biz was getting frantic because I would not come in to breakfast. It turned out to be because she had a marvellous present for me. In the middle of the table there was one small guinea pig in a very small Swiss gentian bowl. There it sat, just fitting in to the breakfast routine, perfectly self-possessed and accepting bits of toast and cornflakes. It was so sweet we think we will have one as permanent floral decoration at meals!

Eric presented me with a lovely box of 4 balls of string coming out through holes and with 'all my love' tied on each. Told him I thought he might have left a little for the rest of the family, but it was nice to feel I still had it after 20 years.

Saturday 3 June
Lina Wood arrived yesterday worn out with too much YMCA.

Our forces are creeping nearer to Rome, everyone on tenterhooks and dare not miss a news bulletin.

We are wondering if the Allies get possession of Rome soon, and it is more or less undamaged, whether the Pope couldn't do something about getting all the Catholics in the Balkans to get right out of the war. He seems such a useless individual. One would have thought with all his power that he would have been able to do something if he took a really strong line.

Monday 5 June
Allies are in the heart of Rome, the first capital of Europe to be freed from German domination. It is bound to have a vast moral effect all over Europe, with or without anything the Pope may or may not be able to do. Few details yet, but it has been too quick for there to have been much destruction.

A great argument about whose flag ought to be flown from the Capitol. I said the Italian, as we were fighting an ideological war and ought to refrain from even this symbol that we had made a conquest. Simmy thought the Union Jack, Eric the flags of all the Allies with perhaps the Italian as well, and Biz, after due thought, the Allied or British flag for just a bit and then the Italian when we had restored order and given it back to them.

Tuesday 6 June
Early morning news reported that the Germans said the Western offensive had begun with
1. Air borne troops on the Seine estuary behind Le Havre
2. The German navy engaged with Allied landing craft
3. Further air attacks on Calais, Boulogne and Dunkirk.

1pm news. Churchill has made a statement in the house to the effect that D-Day is going to plan. No details yet.

Could hardly attend to all the patients in Bath who crowded in, worried about this and that. Busy all day but bits of news kept filtering through every hour. 4000 ships with several thousand smaller craft seem to be making smaller landings along the Normandy coast. 11,000 first line aircraft said to be supporting.

Nearly everyone kept awake with planes going over in the night and now saying they knew it was IT.

I am incredibly tired tonight, probably with suppressed emotion. Cannot seem to get down to peoples' fuss-worries, though I bless the iron medical discipline that drives one on with any patient who has an acute problem, whatever is happening in the world.

Wednesday 7 June

Have discovered for the umpteenth time that I cannot write. It's all right about the lack of butter or petty irritations of patients, but when anything big happens with emotional content either personal or world shaking, my immediate instinct is to shut up like a clam, feel or say nothing and become quieter and quieter in every way. It has always been so. Mummy used to say I talked freely about all my men friends while I was not serious about anybody, but as soon as I ceased discussing anyone it was a danger signal. Eric realised early that when I said least I was feeling most, and the fact that he knew this was always one of the most marvellous things about him. Enough about me.

The point being that I cannot write about the Invasion, though I feel it is just the sort of thing that might be of interest to the children and their children in future years, to know what we were doing and feeling in these momentous days. The trained journalists are just the opposite, rejoicing in having so much 'copy' at last and being able to pour it all forth in a spate of words and impressions. I shall have to put in newspaper cuttings as I have dried up so much. I can feel nothing except slightly sick, and do nothing except what I have to do.

[From this point the entries in the diaries are less frequent, being interspersed with many newspaper cuttings.]

Thursday 8 June

Bayeux is in our hands with hysterically enthusiastic welcome from the French. Fighting round Caen heavy.

An American doctor came to borrow a book and stayed to

tea. He was completely confident and optimistic and pleased with himself, and thought they would go straight on and win the war with no setbacks and that he would be going home soon. Their self-confidence is a bit frightening, but then they have had no Dunkirk, no Singapore or Burma, and have not had to fight for four years completely outnumbered with totally inadequate weapons.

Friday 9 June
Counter attacks have started around Caen, which we do not seem to have captured yet, and the lovely old Norman town is said to be mostly destroyed.

A full and busy day with not much time to think. News on at hurried intervals, but nothing on it except a lot of words about nothing and endless 'Stories from the beachheads' which tell us nothing of what is happening.

Charles to supper very hurriedly after operating. Have invited him next Saturday to meet Sir Arthur[2] (whom the Awdrys are producing) and who actually wrote the proposed Health Service White Paper. Charles was rather bowled over that I was going to meet such a person!

Saturday 10 June
Was prevailed upon by Lina and Biz to go to a gymkhana in the afternoon for 'Salute the Soldier' week. Of all the mad races the British do seem the maddest. On the way we passed squads of American troops doing machine gun training and drilling and pointing their guns at us, all mixed up with the crowds who appeared to be wandering about quite aimlessly. The sun shone, bomber crews going out to France zoomed overhead and children and ponies wandered round in a sunny English park intent upon their races, quite oblivious to the preparations for death and destruction all around them. Is it our weakness or our strength that we as a nation persist in keeping on with this sort of thing in the midst of the most frightful war in history?

Sunday 11 June
Story on the radio of six Canadians captured in Normandy and taken as prisoners to a cave with one hundred armed Germans. The Canadians talked to the Germans and quite soon persuaded them that they (the Germans) would be certain to be captured soon, so the roles were reversed. The six Canadians marched out towards our lines escorting the hundred Germans whose numbers swelled to a hundred and forty before they arrived! Looks as if German morale is not quite what it was.

A BMA meeting at Devizes where we should have been discussing the report of Council but actually never reached this as we went right back to Eric's resolution of last time, discussed it again and passed it again with a further resolution added.

Thursday 15 June
The county nurse at Devizes clinic said that about 1000 prisoners had been marched through the town a day or two ago, and that they were very arrogant, all doing the Nazi salute, several turning round and putting out their tongues at women on the pavements and some spitting at the Union Jack as they passed. Most of the onlookers just laughed but it did not seem a very tactful way of ingratiating themselves to their captors. Looks as if German morale had not suffered much and that they still think they are going to win. If any of our prisoners did that sort of thing in Germany they would be shot immediately.

At 7.30pm last night I was doing my hair which was all down when I heard Bertha bark. It was obvious someone had arrived, so went to the top of the stairs to see who, and there was Arthur, complete in Naval Ratings uniform! I shrieked and flung my arms around him, to his acute embarrassment as he was accompanied by a friend who was the cause of Bertha's bark. They had two nights' leave (unofficial as no one is allowed any leave at the moment), in between finishing the bit of the course at Hensridge Royal Navy Air Station and going to Loughborough. He was looking tanned and fitter than I had ever seen him, having been occupied in putting up barbed wire round the camp for the last three weeks, which though dull, was at any rate in the open air and far better than cleaning latrines. Unfortunately I had just given most of the strawberries and all the asparagus to Daphne Awdry for Sir Arthur Rucker tomorrow night, but hastily scrounged a few more strawberries, which were much appreciated. They were both so fit and well and had hearty appetites which was a bit difficult as we only had dried eggs for supper, but with the addition of a tin of beans it was fairly adequate. They were more than glad to get hot baths again and sheets on their beds. It was marvellous to have him, even if only for two nights. I had never thought that he could look so nice in Naval Ratings uniform, which I always thought rather awful before.

Friday 16 June
Rather unfortunate that the one day Arthur was home should have been a Friday as I was busy all day. Had to rush off and leave them before they had even come down to breakfast.

The main news today has been the launch of the much-threatened German 'secret weapon'. This turns out to be an aircraft without a pilot, set to a certain course at the end of which it falls and explodes. Evidently there have been some quite nasty raids with it in the Home Counties though not much is being said about where, only that 'damage and casualties have been reported', which always means there have been a good many.

Saturday 17 June
Sir Arthur Rucker has cancelled his visit, much to our disappointment. We don't know why, but feel a bomb on the Ministry of Health might be a good thing. It has meant a dozen more telephone calls to put off the selection of doctors we had collected to meet him. Pretty tired by evening – partly emotion at having our Arthur and his going again in so short a time.

Tuesday 20 June
Nixon came in full of stories about the new German weapon.

He says that 5 or 7 are controlled by one plane with a crew who control these things by certain wireless beams, and can direct them from this central plane. Our people are now going for the central plane but this is made more difficult by the Germans varying their position in the formation. He says it needs a two-mile ramp leading up to a cliff to launch it. Most interesting if correct, but with Nixon's stories one never knows!

Wednesday 21 June
A picture in the paper shows how the plane without a pilot may be launched, with no suggestion of Nixon's control plane or a two-mile ramp. No news of us having shot down a control plane, though various pilots have told stories of shooting down the 'doodlebugs' themselves.

Thursday 22 June
A very long and annoying clinic at Warminster, which included a brush with a Roman Catholic mother. A very delicate little boy with congenital cataracts had been dealt with fairly satisfactorily over the years and he was just beginning to see a bit. He had been thrown into a very primitive village school and was of course hopelessly backward and quite unable to cope or be coped with in a class of 40 or more tough village children. When I suggested that he should go to a special school the mother said 'Oh no, he would fret, and his father would never allow it.' I then suggested she should try to teach him to read a bit herself in the evenings as I thought that with a little bit of individual tuition he might soon catch up the others of his age. She replied that she had so much to teach him for the priest each week that she had no time to teach him to read!

I nearly boiled over, but controlled myself and said very coldly that it was for her to decide which was the more important for the child's future. I wish now I had told her that I considered her most wicked and unchristian but suppose she might have had me up for libel. But it seems time somebody said something to these bloody

Catholics. They just get their own way right and left and squeal if anyone says a word against them, while they continue on their mistaken course far more unchecked than anyone else.

Friday 23 June
Cherbourg has not fallen yet. If we don't get it by Tuesday it will be a month since the invasion and the time set for the Germans that if they could prevent us getting a port we should not be able to keep our armies fully supplied.

Charles to supper. Rather a strange one as we seem to have run out of everything. A mashed bean and bacon mixture with sardine patties, but he ate it without complaint.

Saturday 24 June
Russians have started a fresh attack round Vitebsk. This may or may not be the beginning of their real summer attack.

Eric and I were woken up at 12pm by heavy planes going right over the house. We got up to watch them and they went on for so long that we wondered if it was a fresh air attack starting somewhere else, or just bombing Cherbourg preparatory to capturing it. Somehow we both felt it was something more than usual. Strangely enough in my semi-comatose condition, thinking of the start of a new offensive, the association came into my mind of what extraordinary accord there had been between us in our now nearly 20 years of married life. (A rather strange 'free association'.) How we never quarrelled or haggled about little things, like how much window should be opened in the bedroom, or the blackout up or down, or whether the other was getting cold or was dotty to get out of bed in the middle of the night and look at aeroplanes. We have so many differences of opinion on a vast number of subjects, yet can always agree to differ on them without quarrelling and go our own way without nagging. Somehow suddenly in the middle of the night I was deeply appreciative of all this and thought of all the haggling about nothing there is between so many couples.

15

STRETCHING THE RATIONS

25 June–28 August 1944

Sunday 25 June 1944
The American naval action in the Pacific is greater than at first appeared. 44 Japanese ships sunk and as many more damaged. This week we have entertained our third consultant to a meal. Prospect of rain at last.

Wednesday 28 June
Another 6am baby for Eric. He is getting sick of these pre-breakfast parties, and has never had so many babies in June before. He seems fated to be called out on his non-surgery days, which he had just decided to devote to teaching Biz algebra. This time it was to a man staying with friends in Chippenham who had collapsed in Devizes with what was reputed to be a heart attack and was brought back in an ambulance. On investigation Eric made a new diagnosis of 'Doodlebugitis'. The man lived at Horsham, his London office had been blown up and he had very little rest night or day for about a fortnight. He came down here for a rest and was given kippers for breakfast and not unnaturally failed to digest them and vomited, fainted and generally collapsed. Some people have no sense. Why have kippers for breakfast and go racketing off to Devizes when completely worn out physically and mentally?

Friday 30 June
It has been raining all the week. In peacetime it would have been Henley week, which is wet nine years out of ten. Rain was of course

wanted, but now we want some sun to dry up the ground and ripen the strawberries and blackcurrants.

Another case of Doodlebugitis for me in pm. A woman who has come down from Croydon worn out and must rush to have her glasses changed after two days. She had no proper sleep for nearly a fortnight and said no one could have a bath or go to the loo in peace. It was far worse than 1940. When there was a bad raid then it was unpleasant while it lasted, but when it was over it was over. Now it goes on night and day at irregular intervals. Finally I persuaded her to go off with a prescription for sleeping tablets at night and benzedrine in the day and not worry about her glasses till she is more rested. Strange how many people think a change of glasses is a cure-all.

Monday 3 July
A damp grey dark day. This weather is ideal for flying bombs as our people can't see to shoot them down. Also the troops in Normandy can't get the air cover they should owing to low cloud, though they seem to be doing pretty well nevertheless. Late at night great news from Russia. The fall of Minsk.

Wednesday 5 July
Devizes Mental Hospital clinic in the morning. All the staff there seem to have had at least one fortnight of holiday and to be about to have another. At any rate people in the state service on salaries do get proper holidays and off-times. Eric has not been away for a night since our fortnight last August, and I for only two nights to Whitchurch.

Thursday 6 July
Warminster school clinic in morning. Got mixed up in an American convoy going south, and never got out of it the whole way. Very delaying and what we expected last March, but didn't get. I suppose they are the second wave now moving down to the marshalling areas.

Trowbridge clinic in pm for Colley, so had a full and tiring day for a Thursday. It has been a hellishly busy week and hot, heavy weather threatening thunder, which has made both Eric and me dead sleepy, so it is a drive to go on. Also there is much fruit to pick. It seems to be my fate to be professionally busy when the fruit is ready. Shall have to take to getting up at 6am to do it.

Churchill made a statement in the house about the flying bombs. Said that in a month since they started 2750 had reached London or other objective, and there had been 2754 deaths, i.e. about one death per bomb. It seems rather an expensive way of killing from the German point of view. Rucker is said to be coming this Saturday.

Friday 7 July
Eric went to see Frankie today who painted a grim picture of Mereworth and her parents down in Kent. There is very little roof left on the house and no windows. London's guns have been moved out to this area to try and catch the flying bombs before they get to London. In this they are being quite successful but it is bad luck on the residents in the vicinity. The guns are almost as bad as the bombs and Pa Champion has a full-time man going round every day making assessments of the damage. But he and Ma Champion refuse to budge and stay in their almost derelict house, at best scarcely able to eat a meal because the rattle of the guns shakes all the plates and dishes off the table. There they stay as an example to the village, bolstering up its morale the whole time. They are a superb example of all that is best in the British character and tradition. They would no more leave the village (though they could well do so) than a mother would fly to safety leaving her young children to be bombed. This sort of thing, the determination of the privileged and those in authority to stick it out and die if necessary with their people and not use their privilege to take them to safety, is one of the main strengths of the British nation.

D is also continuing to go up to London each day because 'If my clerks can, I can.'

Saturday 8 July

Rushing and tearing my hair all day to get through the work for the meeting with Rucker this evening. We had about a dozen doctors here, counting us, all men who had made their own practices and not entirely without the power of independent thought. It is impossible to summarise all that was said. Suffice it to say that we talked from 8.30pm till 1.30am without stopping. The discussion developed between Dr Ede, who was a good spokesman for the GPs, and Charles for the voluntary hospitals and consultants with Rucker answering back. Altogether a most successful party, and I really felt I had held my 'salon' and was right in it as one of them. Though the only woman I think I looked rather nice and wore my crepe de Chine as being summery and young looking.

Monday 10 July

Russians are over the borders of Latvia and Lithuania and look like cutting off a lot of German divisions in those states.

A major domestic crisis today. Mrs S, the daily cleaner, who never cleans anything and has even left hair combings on my dressing table, 'in case you need them', decided to wash out a glass which had been left in the boothole ever since she had been here. There was a bit of vague dirt at the bottom. If fact it contained Elizabeth's very precious chrysalis of a lakky moth just due to hatch out, and carefully watched every day.

A letter from Hargreaves saying his wife was going to have her fourth baby and must get out of London. Could we do anything about it and what about the other three children? Also by the same post one from a cousin of Eric's whom we have never seen anything of, to say he now has a wife and two children and could we do anything to help them? Also Scoot wants to come here for some leave. Also we may have to put up the new assistant at Corsham if he comes. Also our very nice temporary MOH[1] is being turned out of his bungalow and has nowhere to live. HELL.

Tuesday 11 July

Eric went up to hospital to assist at 8.30pm and arrived back at 3am. Just as they were finishing the operation they were doing, casualties of a smash between a lorry, driven by an Irishman and containing WAAFs, and an American vehicle were brought in. The result was:

1 Irishman – died 10 minutes after admission
1 American – fractured patella
1 WAAF concussion and cuts
1 WAAF fractured skull and severe head wound.

Thursday 13 July

Assistant for Corsham here for the third time this week for tea, but fortunately he doesn't eat much. Went into the garden for a bit after tea and was thoroughly dirty when Eric rang to say the head injury man for the West of England, who came in the morning to see the WAAF, and his ATS driver would like supper in 10 minutes. Dashed in to break the news to Daisy. Upstairs to clean and change but caught in the act. Luckily Biz did the honours till I could get down. They had been to London and back since visiting the hospital here at 8am. A nice pair but the driver pretty dead beat.

We have had someone in to a meal every day this week, though all more or less professional. A bit hard on the rations but we are just surviving.

Friday 14 July

Several patients here in pm and only a few turned out to be eyes. One a baby with a feeding problem, another an old patient, a friend of Granny's that I tried to push onto Eric but quite unsuccessfully. She feels exhausted and wants to weep all the time, and told me she knew she ought to go back to her husband in London but didn't feel she could while she felt so ill. A mental conflict of a classical nature. I couldn't quite explain the nature of the conflict to her. 'I don't want to go back because I am afraid, and therefore I shall be ill and then no one can possibly expect me to go back'. After all it is pretty easy for us to say anyone should go back not having been in it ourselves. So I propped her up a bit and said she was not fit to go back and must face this fact, which was what she wanted. Eric said his mother used to prop her quite a lot so I suppose I must take this on as a legacy from her, or as war work.

Lately we have done nothing but prop up other people and arrange for them and tell them what to do. So many doctors' wives all having babies and where to go and how? We are sick and tired of all this, which is so much more than medicine, yet perhaps general practice at its best. But we are tired and want a good holiday away from it ourselves. Just to be left alone for a bit (preferably with a bit of petrol), and not have the phone ringing and people clamouring, 'What are we to do?'

Friday 21 July
Through a blur of sleep at 7am heard 'This is the news. It is sensational. There has been a revolt in high quarters of the German army against Hitler.' I was awake in an instant. The bomb against him was the symbol of what may prove to be the beginning of the real crack. The Nazis talk of the 'usurpers' who had planned to seize power and say they are to be shot at sight by anybody. Looks as if there could soon be complete anarchy in Germany with the army shooting at each other. Found Colley on top of the world, and thinking it will now be over within a month – in fact he got so worked up with it all that he shortened that to 'A week with luck'.

Rushed through my work to turn on the news but the Germans are not giving much away at the moment. Americans have landed on Guam, the first of their territories seized by the Japanese.

Sunday 23 July
The Russians are sweeping along on all fronts at an incredible rate, almost unnoticed with the news concentrated on wild rumours from within Germany.

Tuesday 26 July
One hell of a day. Scoot came with me to Bath. Shoals of patients pushing and crowding in. After about half an hour I realised I had started to menstruate heavily and was completely unprepared. Managed to get a child into the dark room and grabbed a tampax and bolted through OPs with everyone staring. Subsequently managed to borrow a sanitary towel from Matron, a tampax being quite inadequate these days. Crowds and crowds of patients and a dentist's appointment afterwards that lasted an hour, so I didn't manage to eat the sandwiches Scoot had bought from Woolworths. She had shopped all this time with much effort, having to stand in queues. I had not seen so many cakes, meat pies etc for years, but very useful as we seem to have a doctor or doctor's relative in to some meal most days.

Tuesday 1 August
Americans have shot forward to Avranche and beyond. Eric, Ruth and I went to see the film *Madame Curie* in the evening. Don't know how accurate it is but said to have been vetted by her daughter. Was the most wonderful and moving thing I have ever seen, I was lachrymose most of the while. Bitterly regretted that I had not taken Biz though she had been tired and it was late. She would not have understood it all, or much of the physical apparatus and experiments, but might have remembered some bits of it all her life.

Wednesday 2 August
Turkey has broken off diplomatic relations with Germany. Naughty old Turkey. When war started the country was loud with protestations of friendship for us. When we were doing rather badly, not quite so friendly, sold lots of chrome etc to Germany, and let her ships go through the Dardanelles and into the Black Sea. Wouldn't hear of our enjoying any advantages. Now she sees Germany is done for so she has stopped sending her chrome and is veering round to our side again.

Friday 4 August
Ruth has gone to Whitchurch to have two days on the river with Miles. It is rather an epoch that I can let her go without feeling it should have been me.

Saturday 5 August
After five patients in the morning I had a hot and lazy afternoon mostly on a rug in the garden with a book and the BMJ. Tried to imagine I was in a punt. This was difficult owing to the bombers overhead, said later to be going out to bomb the submarine pens at Brest, so as to stop the subs getting out before the Americans got there. The latter are making spectacular progress and most of the places mentioned are familiar to Eric or me and associated with holiday events. Dinan I remember so acutely from my first trip abroad without my parents about 1920. Helen and I were staying there and met a Breton farmer who said he knew from a distance that we must be *'des jeunes filles anglaises parce que vous marchez tout droite commes les hommes.'* Fresh from St Felix, with its emphasis on deportment, that was a great compliment.

Sunday 6 August
Ruth arrived back having had two perfect days on the river in the skiff, one to Cleeve, one to the Beetle and Wedge. Strangely I minded more not being there when she came and told me about it than I did when she went. I almost couldn't bear it. August bank holiday weekend and for once perfect weather, and me not there. I asked her if Mummy and D missed me and she said no. I think they must have just accepted her in my place. If I cannot get there before we go away I shall not have been on the river at all this year, which simply hasn't happened since I can remember.

The river is constantly before me and anything such as the plash of someone diving into the pool brings up the most vivid pictures. It is the perfect weather really that is biting me this way. I cannot remember being homesick like this since just after Arthur was born 19 years ago.

Wednesday 9 August
Daisy goes on holiday on Friday and I have just heard Arthur is coming home on leave that very day. Being in Bath that morning would not have mattered so much, but Hargreaves also rang to ask if we could have his wife for the weekend. They have got the other children to Penzance but had a frightful crowded and tiring journey with them in the heat and she had not slept for three nights with doodlebugs. Her 4th child is due to arrive at the end of September. So she is completely worn out. I couldn't say no, though it will muck up Arthur's leave. I shall be firm about doing things alone with the family, and as a psychologist's wife she should understand and will probably want to be in bed or just sitting in the garden most of the while. At any rate she will be able to stay in and answer the phone if we want to go out.

Thursday 10 August
Americans in Le Mans, well on the way to Paris, but violent counter attacks from the Germans further north.

Friday 11 August
Ruth did a big food shop while I was at the hospital as the prospect of Arthur and Eva Hargreaves arriving on me at any minute, and not bringing rations, filled me with horror. Ruth stood in queues all morning and almost filled the back of the car with 2 cakes, fish, meat pies, 6 jam puffs – things we haven't seen for years not being given to standing in queues.

I also had to take a patient into the hospital that I couldn't diagnose. Almost complete loss of vision following a blow in the eye with a horse halter. I thought she must have a small macular haemorrhage but couldn't find it, which worried me as I thought I was missing something. However Colley confirmed there was nothing to see, but thinks she has retrobulbar neuritis,[2] probably nothing to do with the injury, or possibly a slow haemorrhage into the nerve as it only came on several days after the blow. He has admitted her, and it was a great relief off my mind that I hadn't missed something obvious.

A telegram arrived later from Hargreaves to say his wife is not now coming till Sunday evening. Perhaps a good thing as Arthur will not arrive to find a stranger in the house. All that food hunt for nothing, though we can do with it all and it will save me having to cook all day on his first days home. Thank goodness for a fridge.

Mima starting to kitten and must have her hand held.

The first one arrived practically on the doorstep with Arthur. The second was 'born in a caul', breathed prematurely and perished in its own liquor. Might have been saved by efficient obstetrics but if only to be drowned later why bother? Still I was glad Biz had gone to bed or she would certainly have been forced to bother.

Eric heard an amazing story from Charles at the hospital today. Fireworks are being made again and shops can already order them in enormous quantities with the prospect of an early delivery, to put away for Peace Night. Suggests this may not be long delayed.

Monday 14 August

A tremendous squeeze going on to try to encircle the German armies in Normandy before they can get back even to the Seine. There is said to be a retreat but no 'rout' yet.

A muddled day spent rushing from cleaning the house to patients, from news to turning out drawers with Arthur. Eric dashing about tearing his hair. Mac at the hospital at 10.30am and Eric had 8 patients he wanted to see with him. A man very ill, undiagnosed but possibly with a cerebral haemorrhage who later died, a naval surgeon's wife who wondered if she was in labour, a fussy old lady's maid gone mad and throwing things at her, Dr P with a temp of 103° after supper, and endless calls from people who thought they were emergencies. Just one of those sort of days when one was on the run under great pressure from morning to night without time to think.

Tuesday 15 August

These are such stirring times to live in, yet life is such a rush domestically and professionally there is barely time to read the papers or grasp it all. Not back till 2.30pm from Bath and Arthur who had driven me in was catching the 3.30pm train to Whitchurch with Ruth to get a day on the river tomorrow. I don't mind so much this time somehow, as I do love them to go off and do things together. Arthur definitely wants to do things now and though I love doing them with him it is all a bit tiring with everything else. Shall miss Ruth terribly. She has been a brick with Daisy away, and is really most efficient in the house.

Landings in the S of France but no news yet where they are.

Wednesday 16–Monday 21 August
One of the most eventful weeks in history, yet so full of chores that no time to take it in. Daisy did not return till Thursday because of an attack of diarrhoea and vomiting which meant I had to continue cooking and cleaning. Have seldom been so tired or so glad to see Daisy. Just no time to write and things happening in such quick succession one forgets which was what day, and have been too mentally tired to make the effort to remember.

Tuesday 22 August
De Gaulle has landed at Cherbourg and is making a triumphal tour of liberated French towns. Perhaps before going to Paris and setting up a new French Government? Almost everywhere the 'Maquis', now known as the FFI (French Forces of the Interior), are coming into the open and seizing power in the towns, overwhelming the small German garrisons left. The Paris populace has risen against the Germans and there is fighting in the streets. A Paris mob, especially when hungry as it is now, is probably still one of the nastiest in the world, with plenty of old French Revolution tradition coming out.

Arthur had left when I got back but his train was apparently late which will make him miss all his connections. Elizabeth out till late riding horses and I am imagining her under the tracks of American jeeps.

Wednesday 23 August
Ruth left for Lancaster in the pouring rain. She does not get there till 7.15pm tonight. It feels as if the family is breaking up.

1pm news. 'Paris has been liberated by the French forces of the Interior.' Just like that. What we have been waiting for, but a bit of a surprise that the French managed to do it all themselves.

[A note added to the diary in 1968 says that the announcement of the liberation of Paris was made prematurely. The rising of the FFI happened then but they were nearly defeated and the Americans and French entered the city on 28th August.]

All of us who love France wept when we heard the news.

Friday 28 August
Left for Whitchurch by train in pm after an exhausting morning in Bath. Train very hot and crowded and a good deal of competition for seats and conversation about who had been standing all morning. It occurred to no one to ask me if I had been. Suppose I didn't look like it, having put on a respectable hat (though a pre-war do-up) for once. Arrived weary, to peace and bliss and two absolutely perfect days on the river. FM's 68th birthday on Saturday. It is quite and entirely incredible that I should be now about the age she was when Miles was born. Going alone like that I just slipped back into being Joan Whitelock again, and it was very pleasant. The river and the company of the parents as always removed my fatigue and irritability in a miraculous way. The only thing was the feeling that it can't go on like that for ever, and with D 75 yrs old any time might be the last. Still it was heaven to have those two days. It must be pretty rare for a hard-bitten professional woman of 45 yrs to crave the society of her parents as much as I do, and to enjoy doing things with them still almost more than anything else in the world. Whatever happens now I shall always have the unforgettable memory of those two days.

Paris not so quiet as it might be. A good deal of shooting and sniping going on but gradually being stamped out. De Gaulle had a very narrow escape in Notre Dame.

16

THE END APPROACHES

30 August 1944–10 May 1945

Wednesday 30 August 1944
Left Chippenham for Manchester after usual rush fixing things up and getting off. Train slow to Bristol and nearly an hour late and very crowded. Two hours to wait in Bristol which we had allowed for lunch though we had taken a few emergency sandwiches. The time was reduced to ¾ hour by late arrival of train. Nevertheless we managed to get an extremely good, comfortable sit-down lunch in dining room at Bristol station. Soup, curry and more vegetables than even we could eat, followed by treacle tart.

Train from Bristol had come up from Plymouth and was VERY crowded but there were through carriages to Manchester. By dint of a bit of luck a first class carriage stopped immediately opposite us and several people got out, so we all managed to get a seat, though it was five a side. It would have been no advantage at all to have 1st class tickets – much better with 3rd class and get in a 1st if the train is full. No ticket collector could have got along corridors to look and wouldn't have cared if he had.

Marvellous to see Sylvia and talk again for the first time since the war began. We took some rations and had lunch out on Thursday so food was all right. Tried to shop (no girls' cardigans or knicker linings at all in any colour).

The news goes too fast to pursue and no time to write it all up quickly enough. All the names of the last war are coming in again: The Somme, Chateau Thierry, Amiens, Arras, Aisne, Marne, Oise etc. There can be practically no fighting. The Germans must be pulling right out of France.

Friday 1 September
From Manchester to Windermere where we shared a car to Grasmere with some other people. A lovely balmy evening and a walk up a hill to look at the lake after tea. Ruth and the Timberlakes came up on Wednesday. She loves it all as I had hoped. It is the first sight of lakes and mountains for both the girls.

Saturday 2 September
Pouring with rain in torrents and blowing. We had ordered lunch to be put up for the whole 9 of us last night so now we will have to eat it in our bedrooms.

The news continues to be breathtaking. The paper says 'Each of a dozen towns would have merited half a column by itself ordinarily.' Now they are old news almost before we get the paper and everyone is straining towards the end.

Great excitement as many of the flying bomb sites in the Pas-de-Calais are overrun, though some may still come from Belgium and Holland.

Sunday 3 September
The fifth anniversary of the outbreak of war. The British and Americans are in Belgium and said to be within 30 miles of Brussels. The Germans are using threats of V2, said to be the most terrible secret weapon, to get some sort of compromise peace.

Thursday 7 September
The papers today contain great news for the ordinary civilian. The blackout is to be considerably modified from Sept 7th, much more street lighting, and no absolute blackout required for windows, only ordinary curtains. This will lighten what has been one of the major burdens and annoyances of war for ordinary people. With a little basic petrol now, our personal slight discomforts would be completely removed.

There have already been rumours from Brussels that the German army had capitulated, but alas only rumours and I suppose there will be many more of these before the actual happening.

We had an early breakfast and started in dull but not actually raining weather to catch the train for Keswick to go to Penrith to meet Helen. The bus was full, and although we were at the front of the queue it would stop to pick up no one, so we went back and got our bikes and managed to pick up a train at Threlkeld. By this time it had started to rain again but we eventually got to Penrith at 1pm and had a good lunch of jugged hare at the George. Marvellous to see Helen again after nearly ten years. She seems almost completely immersed in domestic life and tied to her chores. It is such a waste that all those people with better brains than mine at school should have let them atrophy.

A fire in the lounge tonight which we have not been allowed since Sunday. Really this continual rain is a bit thick. It has been persistent with not more than two hours' break at a time ever since our arrival nearly a week ago.

[It rained for most of the rest of this holiday, but they did manage to climb Helvellyn and do some long bicycle rides.]

Sunday 17 September
Got home yesterday to find the garden very sunny and peaceful and far from the horrors of Europe, and even from the mountains, which can be cruel themselves in a storm.

We have landed a large airborne army in Holland. Some more flying bombs have come over, and rumours of the V2 abound. Meanwhile evacuees have been streaming back to London thinking it was all but over.

Thursday 21 September
Boulogne and Brest in our hands. The road bridge at Nijmegen still intact. Now the crucial point is Arnheim over the second branch of the Rhine, where airborne troops were dropped and have been

fighting alone for three days. Must be having hell. This is absolutely the gateway to Berlin and the end of the war as we would outflank the Rhine and the whole of the Siegfried line.

Sunday 24 September
Packed Elizabeth's trunk and frantically sewed on name tapes. Found rather surprisingly that she really had quite a lot of things that were on the school clothes list, mostly Ruth's cast-off things, with a few things from Arthur and Scoot's green bonnet!
We can't get air supplies through yet to paratroops at Arnheim, but some Poles have got across the river on rafts and taken supplies at night. They are still in a pretty sticky position.

Monday 25 September
Very last-dayish. Biz keeping up wonderfully though can hardly be parted form her animals for a minute. I loathe it more each time, and now with Biz going away to school as well it will be grim.

Wednesday 27 September
News that remaining troops at Arnheim have been withdrawn across the river at night. All pretty desperate.

Thursday 28 September
Long speech by Churchill in the House on the war situation. Fairly cheerful on the whole, but said the war might go on into 1945. Arnheim figures given. There were 8000 dropped of which only 2000 have been brought back, and 1200 wounded known to have been left as prisoners. They fought for ten days alone and surrounded, and with all the German resistance rallied and concentrated on this one point. It is said that by their stand they prevented supplies going down to the other great bridge at Nijmegen and so enabled us to keep this, and that the operation was 85% successful, which actually means of course that it was a failure. It will go down as one of the great epics of history.

Monday 2 October

The first much wanted letter from Biz but more about chrysalises than St Felix.

The German army definitely seems to have pulled itself together again, has stopped the rot and is resisting everywhere on its own frontiers enough to hold us up. We are beginning to be depressed about ending the war before the winter.

Friday 6 October

We have landed in Greece and captured Patros and several other islands without much opposition. We are not being told much about what is happening at the moment.

I had to help in evening surgery as Simmy has gone on holiday for a week. Wanted to go to a Labour meeting at 7.30pm where Tomlinson (prospective Labour candidate and head of Beltane school) was speaking, but of course we didn't finish till 7.25pm and Eric said he was too tired to go without supper or hurry over it. Felt rather desperate and that our profession was assuredly the most exacting and tiresome. However we strolled down at 7.50pm and were almost in time. There was a very poor attendance and not a very enthusiastic audience. Most of Chippenham is extraordinarily Victorian and reactionary. Would have asked Tomlinson back after but felt too tired for more discussion.

Saturday 7 October

Mrs Gillard left to go home to Portsmouth after over 4 years with us. At the end she really didn't want to go, though was anxious to see her own bed again which is a feather one. Truly nobody could possibly have had a more congenial or useful evacuee, but though we will miss her sewing we will be glad of her room for Biz.

Grim accounts in the papers about conditions in Holland. Before our Arnheim expedition failed it was expected that this would all be liberated within a week or two. Since then the Germans have refused to do anything about food to all the western part and are threatening to flood most of the country from sheer nastiness.

Tuesday 10 October
Painter arrived to paint greenhouse, much to our surprise. We asked for it to be done last spring, but since then nearly all the builders' men have been shifted to London to cope with damaged houses, and practically nothing is being done locally. However he was a patient of mine so said he would do windows and doors of workshop as well, and can get them all in green. Let us be thankful for small mercies!

Aachen is now surrounded by American troops and they have called on the military governor to surrender or it will be blown to pieces. It will be interesting to see what their attitude is, now one of their own towns and their own civilian lives are at stake.

Wednesday 11 October
No news of Aachen being surrendered. White flags were hung out which looked as if the civilians wanted to, but then they were taken down again.

Thursday 12 October
Ruth's 15th birthday. I have written to tell her she had better stop now as she is very nice as she is. I adore the daughters now at their respective ages more than I ever did before, and probably more than I shall later.

Daphne Awdry looked in after tea. Daniel is now definitely with the 5th Army on the Adriatic coast of Italy. On dear.

Friday 13 October
Fighting in the streets of Aachen. Russians have taken Riga. Athens liberated by Greek patriot forces and British troops in Corinth receiving a great welcome from the nearly starving Greeks. The news doesn't stand still, though after so much movement at the beginning of September we are inclined to think things are stuck or too slow.

Friday 20 October

Quite a normal day, with Bath in the morning and people here in the afternoon. Aachen definitely captured. They do seem to have fought to the last house for this town at any rate. People now seem to think that if there isn't a big offensive soon things will drag on all the winter, and that we are being held up by the weather. All through April and May when we were doing nothing (in reality I suppose frantically preparing) it was perfect invasion weather. Four days after we had started in June there was the worst storm in the Channel for 40 years. Now, when it is fairly usual to expect a fine October, it rains every day.

Friday 17 November

My interest in writing this account seems to have evaporated. Actually I am rather surprised that it lasted so long. I am out or busy here all day and every day till teatime and it really isn't interesting whether there were a few more or less patients at the eye Hospital. After tea it takes more than an hour to feed all the animals, then the 6pm news and time to look at the morning paper. Twice a week there is the supper to prepare and wash up. Then three letters to the children in addition to all the odd ones. I never cease to be thankful that I do not have to do evening surgery any more. That 6–7pm for writing, reading and domesticities is the most unutterable boon and I cannot think how I did without it for 17 years while the children were young. I never finishing till after 7.30pm, by which time I was dropping with fatigue.

We seem to be thoroughly dug into the sixth year of the war. It goes along, more up than down, with occasional plums like the sinking of the Turpitz.[1]

The powers that be are at last releasing a bit of news about the V2 rocket bombs, which have been hitting London since September. Nothing whatever in the papers but people coming out of London have been telling of other different 'explosions' which come without warning. Now the news has at last been released that these are V2 rocket bombs, which travel to a great height (60–70 miles) and that there is no sound of them coming. This must be most eerie. Some say they are less frightening than the V1s as not hearing them coming you don't have to think about taking cover or getting out of the way. Others say they are worse just because of this.

Sunday 10 December

A depressing week with civil war or as near as dammit in practically every liberated country in Europe, and the British consistently backing the wrong side. Colley always said that there would be left-wing revolutions in every country liberated, who would refuse to have anything to do with their kings or exiled governments who got out to England, that the people would want the resistance leaders to run things.

End of 1944

On the 12th December I went to Bristol with Colley to an ophthalmological meeting. Returned home at 7pm to hear the news that Daisy's mother had been taken seriously ill and was not expected to live, and Daisy had dashed off leaving us with no one. Then followed the most hectic week I can remember. Mrs Harlow couldn't help much as she went up to Lynham to take alternate nights with Daisy. April (Daisy's niece who has been living here and helping after school) did what she could, but she is after all only 13 yrs. I had distant clinics and was out almost all of every day. It was a particularly muddled week and the surgeries were full to overflowing. Ruth and Elizabeth and two of Ruth's friends arrived on Thursday and Arthur on Friday. Found myself getting bedrooms ready or doing surgeries or washing up at 10pm. However the girls were really good when they did come and various other people came in 'to oblige' for an hour or two, and we managed to enjoy our Xmas with just the family and no staff to think about. Ruth was a perfect brick the whole holidays and had the alarm and got up and cleaned the sitting room before breakfast and did a lot of cooking and most of the washing up. I felt a bit guilty about her doing so much when she should have been working for her school certificate. The mother who kept her daughter at home to slave and so ruined her career!

Politically things were very depressing over the end of 1944. Just before Xmas a counter attack in the West had some success and rather caught the Americans napping. It was said that they had allocated too many of their resources to the Far East before Germany was beaten. Only history will show if that was true.

Fighting continued in Greece and everyone was terribly depressed about this and the general muddle and mess of Europe. Altogether 1944 ended on a note of gloom.

1945

In the middle of January the Russians struck through Poland faster than the Germans had gone the opposite way in 1939. We hung on the wireless again and stuck pins on maps until they were at the Oder, less than 50 miles from Berlin. Then in mid-Feb the long awaited meeting of the 'Big three', Stalin, Churchill and Roosevelt at Yalta. They seemed to have reached a greater measure of agreement than some people thought possible.

Domestically things are still pretty hard. All through January I worked a 14 hour day with only the briefest intervals for food and never dared sit down, but got through it with the aid of sleeping pills at night and benzedrine in the day.

Eric excessively busy both with babies and winter ailments. He often had about 6 visits left to finish after supper – apart from emergencies. The prevailing recollection of all this time is fatigue. For the first time since we were married we had to leave the house with a notice on the door and no one to answer the phone while Simmy went to her lunch which was always before Eric or I were in.

February 1945

We started an attack in the West to drive up to the Rhine. Churchill made a speech in the Commons and gave the results of the Yalta conference. From what was said it was evident that the war with Germany was expected to be over last autumn and they were not expected to make a last ditch stand and let all their own towns be destroyed. Consequently too much shipping was diverted to the Pacific. The war against the Japanese is going much better and faster than expected, while that in Europe is dragging on longer. There are still V1 bombs and V2 rockets on London. Enough to make it pretty unpleasant for anyone living there and deter people from going up just for fun.

Friday 23 March
Montgomery's order of the day: 'We will now proceed to cross the Rhine.'

For the first time ever in our offensive we have marvellous weather. The 6th Airborne Division dropped again over beyond Wesel. This time they quickly linked up with ground forces – no second Arnheim. Though all the wireless commentators have been warning us that it is not all over, we can't help feeling that the end in Europe really cannot be long delayed. Though the end of the fighting will only mean the beginning of the cleaning up of completely unimaginable amounts of misery and devastation.

Sunday 1 April (Easter Sunday)
At Whitchurch. It sounds as if the end might come at any minute, but when and how? Who will have the authority to give the German surrender, or will it just be a question of individual units being mopped up until there are none left?

Friday 13 April
Sudden death of Roosevelt from cerebral haemorrhage, probably the greatest single loss mankind has ever sustained, not from the point of view of finishing the war, but for the remaking of a new world. With the development of the rocket shell, jet propulsion etc. a new war in the future might mean the extinction of mankind.

Roosevelt was one of the few Americans with really wide vision, right above party politics or big business, with complete integrity and a big mind. He was a visionary who could think in terms of the world. No other man could have headed the new World State, and the prospects of this ever being formed in the future now look grim without him to lead it.

Sunday 15 April
The *Observer* says events in Europe are much further advanced than we have been allowed to know about, and an 'important announcement' may be expected at any moment, certainly within the next week or two.

Resistance in Germany must by now be quite pointless and the general chaos in civilian life unimaginable. Individual units of the army seem to be fighting on. There seems no longer to be any proper direction from above. The whereabouts of the Nazi leaders is unknown.

Monday 16–Friday 20 April
The news coming out of Germany this week both from the British and American armies are of concentration camps both for German civilians and foreign workers which have been overrun by the advancing armies. The conditions were so horrible that I am keeping some journalists' descriptions. Though I hate and loathe all horrors and avoid them if possible, I feel it is so dreadful that any human civilisation could have come to this in the 20th century, with all the knowledge that we have, that there must be a printed record wherever possible, in case the next generation forget, or do not realise or see the necessity of keeping Germany unarmed. Not that other people's experience does any good or makes anyone the wiser. But someone might say in the future 'The atrocity stories were made up or grossly exaggerated', or 'Such things could not have happened really.' The children or the children's children, who may have to vote for equality of armaments for all countries or some such thing, should be able to assure themselves that it did really happen.

Sunday 29 April
Many rumours rampant. Himmler[2] has sought unconditional surrender from the Western Allies but not from Russia. A last minute attempt to try to cause a split. Mussolini is said to have been captured by Italian partisans and shot. Goering[3] said to have resigned owing to 'ill health'. Hitler said to have had a cerebral haemorrhage and not expected to live many days. Now, Himmler said to have been shot up in his car, but if so could hardly have made any peace offers.

Monday 30 April
Mussolini has definitely been killed and hung upside down in a Milan square, which would not seem to be very helpful to anyone.

There does seem to have been a definite surrender offer, which has been refused because it did not include unconditional surrender to Russia.

The RAF is now switching some of its bombing force over Holland to drop food. Bombing with food would seem to be such a satisfactory thing to do, and so good for the psychology of our boys as well as doing physical good to the Dutch who are said to be at concentration camp levels of starvation.

Wednesday 2 May
Hitler is DEAD. This seems to be fact, though the stories of the mode vary.

Admiral Doenitz[4] appointed as the new Fuhrer to succeed him, apparently by Hitler himself on Monday. He has made a statement to 'Fight On' and will have nothing to do with Himmler's surrender.

Hitler's death leaves us all completely drained of emotion. Now that the end is coming and coming fast one cannot get het up in any way. We are all too tired after 6 years and so many long drawn out expectations and anticlimaxes, and all too conscious of the terrible and awful mess and suffering all over Europe.

Hugh Meredith's translation of Sophocles' *Ajax* in 1939 seems now more than ever to apply to Hitler:

When shall the tale of years be ended
That last so long, that bring no joy,
But wear and tear of war extended,
For us to tramp the plains of Troy,
Where frowning fates the Greeks annoy?

Had he but been caught up to heaven,
Or snatched by death's all-gathering gate,
Who kneaded Greece with ghastly leaven
Of war, to breed us pain and hate,
And all mankind to decimate.

Who dashes from each lip the treasure
Of wine and talk, who damps the sound
Of flute, who mars the dance's measure,
Who treads at night a grisly round
When joy and kisses should abound.

No room for love, no bed for lover;
I rest not soft, I sleep not dry!   *Concentration camps*
The dews that wet my hair, that cover
My face, remember that I
Am neighbour to distressful Troy.   *Holland*

Time was, to fend from me the terror
Of night and battle, I could hold
Tempestuous Ajax: Foolish error!
Today has stretched him stark and cold!   *Apprehension for*
What now remains to make me bold?   *the future*

Oh to be back, where steeply wooded
The sea-washed cliffs of Suniun stand!   *The promised land*
To round the fore-land forest-hooded   *of Socialism?*
Strain my eyes and reach a hand
Towards Athena's holy land.

Later – News that the German forces in N. Italy and Western Austria have surrendered en bloc making about a million men. This extends right over the Brenner pass to Innsbruck and Saltzburg. Berlin now considered completely occupied by the Russians.

Friday 4 May
Mass surrender of all Germans in NW Germany, Denmark and Heligoland. This will mean about another million men to feed on 'ample rations' which are about double what the British civilians get, and many more times than any civilian on the Continent. This seems frightful, but if it is international law that prisoners have the full rations of the opposing army, and we are fighting for the keeping of international law and agreements, there is a case to be made for it.

Monday 7 May
Everyone on tenterhooks all day, waiting for the announcement of cessation of hostilities in Europe. The wireless keeps saying it will not be very long, so we dare not turn it off but kept popping back between patients to be greeted by the most futile of radio plays or music. Finally at six it was said that 'No further announcement was to be made tonight', so we turned it off. The result was that at 8pm it was announced that Churchill would speak at 3pm tomorrow which would be celebrated as VE day, but that the Germans had actually already signed the 'Unconditional surrender to the British, Americans and Russians'.

As usual I am completely drained of emotion and can feel nothing.

A bit of drunken singing in Chippenham but not much. One broadcast said 'In the hour of Victory let us be humble.' This was followed by the playing of 'Land of Hope and Glory – Make us mightier yet'. A bit incongruous.

Tuesday 8 May 1945: VE Day

A mucky sort of day, officially a national holiday. Surgeries of course open with a few patients strolling in. Everyone hanging out flags and doing as little work as possible.

Went to Bath rather late to find no patients at the Eye Hospital apart from a few casualties. Had to wait till 2pm as had been told my afternoon clinic would be held as usual. Went there but found everything locked up, the caretaker not even arrived and not a sign of a patient. Not many crowds in Bath though a good many flags. Thought again of Armistice Day 1918 and being in the lab with electric wires onto frogs' muscles. Then the maroons were going, to celebrate no more war ever again, peace in the world, let us make merry.

Today one can't find any general relief or trust in the future. Quiet thankfulness that the immediate killing is over – yes, though perhaps not for those of us with sons who will have to help beat Japan. No sense of security that civilisation is fundamentally decent. Starvation and chaos and physical ruin indescribable all over Europe with typhus and TB rampant. Already people voicing suspicions that 'It will be Russia next time' and that next time may mean the complete obliteration of a country by V bomb and rockets before even war is declared.

I can feel nothing but gloom and depression and apprehension about the future. Is this merely my age, having a son in the Navy destined for Japan, or more insight than some? I hope not the latter.

Wednesday 9 May

Went up the town last night to see what people were doing. Crowds everywhere, dancing and singing in the market place. There was very little drunkenness and no hooliganism or 'Mafeking', not even a broken window. On the whole people showing their good taste and sense. Family parties out for the evening to enjoy themselves and to show their children the lights in the trees on the islands by the bridge, all reflected in the water and very lovely. Few children have ever seen any lights at night.

Thursday 10 May

King and Queen starting to make drives round London, just as they did after the 1918 armistice when the UCH medical students in filthy, once white dissecting room coats took Phineas out to greet them. This was the first time women had been allowed to take him anywhere. The King and Queen looked quite alarmed when he surged forward to greet them. They probably thought he was a bomb, not a hospital mascot!

Back to normal with Devizes clinic and a chat about getting a new clinic going 'After the war'. Suddenly realised we should not be saying that and substituted 'When things have settled down a bit'.

It is certainly going to take time to readjust, and for the moment there is a certain flatness and lack of anything specific to do, just as there was during the first few days of the war. For the moment people have forgotten their ailments as they did then, though they will surge back next week.

A typical day in the life of two doctors 'After the war':

2.15pm: Joan has a patient that could not be fitted in any other time.

2.30pm: Eric goes to hospital where he assists Leech-Wilkinson to operate and see OPs all day. Joan having finished her patient would like to garden but as it is raining she turns out two cupboards instead.

6pm: Eric having had no tea, dashes back for the news. 'Seems hardly worth while putting it on,' says Joan, 'there won't be any now the war is over.' She was wrong as it was full of nuggets.

1. Surrender of Channel Islands.
2. Basic petrol next month. Five gallons a month for my car and six for Eric's. Joy and rapture unforeseen and unbelievable. Now we shall be able to go out every other Sunday and see Ruth, Whitchurch and Swanage, go to the theatre in Bath on a Thursday if we want to, meet our visitors at the station, fetch dogs' meat etc. Nothing bar the actual cessation of killing could have been more joyful for us.
3. One pound of sugar per ration book to be allowed to make

jam from soft fruit. (The only fly in this ointment is that the devastating frosts of early last week have ruined practically our entire fruit crop). But . . . Oh the joy of some petrol to go where one likes again. Have had to control claustrophobia for the last three years.

6.30pm: Eric goes to hospital committee. Joan joins Mr Bridgeman who has come to do a few hours' work levelling his ex-allotment for her rose garden. Pretty good in the 6th year of war to find someone who will do this sort of complete luxury work for one. It means digging out feet of clay. The rain having stopped, Joan feels she must go and barrow it away for him or it will never be done.

7.30pm: Joan comes in to clean and change, by this time with a bit of a backache.

8pm: Eric comes back from the hospital. Supper.

8.30–10pm: Eric spends time on and off the telephone about an American soldier he has in hospital who was stabbed in the chest with a penknife by (I fear) one of our marines during a dust-up about a girl outside a pub on V night. The American authorities don't seem to be taking any interest in him or removing him, so we have to do something. Finally contacted Belsey, the S-W regional chest expert, who says he will come out at once via Bristol where he will have to pick up a car and driver.

J: That means he will arrive about midnight and will have to be fed. Egg sandwiches I think.

E: What about that bit of asparagus that was left over from supper?

J: Oh, that went into the soup for tomorrow. It would have been nice in sandwiches.

E: Well, I'll go and cut a bit more and we can cook some.

J: Don't be silly, it's pitch dark.

E: Never mind, I can do it with a torch. We only need about 6 sticks.

J: Darling you are sweet, but rather batty. Whoever heard of anyone going out to cut asparagus at 10pm in the dark to put in midnight sandwiches?

Exit Eric. Joan busies herself putting an egg on to boil, and getting tray with whisky, cider and grapefruit squash. Re-enter Eric with very small collection of asparagus.

E: Here you are. It can go on with the egg.

J: Well tie it up then. Have you any string?

Eric produces string from his pocket, ties up asparagus and carefully lowers it into saucepan with pair of Spencer Wells forceps. Then proceeds to cut and spread bread and butter.

J: Easy on that butter, we've already eaten nearly half our week's ration in two days. Oh won't it be nice when we can give a friend a decent amount of butter on his bread?

E: Isn't that water boiling yet? Those eggs have been there nearly 20 minutes.

J: Well it isn't a proper Aga saucepan. The Aga is horribly low. Hope it isn't going out without Daisy here to get it going... the asparagus is getting soft but I don't like to prod it too much with a Spencer Wells or it may disintegrate.

E: Why don't you use a fork then?

J: Oh, a Spencer Wells seems to come handier.

E: Well, drain it off then while I chop this egg.

Joan fumbles with the string and is rescued by Eric who uses the forceps to remove the bundle and prop it against the edge of the sink to drain. 'Darling, I do love you so.' They embrace.

11.15pm: Sandwiches are eventually made and taken into the sitting room.

J: Well, I don't think I shall stay up even for Belsey's lovely green eyes. It's going to be a hell of a day tomorrow with everyone coming to the Eye Hospital who didn't come Tuesday or Wednesday, and a full afternoon here. I'm just too old to burn the candle at both ends now even for an attractive boyfriend. Joan goes to bed.

11.45pm: Belsey arrives and eats with Eric. They go off to the hospital where they aspirate 35ozs of blood from American's chest.

12.15am: Telephone rings.

J: (who has just dropped off to sleep) Hell. (Lifts receiver.) Yes,
     who is it?
Voice: Is that Dr Cox?
J: No it ISN'T.
Voice: Sorry to have troubled you.
J: (sotto voce) So you damned well should be. (Rings off.)
1.45am: Eric returns and goes to bed.

EPILOGUE

by Elizabeth Murray (*née* Hickson)

My mother's most important legacy is surely how to keep going under difficult conditions. This diary shows her doing this during the war, but she also kept going on during the rest of her life and into old age.

At the age of eighty-seven she took my sister and me to Venice. My father had died fifteen years before. The marriage had been very happy and she missed him enormously, as we all did. But her life continued, much of it outside the home. Her immediate surroundings contracted from a large to a smaller house and then to a two-room apartment at the back of my sister's house, all of which she designed herself. She always insisted on a garden, which she maintained and enjoyed. Wildlife was encouraged and fed, somehow compatible with the resident cats and dogs.

People were not forgotten. Exchanges with neighbours, relations and friends were important. Inescapably, the long-lived must watch the painful decline of their contemporaries. My mother was a pragmatist, trying to find feasible solutions to problems. She visited people who thought they could not visit her. Sometimes she persuaded them that they could, perhaps by the example of a difficult bus trip or long rainy walk. Always she went on, without complaint.

Her popularity with her grandchildren was for herself, her humour and her modern concerns. She was genuinely interested and her input, whether welcome or not, was offered lightly, thoughtfully and with imagination.

My mother was not always an easy person. She made demands, on herself and others. We seldom saw those she made on herself. Certainly, with the inevitable failings of age, they must have increased. But any struggles remained largely hidden. When she banged her leg getting off a bus her concern was about rudeness to a neighbour. 'I was rather short with her,' she sighed, 'but I was hurrying home before the blood soaked into my shoe.'

My sister and I stopped resenting her demands. When she yearned to revisit the chateaux of the Loire we all three went, for an exhilarating vacation. The culmination came at Chenonceaux, after we had walked up a half-mile drive and all round the chateau. My mother sat down on a wall saying 'Well, if the Taj Mahal is the most beautiful building in the world, this must come second.'

Venice was more complicated. My mother had not been there since 1930 and feared that in another fifty-six years either she or Venice would not be there – so to Venice we went.

She had never hiked much and by this time she confined her walking to level ground. Steps were difficult. At the airport the water taxis were four steps down and swaying with the tide. 'She can't,' whispered my sister behind her back.

'She can,' said my mother and the Venetian boatman – and she did.

She had forgotten the stepped, hump-backed bridges that pass over every canal in Venice. The first afternoon, during her only daily rest, my sister and I developed some rules. Each supper destination must be no more than two bridges from a water stop, and always in a different part of Venice. The long walks to find those places were a bonus for us.

On the morning of our departure my sister developed acute sciatica. She lay stricken, swallowing painkillers and coffee. I was going on to Rome and worried about my mother's stability without an arm from either of us to steady her. At the hotel desk I said I would help them to the water taxi (one bridge and one square), but they must be met by two wheelchairs at the airport.

We started out. My mother moved ahead. I pursued her over the bridge and we found a table to sit on. Venice is full of beautiful things but lacking benches. I grabbed her stick and rushed it back to my sister who was following more slowly. When the water taxi came we saw that the tide was two feet lower than when we arrived.

'Never mind,' said my mother as she started sideways along a three-foot wall towards the boat's deck, clinging to the railings.

'Arrivederci,' I said reluctantly as they both settled gingerly into their seats.

At the airport half my message had been relayed – there was one wheelchair. 'Good gracious – not me,' said my mother scornfully as they tried to push her into it, 'that's for my daughter.'

She continued to visit friends. Her concern was to cheer without provoking wistfulness for what was denied her listeners. Her boast was that getting out of the bath was easier since she went to Venice. She remained mobile and alert till her death in November 1988.

We too go on, more vigorously because of her example. My mother would find it unlikely that there could be any stimulus in one elderly lady's story. I cannot agree.

NOTES

1 The Bath Blitz: 27 April–7 May 1942

1   At that time the Eye Infirmary occupied a house on the corner of Lansdown Hill and Julian Road.

2   Walter's nurseries were on the A4 just east of Batheaston.

3   Cranhill Hotel: in Weston Road leading out of Bath towards Bristol.

4   WVS: Women's Voluntary Service.

5   OPs: outpatients.

6   Queen's Messenger canteens: mobile vans set up with gifts from the USA and the Queen, to be rushed at need to any blitzed town.

7   Fortts: a well-known restaurant in Milsom Street.

8   At that time consultants from Bath came to see patients and do less serious operations at the Chippenham district hospital. A local doctor gave the anaesthetic and another usually assisted.

9   KP: keratic precipitate, fibrous deposit on the posterior surface of the cornea.

10 pilocarpine: drops to contract the pupil.

11 Eric and Joan had put their caravan by the river Avon, in a field belonging to Mr Self, a patient. It was a place to escape from the telephone, and when there was no basic petrol they could use the excuse that Eric was driving to see a patient.

2 . . . And Afterwards: 8–19 May 1942

1   Miss Brabazon may have been one of the clerical staff at the Eye Infirmary.

2   Battle of the Coral Sea: a major battle in the Pacific between the Imperial Japanese Navy and the Allied naval and air forces of the USA and Australia.

3   *German Spies at Bay*: a factual record of German espionage in Great Britain 1914–1918 by S.T. Felstead (published 1920).

4   Rep. Mist.: repeat prescription.

5   Joan had several accounts at the grocer, butcher etc which she paid by cheque each month.

3 Life Goes On: 20 May–11 June 1942

1   British Restaurants were communal kitchens set up by the Ministry of Food to ensure people did not starve if they ran out of food coupons. Main courses cost about 9d (the equivalent of £1 today). No restaurant could charge more than five shillings for a meal.

2   Before the establishment of the NHS consultants got much of their income from private practice, which was dependent on GPs referring patients to them.

3   Eric and Joan had dug a swimming pool just before the war with the help of the gardener, a handyman, and their children with their sandpit spades.

4   Quotation from Rudyard Kipling's 'If'.
5   Eric's youngest brother had taken the pupils who still attended the school to Canada.
6   NHI patients were covered by the limited health insurance available before the NHS.

4   Patients and Petrol: 15 June–12 July 1942

1   WAAFs, members of the Women's Auxiliary Air Force.
2   The North African campaign was a see-saw battle fought bitterly between 1940 and 1943.
3   The Free French Army under General de Gaulle fought for the allies in North Africa.
4   Sevastopol: a strategic position on the Crimean Peninsula.
5   Tobruk: an important town on the coast of North Africa.
6   Rommel: commander of the German forces in North Africa, who was known as the 'Desert Fox'.
7   Induction is a medical procedure to start a woman in labour.
8   GMC: General Medical Council, responsible for the professional standards of doctors.
9   Every quarter Eric and Joan spent many hours going through the clinical records to decide how much to charge each patient according to their ability to pay.
10   In this context trephining is to drill a hole to reduce the pressure in the eye.
11   POP: persistent occipital posterior, where the back of the baby's head is lying towards the spine which can make the delivery more difficult.
12   Field Marshall Auchinleck was in command of our Middle Eastern forces from July 1941.
13   the Don: a major river in Russia, which rises south of Moscow and flows 1220 miles into the sea of Azov.

5   A Family Funeral: 13 July–3 August 1942

1   atropine: drops to dilate the pupil so that the doctor has a better view of the inside. This is especially necessary with a wriggling child.
2   The lay: term used here for those people who were not medically qualified.
3   Quotation from Lewis Carroll's 'The Walrus and the Carpenter'.
4   Tennyson Jesse: an English criminologist, journalist and author.
5   Timoshenko: a senior officer in the Red Army at the beginning of the German invasion of Russia in 1940.
6   I have been unable to trace the source of this quotation.
7   primipara: a woman expecting her first baby.

6   The River Holiday: 4 August–4 September 1942

1   In those days midwives did not stitch the perineum.

2   The Congress Party committed themselves to an aggressive policy, taking the form of sabotage and of fomenting riots and disorder.
3   Government of India: the Viceroy's Council.
4   Kelmscott: the home of William Morris who founded the arts and crafts movement.
5   Mrs Gordon Snell: presumably the owner or tenant of Kelmscott at the time.
6   The Armstrong Whitworth Whitley was a heavy bomber used by the RAF between 1937 and 1942, said to be ugly yet robust.
7   International: a chain of grocers widespread during the war.

7   Back to Work: 15 September–21 October 1942

1   choroiditis: an inflammation of the choroid layer of the eye behind the retina.
2   Biz had moved from the Beltane school to Buckswood Hill Grange, evacuated from Surrey to a large house just outside Lacock.
3   Unna's paste: an impregnated bandage that hardens on exposure to air, used by Eric most successfully for the treatment of various ulcers.
4   epulis: a benign tumour of the gums growing from the covering of the jaw bone.
5   The Forbes Fraser Hospital is in the grounds of the RUH and at that time was a private hospital.
6   the Thetis: a US coast guard cutter which had been sunk on 10 June 1942.
7   Jan Smuts had led commando forces against the British during the Boer War but then served as commander of the South African Defence Force against the Germans.

8   The Tide Begins to Turn: 22 October–31 December 1942

1   Sir Bernard Pares KBE was an English historian and academic known for his work on Russia.
2   Tank Islands were designated areas, a town or a village, at strategic positions with fixed defences including special road blocks, pillboxes and tank ditches.
3   the *Internationale*: a widely sung left-wing anthem.
4   heterophoria: a dissociation of the eyes which may lead to a squint.
5   General Giraud (1879–1949) was a French general who was captured during both world wars. He escaped in April 1942 and became commander of the French forces in Algeria.
6   Darlan (1879-1942) was Admiral of the French fleet who cooperated with the Germans.
7   Vichy France was the French State formed after the defeat of France by Germany in 1940 and headed by Marshal Pétain.
8   maroons: noisy fireworks that were used as a warning or in this case to tell the people that the war had ended.

9   Simpsons: historic landmark restaurant in the Strand opened in 1828.
10 back lamp and letters: standard eye testing equipment.
11 Luftwaffe: the Nazi air force.
12 The Beveridge report: Report of the Inter-departmental Committee on Social Insurance and Allied Services, an influential document in the founding of the UK welfare state.
13 See note 11 to chapter 4.
14 Panzer divisions were armoured (tank) divisions of the German army.
15 Tripolitania: a region of Libya.
16 ARP: Air Raid Precautions.
17 Potts fracture: term, used less frequently now, for a variety of fractures involving the ankle.

9   Loves and Hates: 1 January–13 March 1943

1   Struwwel Hitler, a play on *Struwwelpeter*, a German children's book of rhyming moral tales.
2   Catty was Biz's favourite cuddly toy.
3   Quisling: a person who cooperated with the Nazis, named after Vidkun Quisling, a Norwegian who helped the Nazis conquer his country.
4   Lord Haw-Haw was a nickname for several announcers on an English language programme broadcast by the Nazis.

10   Country Practice: 4 April–21 May 1943

1   FT: possibly a previous boyfriend who was killed in the First World War.
2   A greenstick fracture, usually seen in children, is a fracture in which the bone bends but does not completely break.
3   WR: a test for syphilis.
4   RAF Lyneham, six miles north east of Chippenham, was the principle transport hub for the service.
5   Some condoms were reusable in those days.
6   benzedrine: an amphetamine that was used medicinally and by those who needed to stay awake for war work.
7   Streatly and Goring are villages on the River Thames.
8   albucid: antibacterial eyedrops containing a sulphonamide.
9   fluorescein: a yellow dye used to detect damage to the cornea.
10 pterygiums: benign growths of the conjunctiva producing white patches that encroach onto the cornea.

11   Family, Friends and Domestic Life: 22 May–4 August 1943

1   Beja: a town in North Africa.
2   Newell: headmaster of Gresham's School, which had been evacuated to Newquay.
3   Lampedusa: an Italian island in the Mediterranean.
4   exophthalmic goitre: staring eyes caused by an overactive thyroid.

5 Sikorski: Prime Minister of the Polish government in exile and commander-in-chief of Polish forces.
6 Victor Cazalet: MP for Chippenham at the time.
7 The King: i.e. the king of Italy.
8 Marshall Badoglio: Italian general and statesman.
9 UCH: University College Hospital.

12 Waiting for the Second Front: 21 August–30 December 1943

1 Joan was in Clough house at St Felix School.
2 Quintin Hogg, Lord Hailsham: an influential Conservative MP and political writer.
3 papilloedema: swelling of the optic nerve at the back of the eye.
4 spam: tinned meat, mainly pork, sent over from the United States in large quantities during the war.
5 GTC: General Training Corps, an organisation for training youngsters prior to being called up.
6 1st MB: the first exam in the medical curriculum, which can be taken at school or in the first year at university.
7 Working men paid in a small sum each week to the panel through their firm and some of the families were covered by 'the club'.
8 M and B 693 was one of the first-generation sulphonamide antibiotics.
9 Field Marshall Wavell was commander of the British forces in the Middle East and became commander-in-chief in India in 1943.

13 The Tension Mounts: 1 January–30 April 1944

1 volvulus: a twisted gut.

14 The Invasion at Last: 6 May–24 June 1944

1 hyperchlorhydria: excess acid in the stomach, usually due to anxiety.
2 Sir Arthur Rucker was a senior civil servant in the Ministry of Health.

15 Stretching the Rations: 25 June–28 August 1944

1 MOH: Medical Officer of Health.
2 retrobulbar neuritis: inflammation of the optic nerve between the back of the eye and the brain.

16 The End Approaches: 30 August 1944–10 May 1945

1 the Turpitz: a German battleship sunk by British forces in 1944.
2 Himmler: an important German military commander and leader of the Nazi party.
3 Goering: commander-in-chief of the Luftwaffe for most of the war.
4 Admiral Doenitz: creator of the fleet of German submarines, who was appointed by Hitler to succeed him and negotiated the surrender of Germany.

Books on Wiltshire and Somerset from Ex Libris Press:

WHERE WILTSHIRE MEETS SOMERSET
*20 best walks around Bath, Bradford on Avon, Trowbridge, Westbury, Warminster &
Frome*
by Roger Jones
Our bestselling walking guide since 1982!
128 pages; Illustrated with line drawings & sketch maps
New edition; ISBN 1-903341-34-5; Price £7.95

THE MID-WILTS WAY describes the course of his 55-mile long waymarked trail across the
county.
by James Alsop
Sketch maps and illustrations complement the guide
80 pages; ISBN 978-1-903341-42-1; Price £5.95

PEWSEY RAMBLES:
Walks on the Pewsey Downs and surrounding area
BY James Alsop
Sketch maps and illustrations; ISBN 978-1-906641-03-0; Price £5.95

EXPLORING HISTORIC WILTSHIRE *Volume 1: North*
by Ken Watts
First published in 1997. This third printing (2008) is available at the original price!
ISBN 0-948578-85-8; Price £7.95

EXPLORING HISTORIC WILTSHIRE *Volume 2: South*
by Ken Watts
ISBN 0-948578-92-0; Price £7.95

*Each of these Exploring Historic Wiltshire volumes consists of 176 pages, is fully
illustrated with photographs & sketch maps and indexed*

CURIOUS WILTSHIRE
by Mary Delorme
Water Meadows; White Horses; Sarsen Stones; Dew Ponds; Blind Houses; Tithe Barns
160 pages; Fully illustrated
Fifth printing
ISBN 1-903341-09-4; Price £7.95

THE MARLBOROUGH DOWNS
by Ken Watts
192 pages; Fully illustrated with photographs & line drawings;
New edition; ISBN 0-948578-15-9; Indexed; Price £9.95

THE DAY RETURNS
Excursions in Wiltshire's history
by John Chandler
256 pages; Illustrated; Indexed; ISBN 0-948578-95-5; Price £9.95

FROM TURNPIKE GATES TO CHRISTMAS WAITS: *Historical Notes from Village Life*
by Alan Dodge
Featuring Freshford, Limpley Stoke & Hinton Charterhouse
Illustrated throughout; 96 pages; ISBN 978-1-906641-43-6; Price £5.95

BRADFORD on AVON PAST & PRESENT
Illustrated throughout; Indexed; 192 pages; ISBN 978-1-903341-30-8; Price £9.95

BRADFORD VOICES: *Life in Bradord on Avon 1900-2010*
by Margaret Dobson
Indexed; 320 pages; ISBN 978-906641-36-8; Price £11.95

BRYLCREEM & BROKEN BISCUITS: *A Street Trail History of Bradford on Avon's Shops in the 1950s*
by Stephanie Laslett
Illustrated throughout; 112 pages ; ISBN 978-1-906641-57-3; Price £6.95

BRADFORD ON AVON'S PUBS AND BREWERIES
by Jack Mock
96 pages; ISBN 978-1-906641-40-5; Price £5.95

FILLING SPACES
by Stan Hey
A crime novel featuring Bradford on Avon's own sleuth, Frank Brennan, written by Bradford-based author and scriptwriter, Stan Hey.
222 pages; ISBN 1-903341-22-1; Price £5.99

HOSTS OF GHOSTS: *Curious Happenings in West Wiltshire*
by Margaret Dobson & Simone Brightstein
Illustrated; 160 pages; ISBN 1-903341-29-9; Price £6.95

WALKS IN THE MENDIP HILLS
by James Alsop
Sketch maps and illustrations; 96 pages; ISBN 978-1-906641-20-7; Price £5.95

WEST MENDIP WAY: *A Guide for Walkers of the 30-mile footpath from Uphill to Wells*
by Derek Moyes
Sketch maps and Illustrations; 112 pages; ISBN 0-948578-45-9; Price £5.95

THE GEOLOGY OF SOMERSET
by Peter Hardy
Fully illustrated with maps, cross-sections and photographs; Indexed
Third printing; 224 pages; ISBN 1-903341-42-4; Price £9.95

Our books are obtainable, post-free in the UK, direct from us via our website, on receipt of net price using Paypal.

www.ex-librisbooks.co.uk

Also available through your local bookshop or from Amazon.co.uk

Please ask for our free, illustrated catalogue describing all available titles from:

EX LIBRIS PRESS 11 Regents Place, Bradford on Avon
Wiltshire BA15 1ED Tel/Fax 01225 865191

Alternatively, visit our website